August Wilson

Twayne's United States Authors Series

Frank Day, Editor

Clemson University

TUSAS 712

AUGUST WILSON.
Courtesy of August Wilson.

August Wilson

Peter Wolfe

University of Missouri-St. Louis

Twayne Publishers
New York

Twayne's United States Authors Series No. 712

August Wilson
Peter Wolfe

Twayne Publishers
1633 Broadway
New York, NY 10019

Library of Congress Cataloging-in-Publication Data

Wolfe, Peter, 1933 –
    August Wilson / Peter Wolfe.
        p.   cm. — (Twayne's United States authors series ; TUSAS 712)
    Includes bibliographical references (p.   ) and index.
    ISBN 0-8057-1631-9 (alk. paper)
    1. Wilson, August—Criticism and interpretation. 2. Historical drama, American—History and criticism. 3. Domestic drama, American—History and criticism. 4. Afro-Americans in literature.
    I. Title.   II. Series.
    PS3573.I45677Z96   1999
    812'.54—dc21   99-14328
                                                         CIP

This paper meets the requirements of ANSI/NISO Z3948-1992 (Permanence of Paper).

10 9 8 7 6 5 4 3 2 1

Printed in the United States of America

With love to my grandson,

Ethan Robert Wolfe
("He starts for most clubs")

Contents

Preface

Is August Wilson as good a playwright as people say? Why is he enjoyed and admired so much by theater audiences today? For several years, these questions kept nagging me. The book you are now holding came into being from a wish to find out why Wilson has won the esteem of so many playgoers since his first Broadway-produced play, *Ma Rainey's Black Bottom,* became an instant hit when it opened at the Cort Theater in October 1984. Unearthing some of the reasons for Wilson's critical and popular success, I soon learned, was reaping other gains, like insights into both the racial tensions vexing the United States and the dynamics of Wilson's art.

Wilson's theatrical prominence is no fluke. Restrained, elegant, and finely observed, his plays include life's imperfections, alterations, and accommodations. The accommodations are often costly. Though wrongs like the underfunding of education and the skimping of social services aren't addressed directly in the work, they disclose themselves through mood, character, and Wilson's ability to keep things moving. Even when his dramatic pace sharpens, Wilson nuances his materials to call forth a subtle response from his audience. Nothing looks fake or forced, either, much of his power stemming from subtext—the tendency of the action to slight the artifices of plot in favor of revealing character through a counterpoint of dialogue, silence, and atmosphere. The characters always come first. And Wilson's engagement with them gives him an imaginative access to their moral selves that overrides moral judgment.

They come to us fresh from life. There are no heroes, villains, or sharp-cut victories in the plays. Wilson has chosen to bypass these conventions. As indeed he might; the right kind of ensemble acting can weave the setbacks, adjustments, and revelations featured in the plays into a compelling, resonant whole. A master of dialogue, he has helped the actors performing his plays achieve this resonance. His plays are extraordinary inventions, their details carefully chosen for their color, texture, and weight. Like other artistic gems, the plays stir in their audiences a new sense of the world. August Wilson has heard black America singing, and he has made the right artistic choices to make us thrill to the music, as well.

Acknowledgments

The author and publisher join hands in thanking those people whose time and energy went into the preparation of this book: Chet Bunnell, Lee Brown, and Ron Himes, artistic director of the St. Louis Black Repertory Company, all of whom generously shared their knowledge of contemporary black drama with me; Chuck Korr, whose expertise in sports history led me to finds that improved my treatment of the plays, particularly *Fences;* Lucinda Williams, for tracking down vital research materials; Dena Levitin, for providing me with important details of theater history; and Sandra G. Shannon, August Wilson's leading expert, for her warm encouragement. Finally, a great debt of thanks goes out to Mr. Wilson himself for his generosity in both making available to me typescripts of his unpublished plays and permitting me to reprint copyright materials.

The combined help of the following people amounts to a major contribution: Selana Cepeda, Carla Britton, Gary Dingledine, Ann C. Taylor, Ira Hattenbach, Logarthur Lane, Del Lord, Dan Pitlyk, Julian Fleischman, and Michael Salius.

Chronology

1982   The O'Neill Center accepts *Ma Rainey,* a breakthrough that leads to Wilson's meeting, that same year, both Charles S. Dutton and Lloyd Richards.

1983   Death of Wilson's mother, Daisy; the O'Neill Center accepts *Fences* for a staged reading.

1984   *Ma Rainey* opens at the Yale Repertory Theater (6 April) and in New York's Cort Theater (11 October).

1985   *Ma Rainey* wins the New York Drama Critics' Circle Award for the best new play of 1984–1985. *Fences* debuts at Yale (30 April).

1986   *Joe Turner's Come and Gone* is produced at Yale (29 April).

1987   *Fences* opens in New York's 46th Street Theatre (26 March) and goes on to win a host of honors in addition to grossing more money in the first year of its run ($11 million) than any nonmusical in Broadway history.

1988   *Joe Turner* opens at New York's Ethel Barrymore Theatre (26 March) and is named the best play of the 1987–1988 theater season by the New York Drama Critics' Circle.

1990   *The Piano Lesson* opens at New York's Walter Kerr Theatre (16 April) and wins the Pulitzer Prize (Wilson's second, after *Fences*) later in the year; marriage to Judy ends; moves to Seattle.

1992   *Two Trains Running* debuts at New York's Walter Kerr Theatre (13 April).

1994   Marries costume designer Costanza Romero.

1995   *Piano Lesson* is performed on CBS's *Hallmark Hall of Fame.*

1996   *Seven Guitars* premieres on Broadway at the Walter Kerr Theatre (28 March). *Jitney* is performed at Pittsburgh Public Theater (6 June).

1997   *Jitney* opens at the Crossroads Theatre, New Brunswick, NJ (15 April). Daughter Azula Carmen Wilson is born 27 August in Seattle.

1998   Second revision of *Jitney* is performed at the Freedom Theatre, Philadelphia, (12 June) and at the Lorraine

Hansberry Theater, San Francisco (21 October) and Huntington Theater, Boston (28) October).

1999   *Jitney* debuts at Baltimore's Centerstage Theatre (8 January).

Chapter One

Introduction: From Street to Stage

New superlatives may have to be deployed to describe the wild success of August Wilson. Both the 1992 judgment of G. M. Berkowitz, that Wilson is "the most important dramatist of the 1980s,[1] and that of Eric Bergesen and William Demastes, that he's "the foremost African-American playwright" of the last two decades,[2] though accurate, need upgrading. Rarely if ever (Bernard Shaw may be an exception) has a twentieth-century dramatist gained the critical acclaim and commercial success that Wilson did with his first three plays. *Ma Rainey's Black Bottom* (1984; all production dates refer to the plays' Broadway debuts) won the New York Drama Critics' Circle Award for best new play of 1984–1985. The Circle Award also went to *Joe Turner's Come and Gone* (1988) for the 1987–1988 season. Finally, *Fences* (1987), said Liz Smith in the *New York Daily News,* won more major prizes and grossed more money ($11 million) in its first year than any nonmusical play in Broadway history.[3] The honors won by *Fences* don't stop here. Besides earning Wilson the *Chicago Tribune's* award as Artist of the Year for 1987,[4] the play won the Circle Award, a Pulitzer, a Drama Desk Award, and four Tonys.

Sandra G. Shannon has judged well to call Wilson "a major American playwright."[5] Essays highly supportive of his art have appeared in the *New York Times Magazine, Esquire,* and *New Yorker.*[6] Nor is Harvard's Henry Louis Gates Jr. the only academic who has discussed him. August Wilson has inspired numerous theses and dissertations along with university press books, one of which (*May All Your Fences Have Gates: Essays on the Drama of August Wilson*)[7] includes contributions from professors at major institutions like Stanford, Michigan, and Wisconsin-Madison. But regardless of their affiliations, Wilson's commentators have granted him canonical status. Bestowing praise that might have looked reckless in 1988, David Barbour ranked him with Eugene O'Neill.[8] Eight years later, John Lahr deemed him O'Neill's superior: "No one else—not even O'Neill," Lahr said in the *New Yorker,* has aimed so high and achieved so much" on the American stage as Wilson.[9] Other comparisons add to the critical juggernaut that has been confirming Wilson as a major leading playwright. Shannon claims that the main character of *Fences* rises to a Shakespearean grandeur (104). Lawrence Bommer, by crediting Wilson with having created "the most complete chronicle since Balzac," sees his man's inventiveness transcending the stage and taking on the resonance of major fiction.[10]

Forecasting the direction of the growing body of Wilson criticism is as problematic as it would have been, as late as 1982, to predict the celebrity the Pittsburgh native would enjoy before the decade's close. Born Frederick August Kittel in 1945, the fourth of six children and a first son, Wilson grew up in the two-room apartment of his mother, Daisy Wilson Kittel. His father, for whom he was named, a red-haired baker who came to the United States from Germany at age 10, rarely visited the Bedford Avenue flat where his family lived. Precocious and bright, his little son Freddie learned how to read at age four, after which he attended Catholic schools. This regimen ended during his freshman year at Pittsburgh's "very prestigious" Central Catholic High School,[11] where he was the lone black in a student body of 1,500. Though at five foot seven and 175 pounds he had enough size, he was kept off Central's football team; he lunched alone in the school cafeteria; and on his classroom desk he'd often find a note saying, "Go home, nigger." This abuse provoked many after-school fights. Wilson recalls the school principal sending him home in a cab to save him from 40 angry fellow students who were waiting to bushwhack him after classes were dismissed.

This ugliness prompted Freddie to change schools—but with unhappy results. He felt so blocked in the vocational school where he divided his efforts between sheet-metal work and "fifth-grade" academic subjects that he transferred to a traditional public high school (Feingold, 117). Here, too, his stay was brief. Frederick August Kittel's formal education ended at age 15 when his history teacher at Gladstone High accused him of plagiarizing a 20-page term paper. In response to the failing grade his teacher gave him, the boy tore up the paper, threw it in the trash, and "walked out of that school forever" (Brown, 120).

It was some months before he told his mother and stepfather, David Bedford, that he had quit school. Each morning he'd leave the apartment carrying his books as if he were en route to class. But he'd divide his school hours shooting baskets in the yard outside the principal's window at Gladstone and reading books by writers like Langston Hughes, Richard Wright, and Ralph Ellison in the "Negro section" of a Carnegie-endowed public library. His development lacked a focus. His 1962 enlistment in the U.S. Army ended after a year. His return to Pittsburgh and civilian life at age 18 set into motion a round of jobs as a short-order cook, a gardener, a porter, and a dishwasher. Much of his spare time he spent at a Pope's Restaurant (which is mentioned in *Fences*)[12] and at Pat's cigar store, where, having discovered that language is the way any people transmits its culture, beliefs, and values, he listened carefully to the sidewalk yarns of the elderly customers, who called him Youngblood (the name he later gave to an important character in the unpublished 1982 playscript *Jitney*). But listening alone didn't content him. He also began writing poetry, affecting the bardic tones and the tweed jackets of his then favorite poet, Dylan Thomas.

The death of his birth father in 1965 accompanied and perhaps gave rise to several other major changes in his life. He moved into his own apartment and bought his first typewriter (for $20), decided he wanted to become a writer, and changed his name to August Wilson. Of equal import was his hearing for the first time the singing of Bessie Smith. In his preface to the 1991 University of Pittsburgh Press anthology of his first three plays, he tells of finding Bessie's "Nobody in Town Can Bake a Sweet Jellyroll like Mine" in a stack of 78-rpm records he had bought for a nickel apiece. The record moved him so much that he played it 22 straight times.[13] It taught him that both the history and culture of African Americans had their roots in an oral, rather than a written, tradition. By stages it would lead to the understanding that this oral tradition consists of an extended riposte to a set of values and codes imposed on blacks by white America.

Though years would pass before this rich oral tradition would seep into Wilson's plays, the cultural forces behind it had caught his attention—and then won his commitment. With his friend Rob Penny, he founded in 1969 Pittsburgh's Black Horizons Theater with the aim of promoting black self-awareness. Nor was this enterprise unique. Imamu Baraka's Spirit House in Newark, Robert Macbeth's New Lafayette Theater in Harlem, and Ed Bullins's Black House in San Francisco all provided venues for the development of African American sensibilities; Bullins spoke in 1972 of "altering the slave mentality of Black Americans."[14] In line with Bullins's intent, Wilson tried to use live drama to promote cultural and political reform. The plays he produced and directed challenged both the aesthetic and the ideological premises of the reigning Caucasian theater. But the greatest influence on Wilson's black cultural nationalism was Baraka (or LeRoi Jones). It was from Baraka that Wilson learned sociology and political commitment. Like those of Baraka, Wilson's plays include anger and violence. They also voice the belief that blacks must control their own capital assets.

Wilson, though, disavows Baraka's belief in violent revolution in favor of developing a collective self-reliance grounded in black history and culture. How to develop this grounding? Because they had little leverage in radio, TV, or the print media, black people for decades had been learning about themselves from nonblacks. Therein lies a huge obstacle to self-being. No people can gain authenticity by either accepting others' judgment of them or looking to others for approval. Black Americans lacked a sense of authenticity in 1927, the time setting of Wilson's *Ma Rainey's Black Bottom*. In a sad but stark recognition of black moral unreadiness, the leader of Ma's band sends for the band's white manager to deal with the fallout caused by a black-on-black killing.

Such moments sadden but also energize Wilson. His search for the roots of black cultural identity has led him to the black oral tradition that helped usher in the blues singing of Bessie Smith, who was, ironically, a contemporary of the real-life Ma. Though a man of mixed race, Wilson identifies with the black ancestry of his mother. This identification has focused his art. In the core of his mind and being, he is a black man who understands the hurdles black America must surmount before doing justice to its legacy.

The Blues and Beyond

In 1988, Wilson told David Savran, "I am trying to write plays that contain the sum total of black culture in America, and its difference from white culture. Once you put in the daily rituals of black life, the play starts to get richer and bigger."[15] This size and richness often stem from speech. Wilson believes his people's history to be "mainly oral" because, in order to cope, blacks in the United States have had to cultivate a gift for subtlety and indirection (Bommer, 16). Verbal agility has helped them survive in a society both made and run by others. Thus Wilson's people often possess speaking styles full of tonalities and rich in idiom and imagery. A figure like the retired Holloway (played on Broadway by Roscoe Lee Browne) in *Two Trains Running* (1992) descends from the African *griot*, or storyteller.

The griot's quickness with words permeates the canon. Wilson will break dramatic flow by inserting a debate about a train schedule (*Ma Rainey)*, an attempt to fix the date of an ex-boarder's time of residence in a rooming house (*Joe Turner*), or a recipe for the preparation of greens

(*Seven Guitars* [1996]). Talk in a Wilson play needn't advance a plot or develop an idea. Its value comes from the economy with which it builds a mood or captures the flavor and robustness of black American speech. Part of this dynamism may evolve from the deliberate lie or the tall tale. Wilson's characters will exaggerate, distort, and falsify if they believe that their fabrications convey a tone feeling that suits the occasion. Caught in a lie, Slow Drag, Ma Rainey's bassist, admits, "Oh, I just threw that in there to make it sound good."[16] Then, rather than taking him to task, all the other band members laugh—as they should. They delight in the freedom governing oral exchange in the black community.

A bonding agent and coping device perhaps even more vibrant than speech for black Americans is music. Any polity shapes its future by imagining and reimagining its past. It builds memorials to itself by giving artistic shape to what happened. Thus Jay Plum called the blues in 1993 "a connective force that links the [black] past with the present and the present with the future."[17] All music, including the blues, abets the forces of renewal and even salvation in Wilson. The song sung by two children near the end of *Fences* eases their father's transit to heaven. A simple tune sung with piano accompaniment exorcises a ghost in *The Piano Lesson* (1990). *Joe Turner,* a play that treats the persistence of bonds, includes a Juba dance, which Wilson calls "an act of tribal solidarity and recognition of communal history" (Preface, xiii).

A lively African dance that includes hand clapping and foot stomping, the Juba sung, danced, and shouted on this Sunday evening pays tribute to the good chicken dinner the boarders at Seth Holly's rooming house have just enjoyed. This surrogate religious rite testifies to Wilson's belief that good food and good company can occasion rituals that prevail over the dramatic structures they skew. In the same vein, Wilson calls the bawdy song that opens *Seven Guitars,* which is sung soon after a funeral, *"a much needed affirmation of life."*[18] Music always warms hearts in Wilson's plays. Spontaneous musical outbursts occur in *Fences, The Piano Lesson,* and *Seven Guitars,* and professional musicians appear in *Ma Rainey, Fences, The Piano Lesson,* and *Seven Guitars.* As guitarist-blues singer Floyd Barton says in *Seven Guitars,* music promotes health and happiness (45), a point made by Shakespeare in *Twelfth Night,* by Mozart in *The Magic Flute,* and by Edward Albee in *The Death of Bessie Smith* (1959). On the other hand, the absence of music can portend ugliness and grief, as is demonstrated by the broken jukebox in *Two Trains Running* and the white merchant who tries to buy old musical instruments from black families in *The Piano Lesson.*

The musical form closest to sources of black vitality is the blues, according to Wilson. Besides serving as a vehicle through which black people interact, the blues provides a cultural focus for the interaction. Paul Carter Harrison calls it "part of the panoply of expressive strategies" that unify black identity.[19] It follows that Wilson's Ma Rainey says, "White folks don't understand about the blues. . . . You don't sing to feel better. You sing 'cause that's a way of understanding life" (MR, 82). This comprehension has African roots. It relies heavily on the call-and-response, or leader-and-chorus, form of singing used by work gangs to coordinate their physical movements. The blues artists who played in carnival tent shows, circuses, rent parties, and juke joints throughout the South would sometimes flatten the third and seventh notes in the major scale of their basic 12-bar format. In a further violation of tonal purity, blues pianists often rearranged both the hammers and strings of their pianos to mimic the drone and the buzz made by African instruments.

A more significant tonal distortion emerged from the overlapping that would occur in work songs between the voice of the leader and the growls, grunts, and howls of the chorus. By varying the call-and-response pattern of the field holler and embellishing it with hand clapping, field workers achieved several important goals. They developed a private mode of communication that evolved from their common past; they kept alive the spirit that was helping them weather the horrors of slavery; they celebrated that spirit. What's more, they managed these feats in an art form completely their own. "Blues singers nearly always sing about themselves," says Paul Oliver;[20] they convey the protest, anger, and joy of the ordinary and the downtrodden rather than the trials and triumphs of public heroes. This humane outlook tallies with the humble origins of the blues. Robert Palmer explains: "Blues in the [Mississippi] Delta . . . was created not just by black people but by the poorest, most marginal black people. Most of the men and women who sang and played it could neither read nor write. They owned almost nothing and lived in virtual serfdom."[21]

The ability of work gangs to sing about their deprivation and torment is a profoundly creative moral act, suggesting the self-transcendence of the religious mystic. By brightening their ordeals with melody, the gangs confirmed the value of their shared suffering. This confirmation occurred in a style, moreover, that eluded the white slave master, a truth that, besides lending the songs some extra charm and bite, primed the singers' sense of self-worth. Though in thrall, they could flaunt before the master a product of *their* culture without fear of reprisal. Wilson calls the blues "the best literature we have" (Shannon, 204), and Albert Murray prizes it as "an agent of affirmation and continuity in the face of adversity."[22] They're both speaking home. Along with having brought the black oral tradition to the white-owned cotton fields, the blues overcame sorrow by mocking it and replacing it with cheer. Blues music fends off the blues. Like all music, it gives ideas and information an emotional charge. Wilson calls its underlying rhythm of confrontation and optimism a "philosophical system" because its repudiation of surrender and compromise endorses the vitality of his African heritage.[23] In 1984, he discussed this confirmation with Kim Powers: "What I tried to do in Ma Rainey, and in all my work, is to reveal the richness of the lives of people, who show that the largest ideas are contained by their lives and that there is a nobility to their lives. Blacks in America have so little to make life with compared to whites, yet they do so with a certain zest . . . that is fascinating because they make life out of nothing. . . ."[24]

In blues music, there's no approach too crude, no argument too simple, no question too naive. All can be elevated or embellished. Players and listeners of the blues have both intuited this article of faith and abided by it. And so have some modern black American playwrights. Wilson's short one-acter *The Janitor* (1985), for instance, justifies Ed Bullins's claim that the blues is part of "the secret language used in Black Theater" (9). A janitor named Sam is cleaning a ballroom in which a youth conference will be held, presumably within hours. Weary of his broom, Sam steps up to the podium and gives an impromptu speech. The absent young delegates to the conference would probably learn more from him than from the honored speaker who will undoubtedly be paid well to address them later that day. But they'll never hear Sam's words.

The janitor tells his imaginary audience that their lives are seamless and continuous, with each moment adding to an ongoing process of self-unfolding: "You are just what you have been,"[25] he says, anticipating Louise's words in *Seven Guitars,* "Wherever you go you got to carry you with you. You ain't gonna all of a sudden be a different person just cause you in a different city" (72). Life contains no shortcuts or radical shifts of direction, runs Sam's Tolstoyan argument; the future grows from the past. Don't squander the riches of youth, Sam continues, because you may need them one day and find yourself overdrawn. Then Sam's boss enters the hall. Ignoring the speech, he tells Sam to "quit wasting time" (*J,* 1902) and to get back to work. Sam's cowed response,

"Yessuh, Mr. Collins. Yessuh" (*J*, 1902), shows the wisdom it has taken him 56 years to acquire running afoul of his pawn complex. Even *he* puts it aside to avoid rankling his boss.

Wilson sees this blues riff as the stuff of tragedy. In 1995, he called Sam "someone whom this society ignores and someone who may have some very valuable information, someone who has a vital contribution to make, and yet you have relegated him to a position where they sweep the floor" (Shannon, 50). The blues, like Wilson's one-acter, calls attention to the extraordinary lurking within the commonplace. There's more to Sam than his job. Just as we forfeit chances for growth by slighting the janitors we see all the time pushing their brooms in school cafeterias and store lobbies, so would we miss the poetry dwelling in subjects like unemployment, high rents, and low wages had they not been incorporated into the blues (Oliver 1969, 103). Another popular blues motif is travel, sometimes for its own sake. Delta bluesman Robert Nighthawk wrote and played a song called "Prowling Nighthawk" to celebrate his wanderlust. In other blues lyrics, the rambling instinct is reviled as a danger or disease that undermines social bonds and moral responsibility.

Often a blues lyric delivers its charge either indirectly or ambiguously. By "signifying," that is, criticizing a practice or a person obliquely rather than head on, bluesmen could extend their range of both reference and popular appeal. Many of them eked out enough money on downtown street corners, at rent parties, or in barn dances to avoid the backbreaking toil of sharecropping. As Oliver points out, blues audiences paid well to hear songs about sexual love (1969, 104), a subject that, in its more frenzied aspects, put a salt edge on the subtleties so popular elsewhere in the blues. As in medieval ballads like "Lord Randal" and "Barbara Allen," love emerges from many blues lyrics as an emotion to be both sought and fled. Texas and Arkansas blues artist Robert Johnson (1911–1938) recounts the pain of unrequited love in "Love in Vain." Its ironic title withal, Johnson's "Kindhearted Woman Blues," like the Lester Young tune "Laughing to Keep from Crying," charts the destructiveness of erotic love; Johnson's kindhearted woman has studied evil to learn how to kill him more effectively and heartlessly.

Blues audiences craved songs dealing with the risks and dangers of erotic love. Eros soon dominated the genre. Prefiguring the deaths of the gangsta rap stars Tupac Shakur in 1996 and Biggie Smalls in 1997, many blues singers absorbed the darkness they sang about. Some did jail time; some died of knife wounds, bullet wounds, or poison. "Blues was so disreputable" in the American South, says Palmer, "that even its staunchest devotees frequently found it prudent to disown it" (17). The denouncers of blues as Satan's music found support for their attacks. Many early blues lyrics included references to devil lore; Petie Whitestraw recorded "Kidnapper's Blues" for Decca. Robert Johnson claimed Satan as an inspiration. Tunes of his like "Hellhound on My Trail" and "Me and the Devil Blues," which was released on Vocalion, included lyrics such as "Me and the Devil both walkin' side by side" and "Hello, Satan, I believe it's time to go." But perhaps his demonic streak cuts its widest swath in "Cross Road Blues," the words of which support Palmer's claim that "the crossroads is the place where aspiring musicians strike their deals with the devil" (126). Johnson's tormented bluesman, who's advisedly called Bob, believes his soul is sinking hellwards. He prays to the Lord in vain. He's alone; he has no family or friends to help him; above all, "no lovin' sweet woman" will assuage his grief.

This grief sharpens when viewed in the context of Western cultural history. Thomas Mann's *Buddenbrooks* (1901) and *Doctor Faustus* (1948) voiced the belief that music is not only the purest and most sublime of the arts but also, because it takes so little of its savor from everyday reality, the most seductive both morally and spiritually. Any listener of Johnson's music should recall that Oedipus killed his father at a crossroads named Phocis. That the victims of the only two onstage killings in Wilson's plays are both professional musicians focuses the many Satanic references in the plays. "God hate niggers!" (98) exclaims a character in *Ma Rainey* after saying, "if there's a god up there, he done went to sleep" (43). Both of these statements reflect Wilson's belief that the white man's god is irrelevant to African Americans and should be ignored by them. Not only does God shrink from easing their woes; he also deepens them. The ex-church deacon Herald Loomis in *Joe Turner* is dragooned into a chain gang while preaching Christian writ to some gamblers.

Why shouldn't Loomis and his kind reach into their African race memory and invoke the devil, a product of the same belief system that gave rise to the tribal songs, juju, and herbal medicine they grew up with? The devil could possibly quiet the pain inflicted upon them by white man's justice. The long-term threat he poses can count less to the downtrodden and the desperate than the benefits he can bestow today. He knows how to promote those benefits. A musician in *Seven Guitars* says, "God speak in a whisper and the devil shout," and he's answered by a fellow band member, "They say God have planned but the devil have planned also" (45). Satan knows how to package his temptations. A pianist in *Ma Rainey* admits, "The devil's strong. The devil ain't no pushover" (45), after hearing a story about a rich Alabama blacksmith who killed a man for warming up to his girlfriend. Because of his pact with the devil, the blacksmith was acquitted—and given a bottle of whiskey by the judge. Hearing this story unsettles the trumpeter Levee, who may have heard others like it. A recurring theme in the blues lyrics of his day, the 1920s, was the belief that Satan would confer musical mastery upon any player willing to hand over his soul.

Wilson's own awareness of Satan finds indirect expression in Sandra Shannon's reading of his commitment to his black cultural heritage: "For Wilson as a black man in America, finding his song means going back to the forgotten regions of his African past, bypassing the influence of his father's German ancestry to confront head-on the painful elements of his mother's history as an African woman who lives in America" (12). Now Wilson couldn't respond to the black experience in America without probing his African roots. The force of his Africanness declares itself viscerally. By unearthing those deposits of his African ancestry lodged in his race memory, he can find wholeness. A key figure in African myth, P. C. Harrison explains, is the trickster, Eshu, whose "wit, cunning, guile, and a godly sense of self-empowerment . . . accords him [the right to perform] extravagant transgressions" (301–2) . This enemy of the status quo calls forth the combat myth of white Western culture. His guile and cunning remind us that one of Satan's specialties has always been the disguise. Satan needs disguises because his role as God's adversary (the name *Lucifer* means *the adversary*) is one of opposition, and he must hide his identity from his would-be victims.

A favorite disguise has been that of the pseudonym. Advisedly, the oppressed outsider August Wilson changed his name, as did Martha Loomis, or Martha Pentecost, of *Joe Turner,* who defected to Christ after losing hope of reuniting with the husband who had disappeared 11 years before. By discarding the riches of her racial unconscious, Martha committed an act of apostasy. But her husband, Herald, is also an apostate. Not only did he join the church; he also became a deacon. Yes, the moral issue he invokes is smudged, but in a way consistent with Western cultural tradition. Like Prometheus, Satan emerges as man's friend. He fosters intellectual inquiry. And because the imaginative freedom he prizes threatens the status quo, the rebellion he embodies—and suffers for—holds the seeds of artistic and technical innovation. This foe of orthodoxy lights up places of darkness.

Precursors and Influences

Some of this illumination could even brighten the outlook for blacks in education, employment, and housing. Wilson's racialism fits somewhere between the militancy of Baraka and Bullins and the multiculturalism of Ralph Ellison, as is seen in his adaptations, especially in *Fences,* of Western stage conventions. Exactly where it fits is elusive. For one thing, his racial anger has remained strong. His insistence on using a black director has held up the filming of both *Fences* and *Two Trains Running*.[26] Being brought up without a father in the home left deep scars. He has never spoken well of Frederick August Kittel, Sr.; he bolted the church, the school, and the army, three authoritarian systems he might have seen as father surrogates; the father-son conflict permeates his work. What's more, a father's death has often freed his spirit. As has been seen, he decided to become a writer the same year (1965) his blood father died. His first marriage, to Brenda Burton, took place in 1969 within a month of the death of a stepfather with whom he often quarreled (Brown, 118). That his marriage lasted only three years, which was also the time span of an army enlistment that was cut short after a year, puts an intriguing spin on his attitude toward male authority. On the one hand, he finds the archetypal father stifling. On the other, he's drawn to it. Most of his plays center on larger-than-life, perhaps heroic, figures who crave the very authority they buck. The subject of the term paper that ended his formal education in the ninth grade was Napoleon.

The surrogate father has resurfaced often in his life. An early example is ex-boxer Charley Burley, who seized Wilson's attention for several reasons, including Wilson's love of boxing. Like Wilson, Burley was a financially strapped Pittsburgh Negro whose talent lacked outlets. His problem was that he couldn't book fights; no middleweight contender wanted to fight him. To support himself in the ring, he had to fight bigger, heavier foes. Even future light-heavyweight champion Archie Moore dodged him after losing to him in April 1944.[27] Another father surrogate Wilson fixed on was also an outsider among his peers, artist Romare Bearden (1912–1988). Perhaps Bearden first captured Wilson's attention because he resembled Wilson in being a mixed-race Pittsburgher. Though Wilson never met him, he admired Bearden enough to write a laudatory foreword to a 1990 biography of the artist (by Myron Schwartzman), and he used Bearden's collages as starting points for *Joe Turner* and *The Piano Lesson.*

In recent years, Wilson's mentor has been Lloyd Richards, director of all six of the Broadway productions. Richards has been artistic director of Yale's Repertory Theater, Dean of the Yale Drama School, and director of the Eugene O'Neill Playwrights' Conference in Waterford, Connecticut, where he helped further the careers of dramatists like John Guare, Wendy Wasserstein, and David Henry Hwang.[28] In 1982, he accepted an early draft of *Ma Rainey* for workshopping at the O'Neill; the intensive rewriting, revising, and polishing he encouraged Wilson to undertake helped launch one of the most productive theatrical teams of the century.

But perhaps Richards's help with the typescript of *Ma Rainey* wasn't the first service he performed for the budding playwright. He had already directed Lorraine Hansberry's *Raisin in the Sun* (1958), the first play written by a black to win the New York Drama Critics' Circle Award. This breakthrough helped other blacks work their way into the theatrical mainstream. The Broadway stage was still white dominated when *Ma Rainey* premiered in 1984, even though black talent had been making inroads in the theater. Lonne Elder's *Ceremonies in Dark Old Men* (1968) was the first play by a black writer to be nominated for a Pulitzer Prize. The prize did go to Charles Gordone two years later for *No Place to Be Somebody*. Other awards followed. Joseph Wallace's *The River Niger* won a Tony as best play of 1975, and Charles Fuller's *A Soldier's Play* claimed the Pulitzer in 1982 without having played on Broadway. Other successes include the musicals *Bubbling Brown Sugar, Ain't Misbehavin',* and, most notably, *The Wiz,* which won seven Tonys in 1975 and ran for nearly four years on Broadway.

The white producers and directors whose support encouraged this success imply a multicultural appeal that Wilson hasn't identified. And neither have most of his non-Caucasian critics. The Indian Kim Pereira speaks of his "structuring his plays around the rituals, folklore, and music of Africans and African Americans,"[29] and Harrison puts him in the same "expressive continuum" as Langston Hughes, Toni Morrison, and Thelonious Monk (294). But his reference to Wilson's use of Egyptian myth in the plays (313) sends out two reminders: first, that the Eurocentric literary tradition Wilson grew up with would have been much more convenient for any American to draw upon and, second, that this Euro-American literary strain would also exert more unconscious influence than the Egyptian on a writer who lists Dylan Thomas, Samuel Beckett, and Edward Albee among his favorite writers (Shannon, 19, 30). Yes, the five Wilson plays following *Ma Rainey* include only one white speaking part (in *Joe Turner*). Wilson can also be trusted when he says that, as a playwright, he wants to look at the most pressing issues facing African Americans in each of the decades of the century.[30] On the other hand, the many similarities between him and mainstream white writers show his imagination vibrating to the same creative spirit that gave life to the literary mainstream. Like Henry Fielding, he'll confront suffering without yielding to it or sugarcoating it. The early nineteenth century also supplies an instructive, if unlikely, parallel. Wilson's sensitivity to mood and atmosphere, skill as a social comedian, and unsparing insight into motives all recall Jane Austen.

Leaping ahead a couple of centuries, we can see Wilson merging the autobiographical and the arcane with the flair of a James Joyce (his mother's two-room Bedford Street flat stood above Bella's grocery store,[31] where Troy Maxson buys bread in *Fences* [7]). The practice from *Ulysses* of "almosting it" finds its way into *Seven Guitars*. Just as Joyce's Everyman figure, Leopold Bloom, comes close to clinching several financial deals, so does bluesman Floyd Barton graze wealth. Had he demanded royalties based on a percentage of the sales of his hit record "That's All Right," rather than settling for a flat fee, his earnings would have equaled his popularity. *Fences* contains an instructive parallel with another great Western writer, Tolstoy. The play's last scene shows all the surviving members of Troy Maxson's family gathering for his funeral. This unity reflects proper family values. Troy, on the other hand, obeyed only the letter of the family imperative. Mostly, he fantasized about extending his freedom. Though he loved his wife, Rose, he also downgraded his 18 years with her as a trap and a dead end. Wilson would dispute his claim that his marriage put his life on hold. Like Tolstoy, Wilson believes that the best life is the one that forgoes some personal freedom to bask in the warmth and depth provided by a loving family.

Admittedly, Wilson may not know *War and Peace*. And even if he has read it, he might not have been influenced by it. Yet perhaps something greater than chance has dovetailed one of his basic ideas about family dynamics with one of Tolstoy's. His treatment of the idea differs, perforce, from Tolstoy's because he uses different character types, writes in a different genre, and anchors his insights in a different cultural milieu. On the other hand, their basic agreement in outlook shows the writers sharing the same family values. This likeness turns the mind to others. Much of Wilson's belief system and aesthetic practice fuses neatly with the assumptions undergirding Western cultural tradition, a fusion that might explain his great popularity with white playgoers (Gates, 47–50).

And the spell he has exerted upon white theater critics, too? Nadel has spoken of his practice of drawing upon "Euro-American dramatic forms, only to reinvent them,"[32] and Savran finds in each of his plays a mixture of "European and African elements"; in all of Wilson, Savran argues, "the conflict between African and European plays itself out . . . in a tension between the structures of the well-made play and an impulse toward jazz-inspired improvisation and poetic form" (290).

Some of the comparisons with Western theater Wilson has inspired are both more pointed and far ranging. His commentators' attempts to place him, to describe his moral and social values, and to account for his greatness have begotten comparisons all over the theatrical map. Matthew C. Roudané compares him to O'Neill, Arthur Miller, and Tennessee Williams.[33] Sandra Shannon credits him with a Shakespearean preeminence (91). But then Holly Hill, jumping ahead some 300 years and invoking a wildly different sensibility, compares some of the verbal byplay in *Ma Rainey* to that found in Noël Coward's *Hay Fever* (89). Switching sensibilities again, one might liken Wilson's juxtapositions of myth and reality to those of Sam Shepard. Both Shepard and Wilson believe that the continuities joining past and present have given today's Americans a unified national history.

A playwright more gentle and lovable than Shepard but one just as deft in portraying his nation's psyche by means of random-sounding but carefully controlled dialogue is Chekhov. But does this kinship imply one between Chekhov and Wilson? Wilson denies any similarity between himself and Chekhov (Nadel, 126). But could he be wrong? Both writers have the rare gift of creating dramatic tension from small events and well-observed details, like the bottle of Coca-Cola Ma Rainey insists on holding during her recording sessions. Then there is the profusion of Chekhovian elements in *Two Trains Running,* starting with the sugar bowl the undertaker West always asks for after ordering coffee but then usually ignores. The restaurant where West sips his unsweetened coffee is slated for demolition in the name of urban renewal. Nor is the demolition unjust. The neighborhood has decayed; gone are the supermarket, the five-and-ten, the cobbler, the doctor, and the dentist that once gave it vibrancy. Memphis Lee's restaurant has lost so much trade that its larder has dwindled to little more than half a box of rice and some frozen hamburger. Yet the razing of this old neighborhood landmark causes the same regret as the flattening and subsequent conversion into dachas of the Ranevskys' cherry orchard.

Other similarities come to mind. Like Chekhov's 1904 play about Russia's doomed aristocracy, *Two Trains Running* is a quiet, relatively plotless work that lacks a central character. Its quietness counterpoints the commotion surrounding it. Antiwar protesters are agitating. The assassinations of both Robert Kennedy and Dr. Martin Luther King took place less than a year before the play's present-tense action, as did the clamorous 1968 Democratic Party convention in Chicago. Yet most of the moody, autumnal characters ponder their lost opportunities while waiting for new ones to come along and lift their spirits.[34] Their wait may be protracted. Much of the dialogue wheels in tired Chekhovian circles, inciting little that's new or fresh. An ex-bank robber turns out to be gentle and sweet natured. Handguns are brandished but not fired.

The same sense of suspended action suffuses *The Piano Lesson,* the main figure of which follows Lopakhin of *The Cherry Orchard* in wanting to buy the very tract of land his slave ancestors had farmed. *Seven Guitars* recalls Chekhov's insistence that a handgun displayed in a story or play must be fired before the work's finale. A character in *Seven Guitars is* shot, though not by one of the handguns displayed in the action. In an irony worthy of Chekhov, the fatal shot occurs both offstage and out of hearing; as a final fillip, the victim never appears before us, not even as a walk-on. A final thwarting of both consequence and closure in the dry-eyed Chekhovian vein occurs in Floyd Barton's death, a loss discussed by his mourners in the play's first scene. Although Chicago beckons Floyd as Moscow did the three Prozorov sisters, he'll never again glimpse his heavenly city.

How closely does Wilson's work hew to the Eurocentric mainstream theater of which Chekhov is a pillar? Are there any other dramatists besides Chekhov that Wilson resembles? Writing in the *{St. Louis} Riverfront Times* about Robert Brustein's February 1997 debate with Wilson on the subject of black theater and race-based casting, Joe Pollack speaks of "Chekhovian overtones" in Wilson's plays.[35] He also cites the belief of Douglas Turner Ward, founder of the Negro Ensemble Company, that the "almost constant" alienation depicted by Sean O'Casey (1880–1964) makes O'Casey's plays natural vehicles for black actors. Turner's statement evokes the uncanny similarity in both attitude and technique between Wilson and his Irish forebear. Both writers avoid using upper- or middle-class settings. *The Plough and the Stars* (1926) takes place mostly in a working-class Dublin pub; Memphis Lee's restaurant, where *Two Trains Running* unfolds, stands in a

Pittsburgh slum. Next, in these plays and elsewhere, both Wilson and O'Casey supply stage directions written with an eloquence and an analytical drive that offset brilliantly the vernacular speech of the players.

Each man, more importantly, rates facts over doctrine. To ensure human survival, political theory must yield to the patience and compassion that brighten the daily plod of living. In Wilson's plays as well as in O'Casey's, those endowed with the gifts of cooperation, support, and nurture are usually women. "Wilson's women embody love and laughter, strength and pathos," said Joan Fishman, citing virtues equally descriptive of many of the women in O'Casey.[36] Mimi Kramer's 1990 statement about gender differences in Wilson's work, finally, applies just as strictly to O'Casey: "Wilson's plays are divided in two—between earth, represented by women and home, and mysticism, embodied in the men who travel around in a world no part of which, they feel, can ever be theirs."[37]

Wilson agrees with Ralph Ellison's belief that "the lower-class Negro family is matriarchal."[38] The men in Wilson's plays shirk their share of the domestic load because of their blindness to nearest things. Like their male counterparts in O'Casey, they embrace grandiose ideals the pursuit of which loosens their ties to their homes in favor of dangerous, life-threatening acts. Sometimes, they go to jail or die. "Who needs that kind of love?" asks a woman in *Seven Guitars* in reference to a niece of hers named Ruby, who was being courted by two men, one now "in the ground and the other in jail" (31). The fight between Leroy and Elmore that killed one of them and put the other in jail started because of the men's overheated reactions to Ruby. By contrast, Ruby knows the pitfalls of such excess. When asked by one of her suitors to define her feelings, she recalls saying, "I told him the truth. I didn't love neither one of them. They both was nice in their own ways" (*7G,* 73).

One of the women she's talking to agrees that passion unchecked by reason can cause havoc. "I tell them [her panting lovers], 'If you got blood in your eye, then you can't see good.' What I want with a blind man?" (*7G,* 73). The same woman had earlier told a lover who had abandoned her for 18 months, "You are one of them special people who is supposed to have everything just the way they want it" (13). Rose Maxson of *Fences* and Berniece Charles of *The Piano Lesson* are widowed because their men, like O'Casey's IRA zealots, overreach themselves. Sometimes, it's sheer wanderlust that breaks up families in Wilson.

Wining Boy, the itinerant blues pianist in *The Piano Lesson,* gave up everything for the road. "Couldn't nothing keep me still," he says. "Much as I loved Cleotha, I loved to ramble."[39] Though he later admits that, in his wife, Cleotha, he "done known a good woman" (32), his rambling proves that the open road meant more to him than the prospect of building a home with her.

Wilson's women, by contrast, enjoy nesting. The wastefulness of their men has forced them to be practical and sensible, even guarded. Berniece's defenses go up immediately in *The Piano Lesson* when her brother, Boy Willie, storms into the house she occupies with her uncle and her 11-year-old daughter. Within five minutes of his arrival, she asks him when he's planning to leave (7). She knows that he has brought disruption with him. Nor can she be blamed for trying to avoid it. Her husband was killed in a heist that Boy Willie helped organize three years before. Like the heroine in *The Plough and the Stars,* who gets shot to death by a stray bullet, Wilson's women often pay for their men's schoolboy heroics. Rose Maxson is content to cook Troy's dinner and keep clean sheets on the bed (*F,* 98), and Bertha Holly, another homemaker, says in *Joe Turner,* "That's all anybody needs. To have love in one hand and laughter in the other."[40]

She takes her own counsel. Friendly and warm, Bertha introduces Herald Loomis and his daughter, Zonia, to the other boarders at her and her husband's rooming house. She offers biscuits and coffee to the Loomises, to her boarder Bynum, and to her husband's trading partner, the white traveling salesman Rutherford Selig. When Loomis's time at the boarding house runs out, she tries to help him find lodgings nearby, and she tells him that he's *"welcome* to some breakfast" (*JT,* 85; emphasis added) rather than being entitled to it. Fortunately for her, her husband leads a stable life, working at three jobs and coming home each night to help with the chores. Other women in the Wilson canon aren't so lucky. One boarder at the Hollys', Molly Cunningham, speaks of the tendency of some men to conceive babies and then flee the nest (*JT,* 62). (A pregnant woman is abandoned by her lover in O'Casey's *Juno and the Paycock* {1924}). The number of men in Wilson who have served jail terms shows their truancy to be often extended, if not permanent. Troy Maxson's 15 years in prison stopped him from raising his son Lyons. But what effect did this long sentence have on Lyons's mother? That she's neither discussed nor even named implies that the ordeal of being an inner-city solo mom might have crushed her.

Coping with Diaspora

Families in Wilson's plays break apart for reasons other than male delin-
quency. Blacks in America have been twice displaced—from Africa and
then from the rural South, where they had created their own culture
after arriving in the colonies as slaves in 1619. The Great Migration
refers to the mass flight by black farm workers to the urban North,
where they expected to find well-paying factory jobs. Wilson believes
that the black exodus from the agrarian South was a mistake (Pettengill,
215–18), even though white southern landowners resisted selling farmland to the offspring of their former slaves. First, this exodus fragmented
many black families. Next, the cities of the industrial North spurned the
new black migrants, herding them into slums and offering, at best,
backbreaking work at low pay. The readiest reprieve from this regimen
was crime. Even Wilson's law-abiding jobholders feel deprived of comfort, security, and a sense of racial pride. A woman in *Seven Guitars* says
after hearing from a suitor that he always keeps his trunk packed,
"That's what the problem is now. Everybody keeps their trunk packed"
(28). How can a couple build a relationship if each of them keeps glancing toward the door? The question of stability recurs often in Wilson.
Most of his people fret over questions of identity and self-determination.
What should their lives be like? they wonder. What do they want? *The
Janitor* affirmed both the value and the importance of menial labor.
There's nothing wrong with being a janitor. No janitor should feel
ashamed of his job despite the tendency of whites and upwardly mobile
blacks to look down on him.

But Wilson's janitor sees *himself* as a victim (Savran, 300). How to
escape the racism and exploitation that creates losers? Blacks *can* better
themselves by assimilating into the dominant white culture. But the
adoption of European values forces them to negate their cultural identity. "Look at the way you dressed," says a blues pianist in *Ma Rainey* to
a colleague. "That ain't African. That's the white man. We trying to be
just like him. . . . We's imitation white men" (94). African Americans
can only buy dignity and prestige by renouncing their defining marks.
But they want to participate in and contribute to American culture as
African Americans. Wilson has explained how both the content and the
style of black America differ from those of the European mainstream:
"They [black people] have African sensibilities, they actually do things
differently, see the world differently. . . . Black Americans—we decorate
our houses differently, we have different values. We value style. We

value linguistic ability. . . . We bury our dead differently. . . . We just happen to be over here in America, but we are still African. Although the geography is different, the culture is strong and very much alive."[41]

This culture needs to be protected and nurtured. Wilson wants his fellow black Americans to accept their African heritage and to behave like Africans, taking pride in their origins. The internalization of African values will lead to a self-definition and empowerment that blacks need to survive. But they can flourish rather than merely survive if they forsake the quick tempo and arrogance of the industrial North in favor of attuning themselves to ancestral origins bound up with the ordeals of slavery and sharecropping. Pereira details some of the issues rising from Wilson's belief that today's blacks ignore the health and wholeness available to them in their African roots: "Pivotal to the theme of reunion in Wilson's plays is the underlying premise to which he constantly returns—that the solutions for the future lie in the past. Clues to the identity of black Americans are strewn along a cultural trail that leads backward through slavery all the way to Africa. Only in spiritual communion with this rich heritage will blacks realize an understanding of their true worth" (5).

Jay Plum calls Wilson's theater "an opportunity for the black community to examine and define itself" because Wilson's people carry within themselves, in the form of ancestral retentions, a mother lode of African myths, rituals, and folkways (562). The subtext of the plays puts forth an alternative history—history that never happened but could have. Harrison's commentary on *Joe Turner,* "The play operates outside the logic of naturalism," defying "fixed expectations of cause and effect," applies to the whole canon (314). Wilson will abandon realism to combine the worlds of matter and spirit, of tragedy and knockabout, in a way familiar to African Americans. It was from Jorge Luis Borges (1899–1986) that Wilson learned how to overthrow the logic of everyday in favor of disclosing the inner workings of reality. The recurrence of portents, omens, and ghosts in the plays emphasizes the otherworldly at the expense of factual verification. Often, facts themselves are disputable. Bertha Holly of *Joe Turner,* for instance, disclaims Rutherford Selig's right to be called the People Finder. But Selig is only called the People Finder by others; he never applies the epithet to himself. Wilson likes to leave such issues unresolved. Opposing Berniece Charles's insistence in *The Piano Lesson* that her brother, Boy Willie, killed the white landowner Sutter to get his land is her uncle Doaker's claim that Sutter was killed by ghosts. Then the numbers runner Wolf defies the others in

Two Trains Running by supporting the white butcher Lutz's decision to withhold the ham that Hambone insists he deserves.

Dissent like Wolf's runs high in Wilson's plays. Rather than resolving it, though, Wilson prefers to give evidence on both sides of an argument in order to rouse the playgoer's mental activity. On this score, he resembles not only Bertolt Brecht but also the Sophocles of *Antigone.* The neutrality of Doaker's remark about the quarrel over the Charles family piano in *The Piano Lesson* posits a clash between two rights rather than one between a right and a wrong: "Ain't nobody said nothing about who's right and who's wrong. . . . Berniece ain't gonna sell it" (46). Still in the sphere of music, the dispute over which version of "Ma Rainey's Black Bottom" will be used to accompany Ma's vocal suggests that both versions rehearsed by the band have valid claims. Wilson's practice of invoking issues beyond the scope of objective truth stems from his belief that vast unseen presences influence and perhaps even rule black lives and that these presences defy the strictures of the Christian-democratic West. Neither reason nor common sense, for example, explains Memphis Lee's prohibition against Wolf's accepting numbers on the restaurant's phone. Memphis uses Wolf to broker his own numbers bets. No careless inconsistencies or cowardly acts of irresolution, the imponderables in Wilson's theater invoke truths beyond the issue at hand. Vera's statement in *Seven Guitars,* "The Bible says some things ain't for you to know" (5), invites larger meanings grazed in the plays.

Her words offer help. One of life's greatest privileges may well consist of living in mystery and doubt. Lacking an answer to every question that confronts us encourages faith, reminding us that God wants the human and divine realms kept separate and that one of heaven's purposes is to answer questions that defy earthly reason. God's impenetrability could well confirm his existence. The Bible often favors paradox over uniformity because, like irony and contradiction, paradox comes closer to grasping those incomprehensible forces that regulate life. Yet the presence in the Wilson canon of conjure men, ghosts, and a 322-year-old prophetess (in *Two Trains*) who speaks in riddles calls up truths beyond the scope of Christian writ.

The African-based magic in Wilson implies that African Americans have both a different savior and a different concept of salvation than white people do. This magic, Wilson believes, will cue a black person to his or her hidden self, which is perhaps the only self that matters. Aunt Ester, the prophetess in *Two Trains,* descends from the witches and enchantresses of universal legend. This foe of male greed dismantles the foundations of her society's capitalist ethic by telling her clients to throw $20 into the Monongahela River. She's testing their strength and spiritual depth. Though she disorients them, her motive is that of the legendary *sauvage;* she's offering growth through the adoption of unorthodox forms of connectedness and radical alternatives. Male counterparts of Aunt Ester in *Joe Turner* and *Seven Guitars* also dismantle the underpinning of the capitalist West, displacing reason with epistemologies rooted in African juju.

Christianity per se is not the enemy, even though its glorification of sacrifice and obedience has encouraged black subservience in the United States. Despite Hedley's perversion of it in *Seven Guitars,* Christian faith anchors Cutler's moral stability and courage in *Ma Rainey;* it gives Rose Maxson of *Fences* an important outlet for her energies after her marriage to Troy sours; and it offers the ex-Mississippi sharecropper Avery Brown a vocation in *Piano Lesson.* Wilson's 1987 statement to Ishmael Reed, "God does not hear the prayers of blacks,"[42] presumes the Judeo-Christian God's irrelevancy to, rather than hatred of, blacks, as is claimed in Levee's shocking "God hate niggers" tirade (*MR,* 98). Though Avery does get the financing to start his church, he fails to exorcise the ghost that invades the Charles home in *Piano Lesson;* only the spirits of Berniece's ancestors can drive out Sutter's shade. Herald Loomis's blasphemous outburst at the end of *Joe Turner* is as angry and shocking as Levee's in *Ma Rainey.* And like Levee's, it voices resentment over having passively accepted for so many years the irrelevancies of Christian dogma. When Loomis's wife quotes the passage from Psalms 23, "Thou preparest a table for me in the presence of my enemies," he counters with the words, "And all I seen was a bunch of niggers dazed out of their woolly heads. And Mr. Jesus Christ standing there in the middle of them, grinning" (*JT,* 92).

This irreverence helps Loomis defy one of the major tenets of the New Testament. He replies to Martha's imperative that he be washed in the blood of the lamb by slashing his chest. Vision comes to him, as it did to Christ, in pain and terror. It also gives him a self-sufficiency that puts him beyond the Christian pale. But, intriguingly, not past the codes and guidelines of Yankee transcendentalism; his act of washing himself in his own blood ("I don't need nobody to bleed for me! I can bleed for myself," he peals [*JT,* 93]) sounds a chord as plangent as any put forth by Ralph Waldo Emerson. The chord recurs in a minor key in *Seven Guitars* in Floyd Barton's lament, "God is in his heaven and staying there" (40). Floyd wants God to show his loving hand by relieving the pain that seems to be everywhere. Either God's not omniscient or he condones our pain, Floyd reasons; otherwise "he would do something about it" (40).

Seven Guitars, which includes a recitation of the Lord's Prayer (50), just as *Joe Turner* does one from the 23rd Psalm, also puts forth in non-Christian terms the notion of death's superiority to life. A believer in natural justice, Canewell faults Jesus for resurrecting Lazarus: "See, all Jesus had done by raising him from the dead was to cause him to go through that much more suffering. He was suffering the pain of the living" (*7G,* 26). Again, a key passage in Wilson invokes New England transcendentalism, Canewell's view of death as both deliverer and friend chiming with Walt Whitman's on the subject. But is this view a morbid exaggeration of Whitman's? Canewell's statement, "Death is fairer than life" (*7G,* 51), implies a pessimism rivaling that of August Strindberg. Yet Canewell gives Vera a goldenseal plant, the leaves of which supposedly have great healing powers. Perhaps he's acting from an ancestral retention. Tallying with the lyrics of Floyd Barton's hit song "That's All Right" is Canewell's belief in the value of unrequited love. Canewell will hold no grudge against a woman who discards him for another man. Accepting the flaws and failings of the human heart, he welcomes love of any kind.

Nearly all of Wilson's plays contain a choric figure, or *raisonneur.* Playing that role in *Seven Guitars,* Canewell helps develop Wilson's portrayal of both the bright and the dark side of the dynamism exerted by the play's African sources. As his 10-play cycle about the black experience in the twentieth century unfolds, so does his awareness of his characters' cultural debt. The compatibility of Canewell's redemptive attitude toward love with the Christian doctrine of turning the other cheek runs aground on the belief that Jesus's raising of Lazarus was a mistake. Perhaps we lack the information to wrest meaning from this apparent contradiction. But what if we do? It's possible that Wilson's future forays into his heritage will either dismiss the contradiction as irrelevant to his people or resolve it in some grand synthesis. If neither step is taken, we can seek out an answer for ourselves. Failing this solution, we can comfort ourselves with the idea, which Wilson presumably sets store by, that certain imponderables will only attain clarity in the forever.

Chapter Two
In Lieu of Justice

Writing in 1997, Carla J. McDonough explains that, in 1990, the job-less rate for black males in the United States was twice as high as that for whites. Hundreds of thousands of African Americans thus lacked the chance to gain self-validation through work. Their frustration has led many of them to prize masculinity over community in the forms of fam-ily, home, and neighborhood.[1] Speeding their quest for social legitimacy is that mockery of Emersonian self-reliance, the handgun. In America today, black impatience over being denied equal rights outweighs Emer-son's impatience with the courtly muses of Europe 150 years ago. Emer-son's exhortation that we be bold and brave and that we trust the uni-verse because God and self are one lacks both the instant prestige and glamour conferred by carrying a firearm. Wilson's deployment of firearms in his work tallies with McDonough's view of them as "symbols of virility and power that compensate for the lack of other more legiti-mate markers . . . such as employment" (156). In *Two Trains*, Memphis Lee indicts those attending a local rally to honor Malcolm X for being unrealistic: "Talking about black power with their hands and their pock-ets empty. You can't do nothing without a gun."[2] The younger Sterling takes his words to heart. Though only days out of jail, this ex-bank rob-ber has already despaired of finding work. The handgun he buys may well land him back in prison within two weeks of its purchase, as Mem-phis predicts (*2TR*, 79).

He won't feel lonely behind bars. "I'll give you a dollar for every nigger you find that ain't been to jail" (*2TR,* 54), says Wolf, who has done time for obstructing justice. Other jailable crimes for blacks, as evidenced by Wilson's plays, include having either too little or too much money (*7G*, 42), busking (*7G*, 23), and assault and battery (*MR*, 49). Troy Maxson of *Fences* spends 15 years in jail for killing a man. His son Cory's outlook may be just as grim. As a marine, he leads a semi-institutionalized life, which exposes him to greater risk of death than he'd face as a civilian. And what if he *does* see his enlistment through without getting wounded or killed? *Fences* makes the point that black combat veterans of World War II, including battlefield casualties, found themselves adrift after mustering out of service. Ex-GI August Wilson includes himself in this sad equation, even though he served in the peacetime army. "Most black talent is wasted," he said in 1987, adding, "I'll tell you honestly, if I weren't doing this [writing plays], I might be out shooting drugs, or probably be in a penitentiary."[3] How can his judgment be faulted? The black-written plays *All White Caste* by Ben Caldwell, *The Breakout* by Charles (Oyami) Gordon, and *Ladies in Waiting* by Peter De Anola all take place in jails.

Ordeals of the Oppressed

Wilson didn't need to go to prison himself to believe that whites have always colonized blacks in America. His Troy Maxson, Herald Loomis, and Boy Willie Charles all wrestle not only with their private demons but also with the spirit of oppression that has fragmented their people for centuries. The fragmentation takes different forms in the plays. The young guitarist Jeremy Furlow of *Joe Turner* loses his first job after being released from prison because he refused to skim 50¢ from his weekly salary of $8 for a white foreman. Now he faces the ordeal of spending nights in a tarpaper shack under one of Pittsburgh's bridges and scavenging for food by day. This same ordeal turned a desperate Troy Maxson to a life of crime, which ended with a 15-year jail term. This term began in 1919. Eight years earlier, Seth Holly of *Joe Turner* was working as a vegetable gardener and a tinsmith while running a boarding house with his wife. Yet he can only get the financing to open his own shop by using his house as collateral. Acting sensibly, he rejects this arrangement. Blacks feel just as stymied in 1927 Chicago, where *Ma Rainey* unfolds. They can't hire a cab, cash a check, or expect promises made to them by whites to be kept. Most of them are stuck in their small, crowded cold-water flats or dingy rented rooms.

The social legislation that tempts Wilson's blacks with middle-class respectability also constrains them. Blacks can't participate in a society whose traditions and institutions have always kept them down. At risk, Wilson told Bill Moyers, is the richness and complexity of black life: "The social contract that white America has given blacks is that if you want to participate in society you have to deny who you are. You cannot participate in this society as Africans" (177). No people should adapt if adaptation requires them to silence their songs.

The fullest analysis of black disempowerment in the plays comes in a long speech by Holloway in act 1, scene 2 of *Two Trains*. The speech opens thus: "People kill me talking about niggers is lazy. Niggers is the most hard-working people in the world. Worked three hundred years for free. And didn't take no lunch hour. Now all of a sudden niggers is lazy. Don't know how to work. All of a sudden when they got to pay niggers, ain't no work for him to do" (34). Holloway is arguing that white people always found plenty of work to keep blacks busy in the days of free slave labor. Even after emancipation, white industrialists paid their ex-slaves a pittance to lay railroad ties, build highways, and sink telephone poles. They invested wisely. By employing thousands at three dollars a day (Holloway's "stacking niggers" conceit [*2TR*, 35]), they created utilities that could last a century. But now that these utilities are in place, they've eliminated several major outlets for black labor. As Toledo says in *Ma Rainey*, blacks have become the leftovers from history (27). The jobs they once did no longer exist—perhaps because they did them so well. Because white society never cared enough about black children to educate them or to house them properly, they can't compete for jobs created by technological developments ranging from the internal combustion engine to the microchip.

Yet black Americans could have done more to resist the fallout caused by this plunder and outrage. A character in *Jitney*, Wilson's unpublished 1982 play about Pittsburgh's gypsy cab drivers, exclaims, "I seen a hundred niggers too lazy to get up out the bed in the morning, talking about the white man is against them. That's just an excuse."[4] Hedley's practice of blaming whitey for his own failings in *Seven Guitars* is another easy way out. A character in Joseph A. Walker's *Odido* says that blacks are their own worst enemies, and much of what develops in Wilson's work supports the character's claim. Toledo of *Ma Rainey* blames the collective black passion for fun: "The more niggers get killed having a good time, the more good times niggers want to have" (41). Later, he argues that black people lack a sense of consequence; blacks are so enchanted by the fun they're having that they forget about the effects it will produce. In the late 1990s, basketball star Charles Barkley and ex-football standout Jim Brown have been warning inner-city youths about the devastation caused by both black-on-black crime and the soaring number of black teenage pregnancies. Wilson's Seth Holly complains in *Joe Turner* that many of his fellow blacks have been misusing the freedom given them by emancipation: "Ever since slavery got over with there ain't been nothing but foolish-acting niggers" (6), he grumps. The folly of Sterling in *Two Trains*, a play set nearly 60 years after *Joe Turner*, portrays the slowness with which male responsibility and

maturity seep into black America. Sterling's dream for the future consists of winning a fortune playing the numbers and then taking his stake
to Las Vegas, where he'll parlay it into a bankroll fat enough to buy a
ranch with horses.

This pipe dream has as little chance of reaching fruition as Hedley's
fantasy about putting a tobacco plantation in 1948 Pittsburgh (*7G,*
24–25). But Sterling will pursue it anyway, if he can, heedless of its
inanity. "Economics is the key for blacks," said Wilson in 1992.[5] So long
as the Sterlings of black America submit to the dazzle of lunatic
schemes, they're doomed. That other dreamer, Hedley, is just as foolish
despite being Sterling's senior by some 30 years. "The white man got a
big plan" (*7G,* 69), he says, defining conflict racially. Yet he's angry with
the world. Before the present-tense action of the play begins, he has
already killed a man, who was, advisedly, black. As with the zealots in
the plays of O'Casey, common sense can't pierce his vehemence. The end
of act 2, scene 4 shows him holding a machete and intoning, "Now
Hedley ready for the white man when he come to take him away" (87).
Hedley's foe isn't the white man; it's Hedley. He *will* use his machete,
but as an attack weapon. His victim, moreover, like his first one, will be
black, not white.

Black-on-black tension runs high in the Wilson canon, as it does in
much of black American literature. Both William Wells Brown's *Clotel*
(1853), the first black American novel, and Wallace Thurman's novel of
the Harlem Renaissance, *The Blacker the Berry* (1929), treat color prejudice within the black community. Zora Neale Hurston's *Tell My Horse*
(1938), an anthropological work, inveighs against the racism directed
by light-skinned Jamaicans against their darker counterparts. But the
flash point for black-on-black aggressiveness in Wilson isn't skin color.
In *Fences,* it rises from the father-son conflict; *Piano Lesson* shows it
pitting brother against sister. *Ma Rainey* also depicts the family as a
seedbed for conflict. But the family in Wilson's first Broadway play is
symbolic rather than literal. Though only 10 or 11 years older than her
maverick trumpet player, Levee, Ma has gone much further in her musical career. She also senses that, like all entertainers, she'll see her popularity wane.

Holly Hill calls Ma's sideman Levee "the first example of many in
Wilson's work of how a black person is thwarted . . . by other blacks"
(89). She's right. Each of Levee's attempts to defeat Ma comes to grief.
As Cutler, her bandleader, says, "it's what Ma say that counts" (*MR,*
37). But even though she overrules every band member or record pro-

ducer who opposes her, this matriarch is tired of conflict; the constant battles of wills are wearing her down. She also knows that when her music goes out of style, it will give way to the hot licks Levee plays— and writes. She's thus both victim and aggressor. The clash between her and Levee probes Freudian depths when she sees her sexual toy, Dussie May, who may be a full generation her junior, flirting with Levee. This coquetry frightens and angers Ma, all the more so because she's fighting off the inference that Dussie May would welcome Levee to her bed. "Levee's got his eyes in the wrong place" (73), she tells Cutler rather than confronting Dussie May with her treachery.

Were such a confrontation to take place, it would lack the long-range destructiveness of the many hostile acts inflicted by whites upon blacks in Wilson's work. Though born after emancipation, Herald Loomis gets pressed into service for seven years on Joe Turner's, or Turney's, chain gang (Barbour, 10). The first part of *Ma Rainey* ends with Levee's juddering revelation that, at age eight, he watched eight or nine white men barge into his family's home and gang-rape his mother. "Them mens . . . took hold of her like you take hold of a mule" (69), he says, foreshadowing the disclosure of Memphis in *Two Trains* that a white man he had taken to court in 1931 retaliated by slitting his mule's belly and then cutting off the mule's penis.

Though such crimes occurred both offstage and long ago, they remain fresh in the victims' minds. "One of Wilson's accomplishments," says Henry Louis Gates Jr., "is to register the ambiguous presence of white folks in a segregated black world—the way you see them nowhere and feel them everywhere" (55). Whites induce force because they often have ethnic names, and they're usually referred to as "Mr." even when they're beyond hearing range. Cory Maxson's football coach is named Zellman, and Cory's boss at the A&P where he works after school is a Stawicki. A Mr. Cohen who's mentioned in both *Joe Turner* (44) and *Piano Lesson* (65) enjoys a career in real estate that spans at least 25 years. But this constancy falls short of that of a Dr. Goldblum who was practicing medicine in Pittsburgh in 1908 (*JT,* 44) and was still seeing patients in 1948 (*7G,* 27). He's even spoken of in 1957, albeit as "Doc Goldblums" (*F,* 60), and again in 1977 in *Jitney* (31). His clinic has even more staying power than the black-owned music lounge and "gambling place" (*JT,* 17) called Seefus, or "Sefus's" (*F,* 45). Mentioned in all of Wilson's Broadway-produced, Pittsburgh-based plays, this dive, where Red Carter of *Seven Guitars* once gambled away a big wad (*7G,* 32), attracts lowlifes, or "thugs" (*F,* 45), and it has been raided by the police

(*JT,* 18). Yet its doors have stayed open, perhaps as a sign of that genius for endurance Faulkner hailed in *The Sound and the Fury* (1927) as patently Negro.

Like the whites in Wilson's plays who make their presences felt without appearing in person (Gates 55), Seefus's exerts a subtle but persistent force. Wilson refers to the place so often because it embodies a working-class black American flair for music, drink, and casual, even rowdy, socializing. Its longevity honors both the inventiveness and the resiliency of the black spirit that suffuses the projects, pool rooms, and taverns of America's ghettos. Wilson discussed the reason why urban blacks deserve this tribute during a 1992 interview with David Savran: "I think blacks are essentially a religious people. Whites see man against a world that needs to be subdued. Africans see man as part of the world, a natural part of the environment. Blacks have taken Christianity and bent it to serve their African-ness" (302). The "religious" worldview Wilson identifies with blacks gains dramatic expression through women like Rose Maxson of *Fences,* Berniece Charles of *Piano Lesson,* and Bertha Holly of *Joe Turner,* all of whom try to maintain domestic harmony by keeping food on the table and love in the heart. Gabriel, Troy Maxson's brother, whose wits were dimmed by an enemy shell, comes even closer to Wilson's "religious" ideal. He won't settle for being on a level with life. By calling his nephew Lyons the king of the jungle (*F,* 47) and by identifying Rose with a literal rose (47), he has created analogies that both unify and amplify experience. Wilson charts the wide gulf between Gabriel's valorizing imagination and the distinction-ridden social code that limits his freedom by making him a brain-damaged Negro. Rose is the only one in the play who listens to him, just as the waitress Risa stands alone in *Two Trains* in extending compassion to the mentally disoriented Hambone, another underdog who, it is implied, has a wisdom we could access to our advantage.

But we won't profit from this wisdom because we prefer to ignore it. White people run America, which means that they make up the rules by which Americans live. Many of these rules stem from a work ethic that includes the passion to subdue and control that Wilson mentioned to Savran (302). A call to service sometimes referred to as the white man's burden, this arrogance grew out of a nineteenth-century rational optimism that made "the march of mind" a popular slogan of the day. The drive to conquer nature, rather than seeking a productive harmony with it, led to ventures like the 1849 gold rush, the Panama Canal, and the destruction of the American buffalo. Helped by the middle-class push to get ahead, it also made material success a pivotal feature of the American dream; God rewards virtue by making the virtuous person rich. And if you're rich, you want to stay that way; what people have, they try to keep. The fusion of high moral principles and loose business ethics in many conservative leaders during the Reagan-Bush years (when most of Wilson's plays were first staged) chilled social progress. Little protest rose from conservative camps. The implementation of progressive legislation might have led to a redistribution of capital assets. Still worse, it could have given have-nots of different stripes some dangerous new ideas about their rights.

White people in Wilson's plays try to build on their advantages. Ma Rainey has no illusions about being loved by the owners of the record firm she has earned more money for than all the firm's other artists combined: "They don't care about me," she tells Cutler. "All they want is my voice. . . . As soon as they get my voice down on their recording machines, then it's just like if I'd be some whore and they roll over and put their pants on" (*MR,* 79). Her metaphor harks back to the white man's drive to fragment and exploit rather than to savor things in their entirety. Although her manager has invited her to his home, he expected her to sing for his friends, not to take a meal. Sterling, the ex-con in *Two Trains,* is deceiving himself when he says, "I can do anything the white man can do" (52). Within moments of his bogus declaration, he's trying to buy a handgun, and the next scene shows him stealing both flowers and a gasoline can. His problems stem partly from within. Like Lyons of *Fences,* who postures like a musician instead of developing musical skills, he wants rewards without toiling for them.

But his problems are also extrinsic. Because whites control the wage-price mechanism, a Sterling lacks the option of placing a value on his services. His being bereft of options has left him nowhere to turn. Although disliked and distrusted, the whites in charge of the distribution of most of the city's goods and services sometimes treat Wilson's blacks better than their black counterparts do. The white syndicate that controls the numbers racket in Pittsburgh cuts Sterling's winning number by half—that is, his number pays half of the promised figure. But the Alberts, rather than singling Sterling out for persecution, have been cutting numbers for years. Furthermore, Zanelli does repair the broken jukebox at Lee's Restaurant. And according to Sterling, a black gas station owner charges three cents more a gallon than a nearby white dealer. (In *Jitney,* Bean charges a nickel more.) Even closer to home, blacks can't expect special treatment from their kind. After firing his black attorney,

Memphis hires a white one who's representing him when Memphis wrests more money out of the town council for his condemned building than he had ever dreamed of getting. It's crucial that this bonanza comes to Memphis through the court system, a conservative institution run by whites. Wilson's blacks *can* sometimes prevail against white America.

In Wilson's plays, racism has caused gross inequalities between the races along with mutual suspicion and, now and again, violence. But it has also given way to suggestions of fairness, a less obvious but very real cooperation, and mutual dependency. It's Troy Maxson who thwarts his son's hopes to go to college on a football scholarship; Cory's white coach and work supervisor both support him. Similar breakthroughs occur elsewhere in the canon. Berniece's 11-year-old daughter takes piano lessons alongside white children (Berniece warns Maretha to avoid "showing your color" [PL, 27] to the other students and teachers at the settlement house). In *Seven Guitars,* a character says, "They letting the colored people in the sanitarium now" (19). Thus Hedley can be both diagnosed and treated for his tuberculosis (76), which gives him an advantage over Levee, who, in a setting 40 years earlier, couldn't even get a veterinarian to stop the bleeding from his wounded chest.

Though the sanitarium where Hedley will be looked after is segregated, the piano in *Piano Lesson* becomes a point of convergence for the energies of both blacks and whites. It was only his emotional stake in the piano that sent the ghost of the white man James Sutter from Sunflower County, Mississippi, to Pittsburgh to stop Boy Willie from selling it. Sutter wants to keep the piano in his extended family orbit, a unit comprising blacks as well as whites. Presumably, the dead in Wilson have their duties. Two people see Sutter's ghost with its hand atop its head as if it accepts its unworthiness to receive the Holy Spirit. Perhaps its translation will occur only after it crosses the color line, a passage made smoothly by Seth Holly, owner of the boarding house in which *Joe Turner* unfolds. Whereas Seth recoils immediately from the black Herald Loomis, he feels relaxed dealing with his white business partner, Rutherford Selig. Selig sells the pots and pans that the tinsmith Seth makes, helping the local economy diversify and cross both state and color lines.

Yes, Seth does fence hard with Selig over the price of sheet metal. But he also keeps the same strict accounts with his tenants, all of whom are black. Seth is deeply imbued with the competitive spirit of the industrial North, where he has lived all his life. But his eye sometimes slips from the main chance. The same Seth who bargains hard with Selig will give him a free head of cabbage (*JT,* 12). Nor does he ever suspect Selig of cheating him. In *Shadow and Act,* Ralph Ellison writes about a jazz club in Harlem in the 1930s and early 1940s called Minton's Playland. "Things were jumping, you couldn't get in for the people" (202), he says. Much of Ellison's joy came from seeing black musicians like Dizzy Gillespie and Charlie Christian jamming with the white Benny Goodman and George Shearing. No such triumphant chord of racial harmony peals from Wilson's plays. But so long as the plays keep using music as a benchmark of health and vitality, it may happen. Speaking of the Charles family piano in *Piano Lesson,* Wilson reminded Michael Feingold in 1984, "It's not coincidence that the piano has both black and white keys" (118).

The Warrior Spirit

Wilson's most famous character type is the "warrior figure" (Roudané, 102). A Levee, a Troy Maxson, or a Boy Willie feels an almost physical compulsion to discharge energy (which explains in part why all three men are highly sexed). Spunky and hot tempered, the warrior wants to act on his own steam. Reveling in his blackness, he also fights the drift to act white. But he does have white antecedents. The larger-than-life foe of precedent and hierarchy intrigued Wilson from the start. He told both Bill Moyers (171) and Holly Hill (87) that he chose Napoleon as a term-paper subject at age 15 because Napoleon was a "self-made emperor." His fascination with the self-starter who succeeded by dint of his own efforts continued. After leaving school, he educated himself in the reading room of a public library donated by the Andrew Carnegie Foundation, an agency started by an industrial buccaneer richly endowed with energy and initiative.

Leaving Pittsburgh in 1977 didn't jade Wilson's fascination for the wild success. While working at the Science Museum of Minnesota from 1978 to 1980 (Shannon, xvi), he wrote scripts about the preeminent Charles Darwin, Margaret Mead, and William Harvey, the seventeenth-century English discoverer of the circulation of the blood (an offstage figure named Harvey is mentioned twice in *Two Trains* [82, 86]). Dark-skinned progeny of these free spirits appear in each of Wilson's plays. Ignoring instructions that he only provide instrumental backing for Ma Rainey, Levee improvises freely on his horn during a recording session. In *Fences,* Troy Maxson never apologizes to Rose for committing adultery. Neither does he show remorse. No penitent, he tells his wife of 18 years that he plans to keep seeing Alberta; he laughs more and feels happier with Alberta than he does at home. In her company, he can forget about repairing his roof or meeting his monthly house payment.

Troy isn't being willfully flamboyant or rebellious. This outsize garbage hauler breaks his marriage vows because he can't live within society's guidelines. The opening words of *Fences,* spoken to him by Jim Bono, his best friend of 30 years, "Troy, you ought to stop that lying" (1), foreshadow the distortions, deceptions, and lies he will later indulge because the laws governing everyday reality can't hold him. But his radical individualism can also help him. For instance, he becomes his garbage collection agency's first black driver despite being illiterate and having no driver's license. Restless and striving, he's forever trampling boundaries. To Bono's remark that he has been eyeing Alberta, he replies, "I eye all the women, I don't miss nothing" (3). Levee is just as opportunistic. When five sandwiches arrive in the recording studio for Ma's four band members, he grabs two of them. Then he takes a third when one of the players says he's not hungry. Ma may be even more voracious; she travels with two much younger lovers, one of each sex. Still another spurner of civilized restraints is Hedley of *Seven Guitars.* "I don't like the world. I don't like what I see from the people. The people is too small. I always want to be a big man" (67), he says, reflecting white America's passion for size. Wilson's blacks can outdo white America at its own failings.

Like the devil, Hedley "ain't never satisfied" (*7G,* 51). His impending clash with Floyd Barton is as inevitable as that of Levee and Ma. "I don't want to hear nothing about no Bible" (40), carps Floyd when Hedley cites a scriptural prophecy to him. In warrior fashion, he decries authority. Although he has lost the voucher granting him wages for his time in the workhouse, he still expects his 30¢ a day. Later, his option expires on the pledge for the guitar he pawned. Yet he insists that the 90-day deadline be waived because he was in the workhouse. If this argument doesn't convince the pawnbroker, he adds, his .38 caliber revolver will do the job (69). His defiance of laws and limits describes him as self-acting as both Ma, who tells her manager, "Ma listens to her heart. . . . That's what counts with Ma" (63), and Herald Loomis, who vents his anger at Christianity by snarling, "What's so holy about the Holy Ghost" (*JT,* 52).

Floyd and his fellow warriors would applaud the words of the black title figure of Clifford Mason's *Gabriel:* "There is no justice, except what we make ourselves."[6] But they might also note that Gabriel dies. Speaking of Wilson's admiration for the renegade spirit impelling some of his leading characters, Roudané says, "This 'warrior' figure is a strong but ambitious man who, frustrated with outer injustices, seeks . . . change" (102). Perhaps more needs to be said about the recoil action of the change the warrior introduces. Some of it is conveyed textually. In one of the two references to Harvey in *Two Trains,* the high-gear Sterling says, "Harvey gave me a ride to the cemetery" (86). Perhaps Sterling's next cemetery visit will be his last. Wilson introduces the possibility with a subtlety rooted in personal experience. The white scientist William Harvey (1578–1657) he wrote about in Minneapolis had a long, distinguished career because he enjoyed freedoms off-limits to a Sterling. This injustice demands redress, and the process of attaining it has been woefully slow. As has been seen, Troy Maxson gets promoted to a job heretofore done only by whites. Still, neither he nor Sterling has the same options as their white counterparts, despite what they say. Only by breaking the law can the warrior attain his hopes. The law may be rearguard and unjust, and the warrior's efforts to change it may thrill us with their boldness and daring. But, as Wilson's glancing reference to William Harvey suggests, these efforts often rain down disaster. Warriors fight wars, all of which produce casualties.

The disaster can be inferred from the warrior's ancestry. According to Harrison, rebels like Levee, Troy, and Loomis descend from Eshu, the trickster of Yoruba mythology who disrupts the status quo (301). Others have put Wilson's warrior in an American cultural tradition. Ishmael Reed's belief, "The apple pie values of self-reliance and the family are at the heart of . . . [Wilson's] plays" (95), squares with the playwright's praise for Elijah Muhammad's plea for black self-sufficiency (Shannon, 210). But this optimism doesn't play out as it should in today's black America; society withholds the wealth of opportunities offered Emerson's white contemporaries. That "opportunity" is one of Floyd Barton's favorite words (e.g., *7G,* 42, 62, 80) foreshadows both Floyd's misreading of his options and his early death. The same status quo that needs changing will fight change.

This stubbornness holds sway in both the black and the white communities. Ma indicts Levee for not playing her song "the way everybody else play it." His answer, "I was playing it the way I felt it" (101), both frightens and angers her, as would the comeback of any innovator to the incumbent he or she is trying to supplant. Levee's impromptu trumpet riffs pervert Emersonian self-reliance as blatantly as does Boy Willie's contempt for the law: "I don't go by what the law say. The law's liable to say anything. I go by if it's right or not" (*PL,* 38). His sense of rectitude, it needs saying, stems from self-interest and not from any vested legal code. He wants to sell the piano into which his grandfather Boy Willie carved the figures Berniece cherishes. And whereas Papa Boy Willie was a carpenter and sculptor, his errant grandson steals wood. In fact, Berniece, who opposes the selling of the piano, lost her husband while he and Boy Willie were stealing wood. That the piano is made mostly of wood couldn't encourage her to sell it any more than Boy Willie's referring to it as "a piece of wood" (52) or his having survived the police raid in which her husband was killed.

The fortune the piano could fetch today stems largely from the exertions of the original Boy Willie, who, as a slave, earned nothing for his carvings. The slave tradition evoked by his cartoonish name survives in his grandson. Wilson's position on the questions raised by this legacy needs defining. The same institution of slavery that oppressed Papa Boy Willie also taught him and his kind how to survive oppression. What's more, though Wilson never tries to sugarcoat the depredations of slavery, he does believe that his warriors' mistakes can bring about depredations as dire as any inflicted upon pre-emancipation blacks by their owners. Boy Willie comes to grief because he disrespects both the property and feelings of others. Harsh and fiery, the warrior spirit he exemplifies scorns reflection, social responsibility, and ambiguity. Troy Maxson defeated Mr. Death in a three-day struggle. Yet he caves in to the lure of Alberta, all the time insisting that he loves Rose. When told by Bono, "If you try to juggle both of them . . . sooner or later you gonna drop one," he can only mutter, "Yeah, I hear what you saying, Bono. I been trying to figure a way to work it out" (*F,* 63). Wilson's killing off Alberta in childbed spares Troy the agony of choosing which woman to drop. It does not, though, block the drive with which Troy's infidelity corrodes his world. The end of the play finds him negated as a husband, a father, a brother, and a friend. Having retired from his job, he can't vent his frustrations in work routine, either. So diminished is he, in fact, that he dies before the play's closing scene.

Do his sharp decline and ensuing death deny any value Wilson saw in the warrior spirit? And does Troy's downfall open Wilson to the charge of inconsistency or, worse, hypocrisy? Shannon's reference to his "controversial sanction of crime and violence as a means of equalizing justice in America for blacks" supplies insight into the questions (182). Both Balzac's belief that behind every fortune lies a great crime and Proudhon's insistence upon the immorality of private ownership presume that capitalism is based on theft. Can a person steal what has already been stolen? one wants to ask. But the question disregards much that is vital in the plays of Wilson, who never recommends a reallocation of goods and money. Besides, racial injustice never steered Troy to Alberta's bed. What *might* have lowered Troy's inhibitions was his ongoing protest against feeling deprived. Despite his steady job, he has never been able to afford a bed for his son Cory. His baseball stardom has landed him literally in a garbage dump doing backbreaking work more appropriate to a younger man. His 15 years in jail have made him feel that he has lost ground to make up, which explains why he likens his affair with Alberta to stealing second base. The baseball metaphor may be sustained. Also gnawing at him is the major league career he never had. The frustrations endured by this fiery competitor make his drive to extend limits natural, if not pardonable. He's kicking against 35 years of repression.

In kicking at invisible foes, Troy has also leagued himself with one of America's most memorable dramatic heroes of the century, Arthur Miller's Willy Loman. Neither man can excuse the injustices that have been robbing him of his rightful place. The stubborn pride of both men turns their anger inward. Like them, the headstrong Levee, Boy Willie, and Floyd Barton all break the law to attain justice. Also like them, these lawbreakers are punished. And has Wilson punished us too for sympathizing with their refusal to acquiesce? Still worse, did he commit us emotionally to these warriors in order to give their punishment an added sting?

Such cunning might look like a fitting revenge upon his white audiences. But Wilson isn't playing the trickster of Yoruba myth (Harrison, 301), as his words about the ex-convict Sterling show: "For Sterling . . . robbing a bank is not simply a criminal act. It can be seen as a noble and heroic thing, a gesture of resistance to the options society offered him."[7] This refusal to settle gains heroic stature from the courage poured into it. Sterling is last seen covered with blood from the wounds he got crashing through the butcher Lutz's window to fetch the dead Hambone his ham. These fresh wounds call to mind Wilson's remark to Shannon, "I think in almost every play most of my characters have scars" (223). In *Two Trains* alone, besides Sterling, there are Hambone and Risa.

In one of Keats's letters is the statement that, though he loathes a street fight, he finds the passions displayed by the street fighters exhilarating. Wilson would credit Keats's exhilaration. Some of the acts performed by his warriors are misguided and wasteful. But the spirit infusing these acts vindicates Wilson's belief that the black man must be willing to bleed to get what he deserves. The rewards this willingness can bring will make him reel. By holding his ground, Memphis in *Two Trains* receives a dizzy $35,000 for a house he'd have gladly sold for $25,000. Herald Loomis slashes his chest to refute the claims made on him by his wife Martha's Christian God (*JT*, 93). The blood streaming from him links him to an African religious tradition more nurturing to him than Christianity. But it brings other blessings, too. His rejection of the blood of the lamb in favor of his own blood expresses his belief that he can find redemption and salvation within himself. He vibrates to the iron string that affirms each individual soul as an offspring of the Universal Soul. This revelation both vindicates the Emersonian decree that every man is his own church and confirms Herald Loomis as an American hero.

The Art of Collage

The sources that feed Wilson's art include exploitation and terror, gloom and bitterness. Yet rather than giving in to the chauvinist, racist ranting that has flattened places like the former Yugoslavia and Rwanda, his writing conveys a feeling of controlled outrage. "There's an anger in the plays, but it never shapes itself into polemic" (291–92), adds C. W. E. Bigsby. Helped by an exacting, intuitive gift for dialogue, Wilson can wrest the epical from the dramatic by concentrating on the details and rhythms of the everyday life of Pittsburgh's Hill, the neighborhood where he grew up. An anecdote like Canewell's discourse on roosters can capture a tone feeling many of Wilson's former neighbors would recognize and prize (*7G*, 60). Wilson, says Rocha, "supplies the American theater with something it never had: an American history that is the product of an African rather than a European sensibility."[8] He's right. Wilson's ability to make the random and the trivial resonate reminds us that daily routines and chance meetings, not great public events, provide the fiber of human life.

Like a surrealist, Wilson has adopted the techniques of collage and the found object, a skill he learned from Romare Bearden, whose painting he discovered in 1977. Bearden's influence on Wilson rivals that of Baraka and Borges. In an essay playfully called "How to Write a Play like August Wilson," the dramatist said that his career took wing only when he began listening to his characters rather than telling them what to say.[9] His characters' words comprise one of the elements he combines to create a play. "I take little scraps and pieces of things and out of them discover and build the world of a play" (Shafer 1989, 165), he said in 1989. Ideally, the finished product will resonate like a Bearden collage (Feingold, 118). Bearden portrays the limits of logic, justice, and reason in a white-dominated society by relying on discontinuity and distortion. Body parts may be unnaturally large or puny. Often, they appear in the wrong places (Rocha 1992, 32). Bearden's influence goes beyond technique. Wilson got both the title and the central incident of *The Piano Lesson* from Bearden's like-named collage. The Bearden painting "Mill Hand's Lunch" inspired *Joe Turner*, in particular a male figure dressed in a hat and coat slouching in an attitude of "abject defeat" (Barbour, 10). This figure became Herald Loomis.

Bearden taught Wilson to write honestly, with a sense of humor, an acute grasp of history, and a fine gift of phrase. Any viewer of a Wilson play (or reader of a Wilson script) is immediately taken by its freshness. Matching Wilson's eye for the revealing incidental is a pitch-perfect ear for speech. He knows his way around a line of dialogue as well as any American dramatist since Tennessee Williams. His apparently effortless mastery of speech rhythms creates a voice that has the virtues of being eloquent, evocative, and tightly controlled. Troy Maxson's description of death as a fastball on the outside corner (*F*, 89) and Aunt Ester's phrase "going back to pick up the ball" (*2TR*, 10) disclose his fondness for sports metaphors. Occasionally, this playwright whose career spurted when he started listening to his characters will sometimes seem to indulge those characters' linguistic flair at the expense of dramatic tightness. But to indict him for shoddy play construction is to overlook his creative intent. Wilson's characters not only live their ordeals; they pronounce on them, too. Besides conveying the warmth, flavor, and nimbleness of black American speech, the pronouncements of a Toledo (*Ma Rainey*) or a Holloway (*Two Trains Running*) describe both the resilience of black American culture and that culture's potential for renewal.

The renewability of black cultural heritage is a recurrent theme in Wilson. Abjuring happy endings and conventional moralizing, he reinvents himself without repeating himself. The process can carry forward in a Joycean framework of repetition and allusion. We've already seen how certain local figures reappear in the canon, like Hertzberger, the store owner and landlord. In addition, the number 651 pays in both *Fences* (21) and *Two Trains* (1–2). *Two Trains* also mentions the amount $20 several times (e.g., 38, 108), presumably because Wilson bought his first typewriter for $20. The notorious lowlife hangout Seefus's has been standing for more than half a century on Pittsburgh's Wylie Avenue, on which West's Funeral Home, Aunt Ester's apartment, and Lee's Restaurant all stand in *Two Trains*. There's also a rooming house on Wylie that Bertha Holly mentions to Herald Loomis in *Joe Turner* (85). Finally, the public library where Wilson first read black American authors stands, in its new incarnation, as a mosque on Wylie Avenue (Brown, 23). Perhaps Wilson's personal experience accounts for the way his plays both extend into and bounce off of one another. A conversation in *Piano Lesson* about killing chickens might have prompted Wilson to make a character in *Seven Guitars* a poultry merchant. And because Hedley sells his chicken sandwiches outside a cemetery, his business thrives on death, as does that of West, the rich mortician in *Seven Guitars*.

Also in *Seven Guitars*, an offstage character dies committing a crime masterminded by the play's main figure, a reprise of Crawley's death in *Piano Lesson*. The offstage character and his mother, who never shows her face either, haunt the action of *Seven Guitars*, as do the unseen Crawley that of *Piano Lesson*, Alberta that of *Fences*, and Aunt Ester that of *Two Trains*. The shock waves sent out by Joe Turner span 10 years and cover a geographical range stretching from Memphis to Pittsburgh. The force generated by these offstage characters bespeaks the rare economy of Wilson's art. But the force transcends craftsmanship. It also suggests the inadequacy of reason to explain the mystery that surrounds us. Wilson's quick warm artistic pulse vibrates to this mystery of unity. The deeper we probe the meanings of his plays, the more vibrant the picture becomes. Sandra Shannon spoke truly when she called him "a prophet of his race" (vii).

Chapter Three
Times Change

A great deal happened in the United States in 1927 to keep America buzzing. The year that supplies the time setting for *Ma Rainey's Black Bottom* saw the execution of Sacco and Vanzetti, Charles Lindbergh's solo flight from New York to Paris, and Gene Tunney's rise from the canvas after the controversial "long count" to decision Jack Dempsey in Chicago, the city in which *Ma Rainey* unfolds. Black America was also making news, both in and out of sports. The Harlem Globetrotters began playing in 1927, Marcus Garvey was deported, and Countee Cullen published two books of poetry. Also in the arts, *Porgy,* by Dorothy and DuBose Heyward, opened as a dramatic play on Broadway, Duke Ellington's radio show premiered from New York's Cotton Club, and pianist Earl "Fatha" Hines joined Louis Armstrong's band.[1] Frank Rich also notes that mainstream America started fastening onto blues music in or around 1927, the same year the real Ma Rainey and Bessie Smith became the first black musicians to sign contracts with the "race" divisions of white-owned record companies.[2]

The so-called race records these singers made sold better in southern towns like Memphis and Birmingham than in New York, despite a potentially big market in Harlem. Ironically, many of these records were cut in Chicago, another northern city where they sold badly, until Bessie (1894–1937) refined the gut-bucket approach evolved by Ma (1886–1939). In 1986, Arnold Shaw said of Ma, who was born Gertrude Pridgett in Columbus, Georgia, "Little known in the North, she had a tremendous following in the South, and influenced the styles of many down-home Blues artists, starting with Bessie Smith."[3] In August Wilson's 1984 play, Ma dismisses Bessie as her protégée before saying, "She got her people and I got mine" (78). Ma's people formed an intriguing group. Besides showing Ma in a photograph with a youth (61), noted blues scholar Paul Oliver mentions "her squat build, her fondness for young men" (63). Actually, Ma was bisexual, as was Bessie. But unlike Bessie, who settled in New York City, Ma rarely ventured north, and her instrumental backing was usually more primitive than Bessie's. Sometimes, she even used a jug band, which may have included a washboard and a kazoo, a whiskey jug to be blown into, and a fiddle consisting of some pieces of string pulled taut between a cigar box and a broom handle. While Bessie developed a cooler, lighter vocal style, Ma would sing with a roughness suited to the minstrel, vaudeville, and tent shows of the South, where her career began.

Vagaries of Power

Ma's power in the circle of people Wilson surrounds her with is absolute. There's no cajoling her. She does what she wants to do and that's that. Grabbing every perk and prerogative within reach, she sets the times for her rehearsals and recording dates, decides which songs will be included and how they'll be orchestrated, and controls all personnel decisions in her group. But she also knows that her circle is small and that its members are aging. And her awareness that trends in music come and go, rather than humbling her, has made her a ruthless careerist bent on augmenting her power at the expense of both rivals and colleagues. This power can be white. A tough realist, she knows that both her white manager, Irvin, and Mel Sturdyvant, the white producer for the firm she records for, value her only for the money she brings in. Thus she keeps threatening to quit the firm unless all her demands are met. This diva is as demanding as a Maria Callas or a Kathleen Battle in a cranky mood. Reveling in the power that comes from her big record sales, she expects her colleagues to fetch and carry for her, meet her deadlines, and excuse her mistakes. Her bandleader, Cutler, speaks truly when he says, "Ma's the boss" (*MR*, 37).

Ma's both boss and bossy. She'll overrule others in a heartbeat, if only to assert her dominance, and she introduces last-minute changes into her song routines that she expects to be adopted, such as having a young friend introduce one of her songs—and then be paid as much for his 10-second introduction as each of her sidemen earns for the whole recording session. She doesn't care that Sylvester's inability to say his lines without stuttering is wasting the studio's recording discs any more than she worries about the money being spent on heat and light during his tongue-tied minutes. Nor will she shrink from a brawl. At the start of act 2, she rejects Irvin's suggestion to table the vexed question of Sylvester's introduction to "Ma Rainey's Black Bottom." But rather than discussing the question, she crushes it. When told that none of the band members believe that Sylvester can speak his lines without stumbling, she snaps back, "What band? The band work for me. I say what goes!" (*MR*, 74). And just when it seems that the hapless Sylvester has lost hope, she buys him some time by refusing to sing without her bottle of Coca-Cola. This pampered diva who arrived an hour late for the rehearsal to begin with delays the session another 15 minutes by sending out for a Coke. What's more, she tells her bassist to accompany Sylvester to the deli. So long as the bassist is out of the studio, the band won't feel tempted to audition a rival version of Ma's song composed by one of its members.

Ma's doggedness calls her ethics into question. Is she sacrificing Sylvester in order to defeat Levee, her ambitious trumpet player and the composer of the rival version of her song? She's certainly imposing her will on Sylvester. But she can be charged with exploiting him to score off Levee only if she knew that Sylvester couldn't manage his lines. This charge doesn't hold up. As selfish as she is, she seems to believe in him. Showing a measure of patience she withholds from all the others, she encourages him gently. "That's all right. That's real good. You take your time, you'll get it right" (*MR*, 76), she assures him after hearing one of his worst flubs. She could also believe her words. Strong herself, she may be crediting her much-younger lover with the grit and the tenacity that helped build *her* career. And she does smooth his diction for a time. So powerful is she, in fact, that she might have willed into existence his ability to glide successfully through his recitation. Wilson has been inviting this interpretation all along. Despite her crudeness, her defensiveness, and her cruelty, squat, dumpy-looking Ma towers so far above the other members of her group that she seems capable of nearly anything.

Her boldness, intensity, and explosiveness can both help and hinder progress. Though called the Mother of the Blues (*MR*, 83), she knows that blues singing didn't start with her. Yet, as her popularity shows, she developed it, advanced its cause, and found a larger audience for it than it had ever enjoyed. She broke off her southern concert tour to record some songs in Chicago because the blues are her life. She's one of the rare happy few whose work and play are one. The blues thicken and intensify what would otherwise be a bleak, empty world, and her singing tightens her grip on this surge. But she'll also reach out for other things. Like a born ruler, she shrugs off the derision of others, and she harbors no illusions about being loved for herself. And despite her casualness in dismissing both her upstart sideman Levee and her rival Bessie, she knows that the popularity that gives her nearly free exercise of will can't last.

Both her efforts to stop Levee from supplanting her version of "Ma Rainey's Black Bottom" with his bouncy update and the audiences Bessie has been winning with her new style of blues singing warn her that her popularity might already be waning. Thus the desperation with which she wields her power makes her both the heroine and the monster Frank Rich claims she is (1984, C19). She forces Sturdyvant to pay Sylvester out of company funds rather than out of *her* wages, as the producer tries to do. Also, by demanding $200 for the recording date, she has set her fee at a figure twice that of her four sidemen combined. But her lordliness can trip her up, too. By accepting cash for the songs she records, she makes the same mistake as Floyd Barton of *Seven Guitars* (1996); like her, Floyd reaches for ready money rather than holding out for royalties based on the sales accruing from, coincidentally, another Chicago-based recording date. Though excusable in a woman whose race prevents her from hiring a cab or cashing a check, Ma's caving in to the allure of cash constitutes one of her rare mistakes in the play.

The first of Wilson's larger-than-life characters, she flouts the restrictions and the boundaries imposed by the prevailing social code. Her rebelliousness declares itself visually, when she walks into the studio with Sylvester and Dussie Mae, two lovers half her age of either sex, both of whom call her "Ma" (e.g., *MR,* 49). But she *can* hold her impulses in check. The same Ma who scorns restraint also understands how calculation can help her. Though she tells Cutler early in act 2 to find a replacement for the maverick Levee (78), she waits until the group's recording date is over before she fires the trumpeter (102). The way she fires him is also richly revealing of her personality. She starts indirectly, by praising her bassist, Slow Drag, who, in turn, credits the skill she admired in his strumming to the group's pianist, Toledo. Only after building this consensus does the streetwise Ma take on Levee, but in terms suggesting that she might be rethinking her decision to fire him (unless she's maneuvering him into talking himself out of his job). Rather than attacking him, she first asks him why he improvised so freely during the session that just ended. It's only when he tells her that his improvised riffs came to him spontaneously that she explains that they skewed her timing. The defiance with which he answers her discloses a mutinousness Ma can cite as grounds for firing—if she ever felt the need to justify herself.

"I know what I'm doing," Levee snarls. "I know how to play music. You all back up and leave me alone about my music" (*MR,* 101). There's not enough room in Ma's band for two radical individualists, particularly two as stubborn as Levee and Ma. Yet her next words to Levee suggest a willingness, even at this late stage, to keep him in her band. Though angry, she's too much of a professional to punish a colleague for demonstrating his talent and musical flair. "You better watch yourself" and "You keep messing with me" (102), she warns him. Levee's the one who keeps forcing the issue. He dares her to fire him even before she suggests that his job is at risk. Foolishly trusting Sturdyvant to keep his word about recording some of his original songs, Levee insists that Ma can't hurt him. He'd have spoken more accurately if he had said that Ma can't hurt him as much as he can hurt himself. Regardless of whether she has lured him into overreaching himself, the hesitation she shows firing him implies some humanizing second thoughts about her decision: "All right, nigger . . . you fired" (102).

That this is the lone time in the play that Ma calls Levee "nigger" directs our attention to the various modes of address used by the people in *Ma Rainey*. These naming practices rest on a strict hierarchy. Both Sturdyvant and Irvin call the members of Ma's band "boys" despite being as much as 10 or 20 years their junior in most cases. Buying into this inequity, the musicians refer to their two white supervisors as "Mr.," even to one another when the supervisors are off the set. Yet Ma simply calls them "Irvin" and "Sturdyvant" to their faces, and she'll refer to herself as "Madame" Rainey when she feels that her dignity is being impugned. Finally, whereas she addresses Levee as "nigger," she's never called "nigger" by him or any of the other sidemen, even in jest.

Ma's noisy, disruptive entrance to the stage midway into the first act foreshadows her imperiousness. Besides showing up an hour after the time she herself had set for the start of the recording date, she's wearing a gown and jewelry more appropriate to a champagne supper on Chicago's Gold Coast than to a working afternoon. Joined by Dussie Mae and Sylvester, she's also flanked by a policeman who wants to arrest her for assault and battery. Sylvester caused a collision because he drove Ma's new car through a stoplight en route to the studio. When a cabdriver refused to drive Ma and her party to the studio, she knocked him down. Then a policeman appeared on the scene. Now Ma can bully Irvin but not the law. Her repeated commands that her manager tell the arresting policeman who she is prove less effective than the money Irvin slips the policeman while giving assurances that he'll soon make everything right at the station house.

Wilson never says whether Irvin keeps his word. But he does portray a more momentous drama. Irvin's rescuing Ma from the law in act 1 looks ahead to the play's finale, in which he's about to be summoned to clean up another mess made by blacks. This later mess, Levee's impulsive killing of the pianist Toledo, surpasses in consequence Ma's assault-and-battery charge. What it has in common with the earlier incident, though, matters as much as this big difference. Both incidents show that blacks have to rely on whites to deal with black-perpetrated crises. C. W. E. Bigsby has explained how the play's physical layout portrays the musicians as part of an underclass: "Set in a recording studio, the action takes place partly there and partly in a basement band room to which the black musicians are relegated. High above is a 'control booth' from which the white company literally controls them" (288). By literally overseeing whatever takes place in the band room below, Irvin and Sturdyvant have turned the musicians into puppets, or cyborgs, whom they control by moving the dials and switches behind the studio's soundproof glass wall. But even this foreshadowing motif is foreshadowed. Though Wilson says in his prologue, "It is with . . . negroes that our concern lies most heavily" (*MR,* xvi), his curtain rises on two white men together, at least one of whom will occupy center stage after the final curtain.

Wilson justifies both dramatically and psychologically Levee's wild outburst against Toledo late in act 2. One major cause would have to be Ma's firing of Levee. Sandra Shannon, though, asks us to suspend judgment on Ma. She rightly calls Ma's music "a continuum of the African tribal drums, the slave chants, and the Negro spirituals of her culture" (87). This continuum focuses Ma's artistry. But Shannon spoils her case by calling Ma "an agent of the past fighting against odds to sustain an endangered cultural element" (82). Musicians have always stood on the shoulders of their forebears. Ma's anger at Levee sharpens when, following the recording session in act 2, she hears him say, "I was playing it the way I felt it" (*MR,* 101). Voicing a sentiment later professed by Troy Maxson of *Fences* and Boy Willie Charles of *The Piano Lesson,* the autocratic Ma had told Irvin late in act 1, "Ma listens to her heart. Ma listens to the voice inside her. That's what counts with Ma" (*MR,* 63). Often in a Wilson play, only egoists refer to themselves in the third person. And most of Wilson's egoists have fragile psyches. The "cultural element" (82) Shannon refers to can sustain itself. Crossover artists like Elvis Presley and Ray Charles have interwoven strains from country, blues, and gospel music as artfully as could be wished.

Ma fires Levee because he has threatened her autonomy. She wants total control of her music. Her shaky ego has been forcing her to deny that her gut-bucket style of blues singing may have to give way to the new rhythms favored by Levee. Even her manager tells her that, because "times are changing" (*MR,* 62), she should perform Levee's more danceable orchestration of "Ma Rainey's Black Bottom." Next, she has intuited the strong mutual attraction building between Levee and her doxy, Dussie Mae. The possibility of Dussie Mae's defection to Levee invokes the threat of Ma's obsolescence in an area perhaps more vital than that of music. It may have even warped the singer's judgment. Ma is mostly protecting or defending her turf, but she's also acting from motives of possessiveness and insecurity. Blues music is more flexible and open ended than her champion Shannon lets on. Ma's bandleader, the church-going Cutler, finds strains of it in the traditional black church (83); he may have even come to it through gospel music. The ease with which the blues assimilated in Ma's own day a range of vocal styles that included the wail, the rasp, and the shout justifies Levee's belief that he can use it as a foundation for his jazz tunes.

Around the time Wilson was writing *Ma Rainey,* Wynton Marsalis was adapting motifs from the sounds of slavery and sharecropping in *Black Codes from the Underground,* his 1985 Grammy Award–winning album. Other musicians adapted blues riffs to forms like boogie-woogie, soul, and rock-and-roll. Ray Charles even infused the blues into Broadway musical comedy, and Aretha Franklin built her career around her highly individualized rhythm-and-blues and gospel amalgams. Such recording artists still have their loyal friends, as did Ma Rainey in 1927. The person Ma hurt the most by worrying about a new generation of musicians ousting her was herself. Probably she lacked a clear sense of how public tastes are formed and sustained. American popular music even in her day was a web of commercial and aesthetic elements too complex to control. The enigma has carried forward. B. B. King's popularity didn't suffer because of his touring partner Bobby Bland's decision in the late 1980s to form his own road company any more than Tony Bennett's rise as an MTV star kept down the attendance at the many live shows around the same time featuring Frank Sinatra. Good music always finds listeners.

The Grip of the Past

Levee betrays his musical heritage, Pereira says, by empowering his white producer Sturdyvant to market his music (18). But is Pereira right? Where else could Levee turn, one wonders, in an age when there were no black record producers or agents? Levee's statement, "You don't see me running around in no jungle with no bone between my nose," denotes a clearer betrayal (*MR*, 32). This "impetuous, hot-headed, selfish villain" has denied his African roots (Shannon, 83). And his denials don't stop there. His insistence on the superiority of New Orleans to Fat Back, Arkansas (*MR*, 54), his scornful words about Slow Drag, who lived happily in Fat Back, "He sound like one of them Alabama niggers" (26), his contempt for the "old jug-band music" he identifies with the rural south (25), and his purchase of a pair of Florsheims to set him off from his ill-shod colleagues: all these responses spell out his rejection of his roots. This rejection matters. Though Wilson's play features Ma in its title, it focuses more sharply on Levee, who enters the action before Ma and remains on stage after her departure.

Spasmodic, edgy, and wired, Levee carries most of the burden of Wilson's portrayal of the combined themes of cultural upheaval and fragmentation. It's fitting that he plays the trumpet, the most piercing, shrill, and strident (he has a strident voice, too [*MR*, 23]) of all the instruments when misplayed. And this man who confuses his skill with his talent needs more technical training than he understands (23). His nagging practice of hitting wrong notes shows that he lacks both the patience and the discipline of the true professional. He may never reach his goals. This brilliant yet warped and tormented 32-year-old dislikes rehearsing and prefers improvising to providing instrumental backup, which is what Ma pays him to do. Yet Wilson extends more compassion to him than does either Shannon or Pereira: "Levee is trying to wrestle with the process of life the same as all of us. His question is, 'How can I live this life in a society that refuses to allow me to contribute to its welfare—how can I live this life and be a whole person?' " (Powers, 53).

These words could also describe Ma, largely because Levee is a surrogate for, or shadow version of, her. The two figures share similar traits. Like her, another Tennessean, Levee arrives late—though not *as* late—to the rehearsal. Though he has put himself in the vanguard of change, he also finds change offensive. Within minutes of his first appearance, he complains about the alterations made in the band room since his last visit (*MR*, 24). He can be as stubborn and as dogmatic as Ma, who refuses to perform until *all* her demands are met. He scorns the advice of others; he interrupts people; wasting no charm or tact, he'll serve notice to any of the other players that he's both better informed and more sophisticated than they. And even though he's always clashing with Ma, he uses her as his standard for professional success: "I'm gonna be like Ma and tell the white man what to do" (*MR*, 94).

He also shares Ma's preoccupation with feet and shoes. He comes late to the rehearsal because he has been buying shoes. In fact, he walks on stage carrying a shoe box which he opens straightaway in order to display his new buy. The shoe motif deserves a close look since being well shod has always been important to Wilson (Brown, 120). Because Levee, perhaps like his author, sees good shoes as a mark of elegance, he fumes when Slow Drag steps on his Florsheims with his "big-ass" countrified footwear (*MR,* 39). What will later make him homicidal is having his new shoes scuffed by Toledo's old ones, which he had scathed as "clodhoppers" and "farming boots" (40).

Late in act 1, Ma takes off her shoes, rubs her feet, and sings a ditty about her worrisome "dogs" (*MR,* 60). Within moments, Dussie Mae complains about *her* shoes, and Ma walks around barefoot during much of act 2, which is also when she does most of her singing. Perhaps being shoeless attunes her to her Tennessee childhood, seedbed of the songs of her maturity. Like Toledo's statement about Levee, "He got to make some money to keep him in shoe polish" (*MR,* 65), Wilson's descendent imagery both alludes to the play's future drift into darkness (the play ends at dusk) and interprets the drift. This legacy from Samuel Beckett's *Waiting for Godot* (1952) reminds us that Ma, Dussie Mae, and Levee all act from the appetites and the instincts. Yet they're also more driven than all the others in the play, with the possible exception of Sturdyvant, by motives of greed, vanity, and selfishness.

Philip E. Smith's view of Levee as "a foolish Faustian individualist searching for money, fashion, fame, [and] sexual pleasure" captures the man's flamboyance along with the contradictions that run so deeply in him.[4] But it overlooks his psychological burdens. Cutler's question to the contentious Levee, "Nigger, why you gotta complain all the time?" (*MR,* 30), implies that the trumpeter is impatient with himself for having reached so few of his goals. In particular, he has been struggling to transcend a hardscrabble rural past disfigured by the sexual assault of his mother and the subsequent murder of his father. This struggle has twisted him, which accounts for Wilson's compassion for him.

In an important expository passage that's delayed till the end of act 1, Wilson discloses the source of Levee's anger. Though unlettered, Levee's father had the savings and the wit to buy some 50 acres of good Tennessee farmland. One day, Memphis Lee Green went to Natchez, 80 miles away, to buy some feed and fertilizer for his acreage. A gang of eight or nine white louts who were offended by Green's thrift and industry took advantage of his absence to barge into his home and gang-rape his wife. Despite being only eight years old, Levee blamed himself for having failed to fight them off. His father's response to the gang rape deepened this bitterness. Green not only moved out of Jefferson County with his family. Wearing a grin, he also sold his land to one of his wife's violators. But his adoption of the policy endorsed in Ralph Ellison's *Invisible Man* (1952) of playing the shuffling minstrel Negro until the time came to strike back recoiled on him. Green's smiles did lull his wife's rapists into false security long enough for him to shoot four of them. Their survivors, though, soon hunted him down and killed him.

Levee claims half a victory from this devastation. "I can smile and say yessir to whoever I please. I got time coming to me" (70), he explains. He will hide his hatred of whitey behind the grin of the proverbial good-natured Negro. Thus he snaps to attention and gives warm, soothing assurances when Sturdyvant enters the band room to see how the rehearsal is progressing. When the time is right for revenge ("I got time coming to me"), he'll know it. And his efforts will be rewarded. Levee's long recitation wins him our sympathy and respect. No mere contrarian, he has earned the right to buck authority. And his grudge against authority, which is personified for him by the white men who both make up and interpret society's laws, has deeper roots than Ma's.

But these roots are twisted. Despite his father's lessons on the benefits of patience and deliberateness, Levee is the play's most brash, headstrong character. His anxiety stems from his recognition that most of his adversaries are black. He denounces Ma's music as "that old circus bullshit" (*MR*, 64). Though illiterate and reared in the rural South, he poses as a slick urbanite, calling Toledo "the most cracker-talking nigger I know" (31). Nor does he try to win women with sweetness. Instead he vindicates Toledo's first-act assessment of him, "Levee think he the king of the barnyard" (59), by asking Dussie Mae in act 2, "Can I introduce my red rooster to your brown hen?" (82)

Ma judged well to fire him. Nobody can relax with Levee prowling around, particularly those in command. His rebelliousness extends to God. After hearing Cutler's story about a black preacher who was abused by a gang of rednecks, he faults God for failing to intervene. A just, loving God would have protected the preacher and punished his attackers, Levee reasons. Then he gives his reasons for God's nonintervention—in terms Wilson would return to in both *Seven Guitars* and his 1987 interview with Ishmael Reed (95): " 'Cause he a white man's God. That's why . . . God take a nigger's prayers and throw them in the garbage. . . . God hate niggers. . . . Jesus hate your black ass!" (*MR*, 98).

So explosive is Levee's attack on God that, rather than worshipping him, Levee says he'd rather serve Satan and the forces of death. Perhaps it's intentional on Wilson's part that Ma first appears onstage within minutes of a discussion of the devil and demonic possession. Despite Levee's blasphemous taunts, God refrains from smiting him, exercising a charity that Ma, God's earthly counterpart or sworn foe, will flout when she fires him a couple of hours later. Wilson keeps Levee's firing in the metaphysical sphere by describing it just after the terrifying crescendo in which Levee, with an Ahab-like rage, repeatedly stabs the air over his head, trying to kill the God who spurned him and his parents in their suffering.

The Members of the Band

In vain would Levee seek the help that God withheld by entreating the two white men in the control booth above. Despite his assurances to the record producer Mel Sturdyvant that he knows how to handle blacks, Ma's manager, Irvin, cares little about the artists who work for him. He *has* invited Ma to his home, but only to sing for some guests. Before damning him, though, one needs to note the terrific obstacles he overcomes to expedite the recording date. Ma's lateness, various personality clashes, and a frayed electrical cord notwithstanding, the group records all the songs on its agenda. And Irvin helps accomplish this feat while keeping three hellishly difficult coworkers, in Ma, Levee, and Sturdyvant, from each others' throats.

Sturdyvant *is* difficult. A tightwad, he turns on the heat in the studio only when the artists are ready to perform. He complains about burning the lights during the hour when the band is waiting for Ma to show up. He lies. By offering to audition Levee's new songs, he's posing as a promoter of new talent. But he finds it easier to settle for the old. Whereas he backs down to Ma, obediently changing the recording disc each time Sylvester stammers into the mike, he betrays Levee. He had characterized Levee's music as the cutting edge of a new jazz idiom (*MR,* 19). Then he claims that the music is "not . . . right" (107). Why does he change his mind? Perhaps he's afraid of siding with Levee against his enemy, Ma. Perhaps he's trying to drive down Levee's asking price for the new songs; he does offer the horn player five dollars apiece for each song Levee wrote out for him. And perhaps he can't explain himself. He grumbles that his job is so bad for his nerves that he'll probably give it up in two years. He may not last that long. He can't sleep, and his wife has been urging him to take a vacation. He'd be well advised to listen to her. So rattled is he by the demands of his job that he has failed to see how much he rattles his coworkers.

Another character on hand during the cold March afternoon of Ma's recording session, about whom critics have said scarcely anything, is Sylvester Brown. Whereas it has been accepted that Dussie Mae is Ma's lover (Cutler calls her "Ma's gal" [*MR,* 89]), Wilson's commentators have overlooked Sylvester. Ma calls him her nephew (49). But the patience and goodwill she extends to him suggests that she's trying to win his favors rather than acting as a caretaker or a mother in absentia. Patience and goodwill are needed to deal with him. Immediately after banging on a piano, he denies having touched it. Though he caused a collision because he drove through a red light, he blames the mishap on the driver of the car he smashed into.

None of this fazes Ma, who had let him drive her new car. She talks about buying him new clothes, as she does with Dussie Mae. She demands at the last minute that he be permitted to introduce her signature song. She protects him from the law. Why? She's not traveling across the country with this Arkansas farm boy with the build of a fullback (*MR,* 48) because of his verbal wit, his driving skill, or his passion for telling the truth. Dussie Mae has no doubts about his services to Ma. Whereas he and Dussie Mae protect Ma, who, in turn, protects both of *them,* the two youngsters will snipe at each other (e.g., 49). They feel insecure. Each of them fears that, because they both offer Ma the same service, one of them may be sent away. Perhaps Dussie Mae feels more threatened than Sylvester, a sign of which is her searching out Levee near the start of act 2. She wouldn't be testing new options unless she were anxious about her future with Ma. And the chief source of her anxiety is the strong-thighed Sylvester and the more socially approved heterosexual bond he offers Ma.

If Sylvester is the play's youngest figure, the oldest might well be Cutler, the leader of Ma's support band. Pereira has described the main traits of this capable, conscientious guitarist-trombone player: "He is the leader of the group by virtue of his long association with Ma. He draws strength from the blues, his friendship with Ma, and his religious faith, and he is zealously protective of all three" (28). Like Slow Drag, his bassist, Cutler is a seasoned pro. Both men's professionalism surfaces early in the play. Slow Drag will give the rehearsal his best efforts, even singing one of the absent Ma's numbers for her (*MR,* 35), and then leave the studio, content that he has earned his money. Neither he nor Cutler complains about the music he's supposed to play; neither shirks his duties to his colleagues. Although Cutler has just gambled away four dollars to Levee, he forgets about this reversal in favor of settling down to work. Levee immediately puts Cutler's four dollars toward the purchase of a new pair of shoes, a transaction that makes him late to the rehearsal. But he'll burden his colleagues with still more delays. After arriving late in the band room, he continues to hold up the rehearsal by working on the songs he wrote for Sturdyvant. Finally, when he keeps insisting that the band rehearse *his* version of "Ma Rainey's Black Bottom," Cutler remains neutral. The playing of music is all in a day's work for him, regardless of whose music it is. Once told by Irvin to rehearse Levee's version, he does so without a qualm.

This capable, limited man has accepted his role as an accompanist; no soloist or arranger he. He calls his group "an accompaniment band" without wishing it were something grander (*MR,* 27). He can also reproach Levee ("You just play what I say" [34]) with a clear conscience. He's the leader of the band, and it's his duty to make sure that the band gives Ma the instrumental backup she expects. Levee's innovative flair, which clashes with this intent, has created an ambiguity as well as a personality conflict. It's material that Levee is the only member of Ma's company who talks about music as art (25). Perhaps equally germane is his inability to spell the word *music* (28). Progress in the arts often comes from eccentrics like Levee (whose very name suggests a frontier or border).

But the Levees and the Charlie Parkers need a body of artistic endeavor to strain against. Steady, no-nonsense practitioners like Cutler keep the arts alive with their professionalism. A Cutler will also have the artistic insight to help the Levees he finds so disruptive. Yes, Cutler bloodies Levee's face when Levee's blasphemy sends him into a rage. But he never attacks Levee with a knife, as Levee does him, because, unlike Levee, he carries no weapon. He's a man of charity, not violence. When Ma orders him to find a replacement for Levee, he reminds her of Levee's value to the band. He also takes the trouble to frame his reminder in terms that are fair, accurate, and nonpartisan: "Levee's all right. He plays good music when he puts his mind to it. He knows how to write music too" (*MR,* 78).

The play's dramatic climax, though, bypasses Cutler in favor of the pianist Toledo, whom Wilson has called "a substitute for the white man" (Powers, 54; see also Bigsby, 289), and whom Levee referred to as "the only cracker-talking nigger I know" (*MR,* 31). These words remind us, first of all, that Wilson portrayed Levee as a surrogate for, or a reflection of, Ma. Then there are the similarities in outlook and background shared by those musical colleagues of 22 years, Cutler and Slow Drag (31). The blacks in the play exist as mirror images of each other or as parts of a series. Thus the outburst of violence at the end foils the chance for a major breakthrough. Writing from a conservative standpoint, Wilson sees Levee's musical pioneering, irksome though it may be to the others, as an opportunity for a black man to break artistic ground.

As a substitute white man, Toledo is the proper target for Levee's rage. Overcome with frustration, Levee stabs Toledo to death rather than Sturdyvant, who wronged him more grievously. Toledo, though, is more than an innocent bystander, as Wilson combines both his death and the events leading up to it with larger moral issues. As has been seen, Levee is crushed by Sturdyvant's refusal to listen to his music. His confidence that his newly written songs will bring him fame and freedom explains his defiance of Ma. Staying in one place, rather than traveling with her band, will help focus Levee's energy on his songwriting. Now he lacks both job and prospects. The only remnants of the elegance he has been aspiring to are his new 11-dollar Florsheims. And Toledo accidentally scuffs one of them with a shoe Levee had earlier derided as a "clodhopper" (*MR,* 40). It doesn't matter to Levee that Toledo's act was an accident or that he apologizes for it. Levee strikes out in "a transference of aggression" (Powers, 54) because he lacks any other available target. His dreams of sophistication and prominence, symbolized by his new shoes, have been punctured by a farming boot, sign of a rural southern past he equates with the rape of his mother, the murder of his father, and a knife wound that nearly killed *him.*

But if Toledo confirms for him the triumph of a brutal, inescapable past, he also stands for the white world that crushed his latest and perhaps dearest hope. For one crazy moment, Toledo incarnates for Levee both the authority he has been bucking and the past he thought he had transcended. This charged moment undoes him. For giving into it constitutes his worst mistake. The same Toledo who provides a ready target for his wrath is also the last person in the play he should have attacked. The only literate member of the band, Toledo discusses matters like race memory, the persistence of change, and the need to improve the lot of blacks. His social conscience and the ease with which he fits his mind to abstract concepts make him the play's most reflective character. He may also be the most tactful. For one thing, he knows how to change the subject of a conversation that threatens to lurch into danger. Responding to Levee's paean to death, he asks Cutler about his St. Louis-based brother.

Toledo is the first of Wilson's philosopher-spokesmen. His forebears include the Greek chorus, the African griot, and the raisonneur of the well-made play of nineteenth-century French drama. Perhaps also owing to figures in recent American plays like Thornton Wilder's *Our Town* (1938), Tennessee Williams's *Camino Real* (1953), and Arthur Miller's *View from the Bridge* (1955), Toledo both comments on the action and has a personal stake in it. Wilson takes pains to make him a person rather than a compilation of ideas and principles. His heart pumps real blood. Having lost his wife and children to divorce, he has suffered. Of all the people in the play, *he* could help Levee the most, a truth which lends his murder at Levee's hands some of the pity and the terror of tragedy. One thinks of the loss inflicted upon Venice when its military command passed from Othello to the less-qualified Cassio. Snuffing out, in perpetrator and victim, two promising outlets for growth, Levee's stabbing of Toledo leaves the black people worse off than they were before. Levee's creativity, his truculence, and the blood he sheds asserting his rights all make him a radiant example of Wilson's archetypal warrior, an agent of much-needed change. He also, unfortunately, enacts Wilson's warning that the warrior's efforts to promote change can have a nasty recoil action.

Predating *Ma Rainey's Black Bottom,* Ron Milner's play *Who's Got His Own* uses the motif of the black child from the rural South whose father dies avenging the brutality heaped on his wife by a pack of white thugs. Milner's play also includes, in a passage of delayed exposition, the disclosure that an innocent has died because he was a convenient object of the pent-up wrath of the play's main figure. Even if Wilson did borrow these plot lines from Milner, he made them completely his own in *Ma Rainey.* Toledo's death, though unexpected, isn't really surprising. Rooted in the events funneling into it, it's both stranger and more ordinary than anything we had imagined.

Critical Overview

The play begins as strongly as it ends, with a portent of Toledo's death. Ma is late for the recording session, prompting an anxious Sturdyvant to warn Irvin twice that he expects the spoiled, irascible diva to be "kept in line" once she shows up (*MR*, 18). The tension brewing between the tardy black artist and the white businessman she has been flustering seizes our attention. Rivaling the depicted action is our premonition of the crisis that could erupt as soon as Ma walks on stage. Sturdyvant recalls the trouble this high-maintenance prima donna caused the last time he worked with her: "She marches in here like she owns the damn place . . . doesn't like the songs we picked out . . . says her throat is sore . . . doesn't want to do more than one take" (18). Another portent surfaces after Ma's sidemen arrive, thanks to Wilson's skillful layering of plot lines. The list of songs Irvin gives Cutler differs from the one Ma told Cutler to prepare (19). Then there's the further worry caused by Levee's lateness. But Levee's not only late; he was also seen chatting up Dussie Mae the night before. The possibility that he's poaching on Ma's turf and, also, that he's challenging Ma's hegemony by being late creates another dangerous direction for the action. By the time Ma comes on stage, everybody is tense and edgy.

Yet *Ma Rainey* is a subtle play with its absence of heroes and villains. No simple depiction of a clash between good and evil, it pits two people against each other who are both sympathetic and hateful. It also drops them in a volatile, highly activated field. The clash between these two southern blacks occurs in a northern city controlled by whites who care little for them or their kind. This multilayered opposition reflects Wilson's appreciation of the problems, both extrinsic and intrinsic, his people will have to face in their struggle for social equality. His 1976 one-acter, *The Homecoming,* features a bluesman, Blind Willie Johnson, who's based on Blind Lemon Jefferson (1897–1930). This unpublished play connects to *Ma Rainey*. Not only did Jefferson write the tune that serves as an epigraph to *Ma;* he also died in Chicago, the setting for Wilson's 1984 play. Such echoes invoke the genius of *Ma Rainey,* a remarkable, expert play that uses the right ingredients and steers them through a fascinating series of events with consummate control. Each of its scenes takes its reality from the people living it. Nothing is abstract; everything varies in importance from moment to moment.

It's always difficult to find the spot where an artist jumps the gap from being a promising technician with some sharp insights into creative genius. Perhaps Wilson made this leap when he and Lloyd Richards were revising and polishing *Ma Rainey*. In any case, his first Broadway production has the distinguishing marks of a genius of the theater.

Chapter Four
The House of Maxson

A play about disenfranchisement and suffering, *Fences* describes the effects of the bans preventing blacks from pursuing the American dream of getting ahead. Like their white counterparts, black Americans in 1957, the time setting for most of the play, want to improve themselves through hard work, thrift, and the furtherance of close family ties, all of which will, they hope, create educational and social breakthroughs for their kids. But Wilson's blacks hope in vain. Society and its laws frustrate the play's main figure, Troy Maxson, trapping him in a past full of indignities. The cycle Troy wants to escape began with his father, a southern sharecropper saddled with debt. The harder Maxson Sr. worked, the more he owed. To vent his frustration, he persecuted his intimate family members, all of whom left him.

Troy's move to the industrial North at age 14 (in 1918) renewed his troubles. Unable to find work or lodgings, he drifted into a life of crime, a process culminating in a 15-year jail sentence for manslaughter. At the time he appears before us, some 20 years after his release from jail, he's living very modestly, in "an ancient two-story brick house" jammed into "a small alley" (*F,* xv) in Pittsburgh. It's just as well that his son by his first marriage, Lyons, has left home, because he'd have no place to stay; his younger brother, a high-schooler named Cory, lacks a proper bed to sleep on. The physical setting of Wilson's 1987 play, the Maxson's shabby porch and backyard, conveys the dispossession and alienation fretting their father, the family provider. Even though he works full-time, he needs the government subsidy from his brother Gabriel's war injury to meet his expenses. And now that the brain-damaged Gabe has moved out and taken his subsidy with him, Troy's exchequer is more pinched than before. A potential escape from the privation that has been dogging him his whole adult life was baseball, which Troy learned to play in prison.

Troy was a great hitter, fully deserving of the chance to become a major leaguer. A friend's statement, that only Babe Ruth and Josh Gibson hit more home runs than Troy (*F,* 9), though possibly an exaggeration, attests to Troy's prowess as a slugger. Most of this prowess,

though, ran to waste. When Jackie Robinson joined the Brooklyn
Dodgers, Troy had already turned 43. Being so far beyond his playing
prime in 1947 that no big league team would sign him has always ran-
kled him. "There ought never have been no time called too early" (9), he
claims, noting that a player's ability to succeed should be based only on
his ability. This reasoning is fit and logical. And so are his disclaimers
against New York Yankee right fielder George Selkirk, who hit .269 the
same year that Troy batted .432 in the Negro Leagues. Yet these events
occurred in 1940, 17 years earlier.[1] Troy has been fuming for too long.
And his creator, August Wilson, has been using sports statistics with
estimable cunning. Selkirk died in 1987 (Reichler, 1444), the same year
Fences opened on Broadway. What's more, another Yankee right fielder,
Roger Maris, also batted .269 in 1961 (Reichler, 1211), the year he
broke Babe Ruth's single-season record by hitting 61 home runs, a
record that had been standing for 34 years when Wilson's play premiered in New Haven. Numbers point to meanings in *Fences*. Troy's
elder son, Lyons, is 34, and Jackie Robinson died at 53 (Reichler, 1401),
Troy's age at the time of the play.

Such data improve our understanding of Troy. Not only has his exclusion from the major leagues poisoned his psyche for the last 17 years.
His dying act consists of playing an imaginary game of baseball in his
backyard (*F,* 95–96). Baseball remained his passion. He may not have
been alone. In 1987, *New York Times* sports journalist George Vecsey disclosed some instructive parallels between Troy and ex-Negro Leaguer
Ray Dandridge, suggesting a possible model for Wilson's character.[2]
Robert Peterson's *Only the Ball Was White* (1970) identifies Dandridge as
a third baseman who played professionally for 16 years (most notably
for the Newark Eagles) before joining the Minneapolis Millers of the
American Association. Dandridge starred as a Miller. In 1949, his rookie
year, he hit .362. The following year, in which he was voted the league's
Most Valuable Player (MVP), he batted .311. His average in 1951, his
final season as a Miller, was an impressive .326.[3]

The New York Giants, who owned the rights to him, resisted promoting him to their roster for two reasons, neither of which referred to his
ability. He was about 40 during his Miller heyday, and the Giants were
already suiting up two black players in Henry Thompson and Monte
Irvin. To dress a third would have violated the "quota system," an infor-
mal yet binding agreement among baseball owners to keep the game as
white as possible. But Dandridge suffered another indignity. The Millers
refused to sell him to the Philadelphia Phillies, where he *could* have won a

roster spot, because he was such a big drawing card in Minneapolis (Vecsey, V3). A final intriguing highlight on the parallel between him and Wilson's Troy Maxson is that another third baseman named *Troy* Dandridge played for the Chicago Giants in 1929 (Peterson, 329). Before dismissing this coincidence as idle and meaningless, we need to bear in mind that, even though Troy's field position is never revealed, the play featuring him debuted on Broadway the same year (1987) that Ray Dandridge entered baseball's Hall of Fame (Reichler, 41).

The Crookeds and the Straights

Sandra Shannon has pointed out that *Fences* "reverses a stereotype" found in black plays of the postwar era such as Lorraine Hansberry's *Raisin in the Sun* (1959) and James Baldwin's *The Amen Corner* (1968), namely, that of the "manless black household" (101). No absentee husband or father, Troy Maxson takes charge of his family's welfare. Asked by his 17-year-old son, Cory, to spend $200 on a television set for the home, he answers that the roof of the home where Cory wants to put the new TV needs tarring and, also, that a leaking roof can rot all the timber in the house. Better to tar the roof as soon as possible for $264 than to replace it together with the beams, joists, and flooring a few years hence. Troy plumes himself on his ability to protect his family from this kind of grief; his wife and son can both count on him to look after their material needs. He takes special pride in his Friday night ritual of turning over his weekly wage packet to Rose and getting back six dollars in street money. His financial responsibility came to him from an otherwise tormenting father. But that father's legacy also includes the withholding of warmth and affection. Troy can't be soft and gentle with his sons. By bullying them, on the other hand, this hauler of garbage believes that he's teaching Lyons and Cory that the world is a hard, fighting place. His duties to Cory, he claims, consist of feeding, clothing, and sheltering him. Love is irrelevant. He provides for Cory because it's his job (Pereira, 44).

Philip Hayes Dean's *The Owl Killer,* a play Wilson directed in Pittsburgh (Savran, 292), also turns on a conscientious blue-collar provider who torments the family he supports. Though Troy is a strong male presence in the Maxson home, his disregard for the emotional needs of his intimates stops him from being a healthy one. But what *does* he represent? Perhaps he eludes or even transcends definitions. Shannon rightly calls him "marvelously complex and contradictory" (104), Wilson's "ultimate warrior" (104), yet also "pensive, sensitive, and lovable" (116). Wilson's layered, ambiguous portrayal of Troy isn't meant to beguile. Appearing to change his mind about Troy and even to withhold judgment, Wilson forestalls our outrage at his domineering, sometimes wicked hero. Troy's toughness hasn't dried his heart. For instance, soon after denying Cory's request for a TV set, he displays a touching openness and flexibility by offering to put a hundred dollars toward a new TV, no idle overture in view of Cory's after-school job at a local A&P.

Troy is thus something more than a heartless beast. He's great but awkward, particularly when it comes to showing love in the home. His size has cost him his emotional bearings. The same patriarch who withholds affection from his son expresses his love for his wife, Rose, through the medium of sex—presumably a great deal of sexual activity plus a near torrent of sexual references directed at her. In his inability to display emotional tenderness, he resembles a force of nature. Wilson conveys this rough vitality as soon as he can, even before the curtain's rise. I'm referring to the cast of characters that confronts the reader in the play's front matter (or the theatergoer in the program, or playbill):

TROY MAXSON		
JIM BONO	TROY's friend	
ROSE	TROY's wife	
LYONS	TROY's oldest son, by previous marriage	
GABRIEL	TROY's brother	
CORY	TROY and ROSE's son	
RAYNELL	TROY's daughter	(xiii)

Secondary and contingent, all of the other speaking parts take their identities from their bonds with Troy. Troy's fellow garbage collector, Jim Bono, has been deferring to Troy throughout most of their 30-year friendship; the force of Troy's personality has blocked outlets for his sons' normal healthy growth; at play's end, just before Troy's funeral in 1965, Rose admits that she sacrificed too much of her freedom and identity to Troy's hegemony. Hegemonic is this bruiser who fathers three children over a 35-year span with three different women. His middle child, Cory, is tempted to skip Troy's funeral because his integrity depends upon his denying his father at least once.

It's easy to see why Cory kept caving in to Troy during Troy's lifetime. Besides invoking his physical bulk, Troy Maxson's last name calls forth his mighty imagination, a quality reflected by his bursts of eloquence. Troy sprung from his larger-than-life self-image. Rejoicing, suffering, and betraying his intimates on a scale beyond those intimates' imagining, this paragon of vigor dominates whatever environment he occupies because of the raw, demanding surge of his personality.

This power asserts itself straightaway. The play's first scene reveals that he has put his job at risk. Invoking a metaphor from Ralph Ellison's *Invisible Man*, Wilson has placed him "on the carpet." Because he has roiled his coworkers by challenging company policy, he has to report to the commissioner's office. This defier of limits and boundaries recently protested through his union his chiefs' policy of using blacks to lift the heavy garbage cans while leaving the easier work of driving the trucks to the white employees. Troy's brush with authority leaves him unscathed. In fact, Wilson's invocation of Ellison's carpet metaphor soon proves itself to be a red herring. Wilson roused worries in the reader that he planned to dispel and even reverse. Protesting company policy, rather than hurting Troy, helps him. Despite being illiterate and thus unlicensed to drive, he becomes his firm's first black driver.

He achieves this breakthrough by acting in keeping with the grandeur associated with his first name. More of an ancient Greek than a modern Negro, he behaves like a classical hero badgered by the Furies, by fate, and by tragic irony. His pride has stopped him from being wiser or kinder than the rest of us. But it has also leagued with his anger, his inner strength, and his thwarted sense of justice to make him much bolder than we. As his protest to his union shows, he undertakes actions that would daunt and dismay all of the play's other characters. This boldness gives him a stature that invites comparisons with Shakespeare's tragic heroes. The poetic streak that infuses his rage evokes Othello; the Lear-like voracity with which he arrogates life's prizes to himself rests partly on his dearth (or slenderness) of self-knowledge; his arrogance has seduced him into a Coriolanus-like contempt for others. Such qualities remind us that tragic heroes can be brutes, as Hamlet's abuse of Ophelia also shows.

Troy's pride gives the play a menace that has less to do with what actually takes place on stage than with what the audience fears is *about* to take place. The fences of Wilson's title evoke the Trojan walls that Troy would raze with his baseball bat if they stood between him and his goals. An allusion to classical literature just as vital as this one from *The Iliad* refers to Sophocles's *Oedipus Rex*. The fence that Rose wants built around the family property is gratuitous. When Cory says, "I don't see why Mama wants a fence around the yard noways," Troy answers immediately, "Damn if I know either. What the hell she keeping out with it?

She ain't got nothing nobody want" (*F,* 61). Troy is both right and wrong. As with Oedipus and the stricken state of Thebes, the enemy is already ensconced within. The same qualities that have lifted Troy above his colleagues—his energy, his exuberance, and his daring—also taint and even reverse his gains. Rose wants to fence in her yard in order to secure Troy and the love he represents to her. But she's too late. He has already clicked with another woman.

Edith Oliver explains Troy's adultery as a function of his loathing of shackles of any kind. So powerful is his antiauthoritarianism, Oliver claims, that he'll sacrifice his most cherished commitments to indulge it: "There is no aspect of his life in which he does not feel constricted—fenced in. . . . He even feels fenced in, it turns out, by his happy marriage to a woman he loves, and he has an affair with a much younger woman."[4] Like Ma Rainey, he'll look opposition straight in the eye and do battle with it unflinchingly. In a recitation that riles Rose as much as Levee's caustic "God hate niggers" speech did Cutler (*MR,* 98), Troy discusses his imagined three-day-long wrestling match with death. The struggle began when the white-robed Mr. Death asked a delirious Troy if, instead of dying immediately, he wanted a year's grace. "Let's settle this now" (*F,* 11), snapped Troy, backing up Mr. Death before closing with him. Decisive and resolute he remains. Recalling Oedipus, he tells Rose in act 2, scene 1, without dithering or trying to sugarcoat his words, that he has impregnated Alberta. The scene may be the strongest Wilson ever wrote. Not content to develop an encounter between a heretofore serene, happy couple forced to admit that their marriage may be over, he challenges himself further. He brings Gabe onto the set within seconds of Troy's soul-wrenching confession. Gabe has brought Rose a rose, the beauty of which he identifies with her. She merits this adoration. Despite the shattering news she has just heard, she retains the charity, warmth, and presence of mind to take Gabe's rose, thank him for it, and send him inside the house for a slice of watermelon. But he has some news to convey first. On his way to the kitchen, he explains that he has been pursuing hellhounds (*F,* 67).

Perhaps his chase led him to the right place. Despite Troy's insistence, "You've got to take the crookeds with the straights" (*F,* 37, 94), he scorns compromise. And why shouldn't he, believing as he does, that he can flout guidelines and rules. "Age ain't got nothing to do with it" (67), he says after Rose tells him that his affair with Alberta makes no sense for a man of 53. His exalted sense of self (which also excused him from practicing birth control with Alberta) transcends the calendar. He is owed. He'll never stop trying to right the injustices he has been burdened with since his baseball career ended. Having known denial and deprivation for so long, he feels entitled to the reprieve he finds with Alberta. She offers him the laughter and joy his duties as a provider have put beyond his reach at home. "I done locked myself into a pattern trying to take care of you all that I forgot about myself" (69), he tells Rose. And though he regrets hurting her, he refuses to walk away from Alberta and the casual fun she has brought to him. No fences can restrain him, particularly because he has always been so straight and decent with Rose about his weekly pay. He has earned a little freedom, he believes.

Troy subscribes to the material and sexual acquisitiveness that, for some American men, measures personal worth. Rather than keeping his instincts in check, he has rejected the social contract, which decrees that, in return for the steady warmth provided by home and family, the individual forgoes certain freedoms. His words, "I ain't sorry for nothing I done. It felt right in my heart" (F, 79), both rate personal gain over the common good and condone aggressiveness. Though not at war with middle-class morality, this erotic egoist has exempted himself from bourgeois norms of conduct and conscience. This attitude toward freedom weakens the strictures upon which freedom depends. Making a cult of selfhood brings family cohesion to grief. Close bonds are scorned as deterrents to freedom, and self-interest enacts itself as a series of collisions.

Troy's buccaneering makes him negative and destructive instead of positive and creative. It also fosters fragmentation at the expense of unity, and, inevitably, this fragmentation corrupts his psyche. Having cast other people as supporting players in his life-drama, he has become angry, bitter, and lonely. His inner world is small and narrow. Deprived of warmth and wholeness, he revels in his animosities. His conversation is antagonistic, especially when he's discussing sports. When Cory mentions that the Pittsburgh Pirates have won five straight games, Troy faults the "all-white" hometowners for keeping black outfielder Roberto Clemente on the bench (F, 33). Wilson has researched the matter of Clemente's playing time in the Pirates' 1957 season. The five-game winning streak Cory mentions must have been rare for the 1957 Pirates. Except for the part-time starter Clemente, the last-place Pirates *did* field an all-white team most of the time. Nor would Clemente's everyday presence in the starting lineup have improved the team's standing. He played in only 111 games with the 1957 Pirates, batting 451 times.

Both of these figures are lower than those he recorded in 1956 (when his team finished second from the bottom in the National League). The decline in his batting average from .311 in 1956 to .253 in 1957 also suggests that he didn't deserve to play every day (Reichler, 841).

These statistics merit attention because, as an ex-Negro Leaguer living in Pittsburgh, Troy would have been aware of them. To provide access into Troy's rancor, Wilson also mentions in the play's headnote that the Milwaukee Braves won the World Series in 1957 (*F*, xviii), when most of *Fences* unfolds. The Braves' all-black starting outfield (of Wes Covington, Bill Bruton, and Hank Aaron) would forestall any complaint by Troy about their fielding an all-white team. But Troy withholds praise from the 1957 world champions, anyway. When Cory mentions the two home runs Aaron hit in a late-season game, Troy grumps, "Hank Aaron ain't nobody. That's what you supposed to do. . . . Ain't nothing to it" (34). Were he told a few weeks later that MVP Aaron led the National League in home runs, runs scored, and RBIs in 1957 (Reichler, 695), he'd have also found a way to minimize *these* feats, probably by alluding to his own bygone prowess with the bat. He even denigrates Jackie Robinson ("I done seen a hundred niggers play baseball better than Jackie Robinson. . . . Jackie Robinson wasn't nobody" [10]).

This malcontent who beats terrific odds to pay off his house even withholds credit from himself. Like Ma Rainey, he needs constant stimulation to fend off boredom or moodiness. Within weeks of becoming his firm's first black driver, he moans about his new job and considers retiring (*F*, 83). Basically, he's unhappy with himself. His complaints in the first few minutes of act 2, scene 1—about Rose's playing the numbers, about a local restaurateur, and about Cory's alleged neglect of his household chores—reflect the mind-set of a loser. The opening words of the play, spoken to him by his longtime friend and fellow garbage hauler Jim Bono, "Troy, you ought to stop that lying" (*F*, 1), foreshadow Troy's maladjustment. Rose's later disclaimers, "Troy . . . don't even know what he's talking about" (12) and "Troy lying" (15), bespeak in her husband a need to lie and distort because the reality that most of us accept, give or take a bit, keeps thwarting him. "I eye all the women. I don't miss nothing" (3), he says early in the play, alluding to the fervor with which he tries to arrogate things to himself. But his constant striving to add to or improve his lot finally defeats him. He lies so much because he's restless with himself. His constant practice of casting Bono in the role of approving outsider (e.g., 8, 11, 18) denotes a self-doubt he has increasing trouble suppressing in his search to extend his boundaries.

Another smokescreen he uses as a diversion from his anxiety is his macho posturing. A feminist's nightmare, he sends Rose away so that he and Bono can indulge their "man talk" without constraint (*F,* 5–6). His words to her in act 1, scene 4, "You supposed to come when I call you, woman" (43), show that he doesn't view her as a full and equal partner. But his addendum, "Bono'll tell you that" (43), implies his uneasiness with these sexual politics. Elsewhere, he'll try to shore up his mannish stance by constantly peppering his speech to Rose with sexual references. Even after 18 years of marriage, his language at home exudes sexual bravado. Nor is he steeling himself to perform his conjugal duties. Like Wilson's other warrior figures, he has a giant-size libido. At the end of act 1, scene 2, he ostensibly goes to a local bar to listen to a baseball game and stays away from home for four hours. Cory's statement at the start of the next scene, that Troy has spent the last four or five Saturdays at Taylor's (*F,* 29), reminds us that Taylor's is where Troy first met Alberta. The various levels of awareness displayed on stage fuse in a masterful irony when Troy answers Rose's question about the score of the game he was supposedly listening to by saying, "What I care about the game? Come here, woman" (30). He can't tell her the score of the game because, rather than listening to it at Taylor's, he has been having sex with Alberta. And now he's making sexual overtures to Rose. The only thing that derails his monumental lust is the chance to ride herd over Cory. And even these two drives dovetail in his psyche.

Troy lacks the security both to be gentle and to share power. He blames himself that his son Lyons, a jobless musician who lives off his girlfriend, has achieved nothing, Troy having spent Lyons's formative years in jail. He also feels guilty that he owes what little comfort he enjoys to Gabriel's war injury. The dimming of Gabe's wits by an enemy shell during the war made Troy his legal guardian and thus the recipient of Gabe's monthly government check, which, till recently, Troy has been using to meet the family's expenses. On the subject of Cory, he's deeply divided. Though he wants his son to succeed, he also resents the social changes that have opened doors for Cory as an athlete that were closed in his own day. Troy has trouble controlling his resentment. Mostly, he's afraid that he'll yield to the destructive impulses he unconsciously directs toward his son. These fears plague him, since he knows that he can't continue supporting both his guilt and his grief over lost opportunities. Troy has inherited his father's Laius complex. The last time he saw his father, at age 14, he had been distracted from the plowing job the father had assigned him to do. What distracted him was a different kind of plowing. He got off his mule in order to enjoy the charms of a local girl. After nestling down together near a creek, the amorous couple was surprised by Troy's fuming father. But the father didn't take a horsewhip to Troy to punish him for malingering. He routed Troy so he could have his son's 13-year-old sexual partner for himself.

Troy's recollection of the beating his lust-crazed father gave him has the expected Oedipal overtones: "I thought I was blind. . . . Both my eyes were swollen shut" (*F,* 52). This recollection conditions Troy's attack 40 years later on Cory: "You done got grown to where you gonna take over. You gonna take over my house. . . . You gonna wear my pants. You gonna go in there and stretch out on my bed" (86–87), he taunts the defiant 17-year-old. Perhaps Cory's ne'er-do-well brother Lyons acted more wisely than Cory. By settling for failure, he both hones his father's guilt and steers clear of his wrath. This wrath drives deeper than Lyons suspects. To defuse it, Troy takes refuge in ceremony. Every Friday, he shares a pint of whiskey and some conversation in his front yard with Jim Bono. Then he gives his weekly salary to Rose, who returns six dollars to him. He'll soon be visited by Lyons, who, acting as if chance has brought him to his father, idly asks to borrow $10. This last ritual veers into darkness. By permitting Rose to give Lyons the money he has come for, Troy gains the satisfaction of not turning it over himself but of feeling entitled, regardless, to browbeat his son. The browbeating, though humiliating, protects Lyons from heavier attacks. Troy's later rejection of Lyons's attempts to repay some of the borrowed money underscores the importance of the weekly ritual scolding to the father. Unfortunately, the father's motives discredit him. By keeping Lyons in his debt, Troy can also keep bullyragging him and thus crush the self-esteem Lyons would need to challenge his father.

Though rusty and tarnished, the protective shell of ritual in which Troy has encased himself does its job well enough till women enter the picture. His wiry libido keeps him from being ceremonial with women. When Rose chides him for allowing himself to be overcharged by a woman grocer who sells on credit, he replies, "I'll do my shopping where the people been good to me" (*F,* 7). But is Bella being good to him or has she duped him? He probably grabs any excuse to avoid patronizing the local A&P, where Cory works. By shopping elsewhere (particularly during Cory's shift), he can teach Cory not to expect favors or even encouragement from others. That the grocer Troy patronizes is a woman makes it easier for him to avoid the A&P. Bella needn't be physically attractive. All his resolve, together with his vaunted sense of family responsibility, crumbles when confronted by femininity. An attractive woman will demolish his defenses. "I . . . tried to throw her off me . . . but she just stuck on tighter. Now she's stuck on for good" (*F,* 63), he says of Alberta. Unable to resist the compulsive appeal of adultery, he has slid quickly from the point where he needn't worry about the danger Alberta posed to his domestic peace to where he is past help. His saying of his attraction to her, "I done wrestled with it" (63), reminds us that death was an easier foe for him than sexual temptation. Whereas he out-wrestled Mr. Death, he caves in to Alberta. It's no wonder that he issued his challenge of mortal combat to Mr. Death in masculine terms: "Bring your wrestling clothes. . . . This is between you and me. Man to man" (77). He knows he'd have no chance against a woman.

But his greatest enemy remains himself. He deceives, exploits, or betrays everyone close to him. By driving a company truck without a driver's license, he puts his employer at great financial risk in the event of an accident. He signs Gabe back into the veterans' hospital in order to reclaim half of his monthly maintenance check. He goes behind Cory's back twice—asking his supervisor at the A&P about Cory's work schedule and dissuading the boy's football coach from sending a recruiter to the home to discuss Cory's hoped-for football scholarship. He deceives his wife with Alberta, who, in turn, would have surely lived longer had she not met him. Perhaps he even wrongs Raynell, his daughter by Alberta, by defecting to death. It's typical of Wilson's ambiguity that Troy dies the same year, 1965, as Nat "King" Cole, Malcolm X, and 34 people during the riots in the Watts neighborhood of Los Angeles. Augmenting this legacy of black courage and artistry were developments in baseball that would have filched some of Troy's main sources of discontent. For the first time in Major League Baseball history, no Caucasian was elected Most Valuable Player. Tony Oliva of the Minnesota Twins, a black man, also led the American League in batting, and his black teammate, Jim "Mudcat" Grant, was baseball's best pitcher with 21 victories and 6 shutouts. What's more, the leaders in batting percentage, stolen bases, and total bases in the National League were all black, as were the league's four top home-run producers. But even if these feats *had* swept away Troy's longstanding quarrel with organized baseball, they'd have played havoc with that warrior spirit that made him so dangerous but also so exciting and memorable. A Troy Maxson without grudges and grievances is beyond imagining. Wilson did well to take him from us when he did.

Barriers with Deep Roots

Although only one wooden fence encloses the Maxson home, Wilson uses the plural, *Fences,* as the title of his 1987 play because the fence has different meanings for each of the home's three occupants. Troy sees it as both a barrier to self-fulfillment and a deterrent to death. To Rose, the fence is a means of safeguarding within the confines of the home what is good, healthy, and loving. Because she values the fence as a shield from loss and pain, she urges Troy to finish building it. Cory has his own vision of it. To him, the unfinished fence (which is completed only after Alberta's death, when it's too late) symbolizes his failure to please his father. Because he and Troy worked on it together, they could have made it a bond or covenant. In its completed state, it represents an insurmountable barrier. During their last depicted encounter, the two men hold the stage alone. The scene is the play's most violent. After they come close to killing each other—with Troy's old baseball bat, no less—Troy orders Cory off his property. To Cory's comment that he'll be returning to pick up his things, Troy answers, "They'll be on the other side of the fence" (*F,* 89).

An intergenerational clash between a black father and a son drove the plot of Leslie Lee's play *First Breeze of Summer* (1975), and Wilson himself had already used a "pivotal father/son conflict" in his 1982 play *Jitney* (Powers, 52). *Fences* lends the conflict a new vigor and authority. Troy limits his fatherly duties to feeding, clothing, and housing his brood. To prepare the boys for an uncaring, even hostile, world, he teaches them the middle-class values of hard work, parental respect, and moral responsibility. Duty for him always outranks love. "Don't you try to go through life worrying about if somebody like you or not. You best be making sure they doing right by you" (*F,* 38), he tells Cory, disregarding the boy's appeal for warmth, kindness, and love. At times, he seems more determined to foist his will on Cory than to help his son. His insistence that Cory learn a trade like car repair rather than going to college is curmudgeonly and mean-spirited. Refusing to admit that times have changed since his baseball heyday, he claims to be protecting Cory from the white sports moguls who denied him *his* chance in the limelight. The differences between the decades when he and Cory began playing organized team sports seriously discredit his claim. Now that sports have become integrated, the Negro Leagues Troy played in have folded. And whereas Troy was a professional baseballer, the career in college football Cory looks forward to will take place at the amateur level.

He has no ambitions to play professionally. Going to college and getting a degree would better prepare a good student like him for the future than would Troy's rough-and-ready agenda—as could football; as a team member, he'd have to master the virtues of loyalty, bonding, and sportsmanship regardless of how much playing time he'd get. What's more, even if he's denied a scholarship—which he'd need to make it to college—the home interview with the recruiter from North Carolina that Troy squelched would have created a healthy breakthrough for the Maxson family in the area of interracial cooperation.

As has been seen, Troy fears being eclipsed by the son he wants to eclipse him. Rose discusses this contradiction with Cory: "Your daddy wanted you to be everything he wasn't . . . and at the same time he tried to make you into everything he was" (*F,* 97). Troy dramatizes C. G. Jung's belief that truth lies in contradiction and paradox through the problems he has handling the similarity between himself and Cory. Similar the two Maxsons are. Both procrastinate; both play team sports; each leaves home after clashing with his father. Finally, both lie, which means that neither can claim moral superiority over the other. Just as Troy deceives Rose with Alberta, so does Cory fib about working weekends at the A&P. During his last fraught encounter with Troy, he challenges his father's right to banish him from the yard: "It ain't your yard. You took Uncle Gabe's money he got from the army to buy this house and then you put him out" (*F,* 87), he claims. And though he's not speaking truly, there's enough truth in his words to rile Troy. Neither can Troy fault him for putting this truth in an ugly light since the boy learned this tactic from Troy himself.

It's both fitting and poignant that their conflictive leave-taking occurs near the fence that Cory and Troy worked on together but did not finish until Troy's defection to Alberta. Eight years later, Cory is still reeling from the shock waves of his violent last encounter with Troy. His malaise declares itself indirectly. He arrives home somewhat later for Troy's funeral than propriety dictates. When asked about the delay, he lies: "You know how the Marines are, Mama. They got to get all their paperwork straight before they let you do anything" (*F,* 92). Then, significantly, he rejects Rose's offer of breakfast. The meal symbolizes communion. It confirms the living bond between people. The rejection of the meal, or feast, denies community. But community is exactly what has been troubling Cory. Missing the funeral, he believes, is his last chance to say no to the domineering father who always cowed him. But he can't stay away, the funeral also being his last chance to farewell Troy.

To miss this chance would be a denial of closure, a major trope in Wilson's next play, *Joe Turner's Come and Gone*. It would also violate the family bond. The gathering of the funeral party at the end both honors Troy and reproaches him. Unlike Troy, who sought to expand his freedom beyond the purlieus of home, his intimates all turn up for his funeral. Cory's presence helps complete the circle.

The circle perforce includes Lyons, now 42 years old (Jackie Robinson's uniform number was 42) and an inmate in the local workhouse. Polite like Cory, he calls his father's best friend "Mr. Bono" (*F,* 13) and his uncle "Uncle Gabe" (100). If Troy taught him good manners, he seems to have also crushed his son's spirit. Troy's statement about him, "The only time I see this nigger is when he wants something" (16), though true, puts Lyons at a disadvantage he can't recoup. It's no wonder that he never brings his girlfriend, Lorraine, to the house. Besides bullying Lyons, Troy keeps resisting his son's attempts to win his support and goodwill. When Lyons invites him to hear him play at the club, Troy claims he's tired. Besides, Lyons's "Chinese music" (68) is not to his taste. Lyons needs to feel solid and responsible. He turns down Troy's offer of a job (17), he misses Cory's high school graduation, and, after Lorraine leaves him, he goes to jail for cashing other people's checks. His being in custody at play's end perhaps vindicates Troy's contempt for him. But it also suggests that a warmer, gentler view of him than Troy's would have been morally preferable and perhaps even more socially productive.

This outlook can be found in Rose. Well past girlhood when she married Troy, she brought into the marriage a history of having been used, hurt, and deserted by men. Her gratitude to Troy for rescuing her from this cycle of wretchedness shows in her many acts of intuition, tolerance, and compassion. Writers like Dante, T. S. Eliot, and Rebecca West have portrayed the rose as God's loveliest creation. If Wilson's Rose isn't lovely at age 43, she still offers Troy the best he can imagine. Her positive, loving attitude refreshes and offsets his longstanding grudge against life ("Don't nothing sit right with you" [*F,* 23], she tells him in act 1, scene 2). Without whines or whimpers, she cooks and cleans, does the laundry, and manages the family's meager finances. Her song, which begins with the words, "Jesus, be a fence around me every day" (21), differs sharply from Troy's. This legacy from his father celebrates a dog who trees a possum in a hollow log (82). But it's more than a celebration. Troy's likening of Rose to the dog of his father's song (43–44) makes *him* the trapped possum.

Such desperation wouldn't touch her. Committed to values that cele-brate life, she finds his talk about death morbid. To fend off friction, she'll change the topic of a conversation (*F,* 17). She offers to feed Bono, Gabe, and Lyons soon after they enter her yard. Forgiving and noncon-frontational, she asks Troy to lend Lyons money (19). Proud that Cory is being recruited by a college football team, she encourages Troy to let him play, arguing with a gentleness and tact that will salvage Troy's huge but fragile ego. Other people's feelings count with her. To shield Cory, she says that Troy "ain't said nothing too much" about her son's proposed meeting with the recruiter (29). She also tells Cory to scrub the house steps on the off chance that the sight of Cory doing his chores might persuade Troy to retract his decision to douse Cory's football dreams.

But during the time that both son and mother are immersed in housework, Troy is fucking Alberta. His love and respect for Rose can't ensure his fidelity. Both his exalted self-image and his resentment over having been wronged most of his life have blinded him to Rose's simple formula for defeating temptation: "You should have held me tight. You should have grabbed me and held on" (*F,* 70). It was Rose's job to give him sex, not another woman's. After saying this, she surprises Troy by telling him that she has been applying this formula to herself for some time. She has known for years of Troy's shortcomings. During this time, she has been compromising her dreams, overlooking her grievances, and suppressing her instincts—all for the sake of the marriage. But Troy remains clueless. His tie with Alberta has halted his ceremony of sharing a payday pint with Bono in his yard. Now he stops at Alberta's before coming home. And Alberta hears the news of his promotion to truck driver before Rose does. Two months later, he's referring to the family home as "my house" (*F,* 84), as if he lives there alone.

Meanwhile, signs of hope and renewal coexist with the damage Troy has done to the house of Maxson. Act 2, scene 3 opens with Rose listen-ing at late evening to the final out of a baseball game. Alberta has just died in childbed. Then Troy enters carrying his and Alberta's baby in his big, clumsy arms. Rose agrees to look after Raynell. She will thus relive the burden of smudged family ties that haunted her early years. Besides raising another woman's child, she'll also interact every day with a man only nominally her husband. Her only birth child, Cory, meanwhile, is stationed hundreds of miles away on a marine base. But living an anom-aly doesn't defeat her. Raynell accepts her as a mother, and she, in turn, loves Raynell as if she were "all them babies I had wanted and never had" (*F*, 98). That this blessing comes from Troy could even boost her love for Raynell, though she could never be expected to admit it.

Alberta's appeal to Troy declares itself in both her Florida roots and her name, which evokes the distant, fertile Canadian prairie. Writing with his usual drive and economy, Wilson makes Troy's attraction to Alberta an issue straightaway. Bono refers to her two minutes into the first act, prompting Troy's confession that he bought her a drink at Taylor's to be polite. Though reluctant to challenge the larger, stronger, more articulate Troy, Bono nonetheless corrects his friend's miscalculation. Troy bought Alberta two or three drinks (which he couldn't afford to do) and has also been spotted walking on her street "more than once" (*F*, 4). Despite the near constant sexual banter he directs toward Rose, he prefers sex outside the home. One can see why. His lovemaking with Rose takes place under a roof that he'll soon have to tar for $264. For unfettered thrills, he goes elsewhere. He feels no remorse. The marriage vows he violates belong to an ethical system that has been frustrating him since he was 14. It's plausible that he'd want to avenge himself upon this system, even if vengeance means having extramarital sex without a contraceptive. Either his sense of family duty can't withstand sexual temptation or his impulsiveness has wrecked his judgment. In either case, he's magnetized by Alberta. The chance to commit an act of social revenge while also sating his huge sexual appetite rivets him to her before either of them knows what has happened.

Victory from Defeat

Alberta's death saves Troy from the ordeal of deciding which of his two women to drop. It also solves some technical problems for Wilson. But it's no flaw. The new direction in which it takes the plot shows Wilson at his most capable and assured. And much of his genius enacts itself through Troy. Alberta's death was no reprieve for him. As soon as Troy started dating her, he also began courting death—the death of the family routine he and Rose had toiled for 18 hard years to put together. This collapse not only includes him; it also hits him the hardest. Less than a minute after telling Rose about his liaison with Alberta, he grabs her arm. Cory comes onto the set, and, acting on impulse, seizes Troy from behind and knocks him down. Troy's physical and moral downfall have coincided—in his very backyard, moreover, the place where most of the damage caused by his liaison concentrates. And though he rises to his feet, he never does recover from either descent. "I'm coming in and everybody's going out" (*F,* 81), he says two months later as he watches Rose take Raynell to church. He's a loner in the house he fouled with his unfaithfulness. "What time you coming back?" (82) he asks the departing Rose, posing the sort of question she used to pose to *him.* Having shifted her moral fulcrum from the home to the church, she replies curtly and evasively. Then he takes out his pint bottle, which he drinks from alone. The brief appearance of his best friend, Bono, in the yard for the first time in weeks underscores his loneliness. Bono's remaining with Troy just long enough to turn down the offer of a drink portrays the extinction of the payday ritual that opened the play (Pettengill, 222). Recalling Ibsen's main character in *The Pillars of the Community* (1877), Troy's elevation in the workplace has coincided with the loss of his private life. Perhaps Pereira was right to say that doing a white man's job of driving a garbage truck helped cause the isolation that seizes Troy in the play's closing scenes (*F,* 48).

He's more isolated than he knows. Cory's words to him, "You don't count around here no more" (85), shouldn't shock him as much as they do. The ending of each scene following his confession of infidelity to Rose widens the rift between him and the controlling realities of his life, making his death inevitable. His destructiveness *is* mitigated, but only briefly. At the start of act 2, he reports having paid $50, or three days' pay, to spring Gabe from jail, where he had been sent for disturbing the peace. This liberality wins back our sympathy only briefly. Before the next scene begins, Troy has already signed Gabe back into the hospital to recover half of his disability check.

His treachery has made him an easy mark for death. Having retired from his job, he finds his occupation gone, like Othello before him. The conditions Rose forced upon him when he asked her help to raise Raynell have also diminished him. "You can't visit the sins of the father upon the child" (*F,* 79), she says, breaking the cycle of anger and displacement that has hemmed in three generations of Maxsons. But her charity has limits. In exchange for mothering Raynell, she wants to exact some revenge. The revenge is swift and absolute. "From right now," she tells Troy, "this child got a mother. But you a womanless man" (*F,* 79). She has scored twice. Three days before, Troy was faced with the problem of juggling two women while deciding which one of them to drop. Now he has none. Nor will he go looking for female company. His sex life is over, an accurate sign of which is the halt of the smutty talk he used to plague Rose with.

Any woman he might approach, however casually, should beware. Though he insists, "You've got to take the crookeds with the straights" (*F*, 37, 90), this furnace of impetuosity has always fought compromise and negotiation. He must have it all his way, and even then he won't be content. He never values what he has. An unexpected sign of his distress is his attitude toward the activity that brought him his greatest distinction—baseball. He tries to justify his affair with Alberta by telling Rose, "I stood on first base for eighteen years and I thought . . . well, goddamn it . . . go on for it" (*F*, 70). But as Rose says, his baseball metaphor is misplaced. The subject under discussion isn't baseball, but adultery. She might have added that, even if Troy were to find a common context for marriage and baseball, his base-stealing metaphor would still be off the mark. A base runner who's thrown out stealing second will be sent to the bench and his team charged with an out. But he hasn't broken any rules. Adultery, on the other hand, violates *all* law, moral and civic as well as marital and religious.

One final turn of baseball phrase Troy uses is so misjudged that the store he sets by it makes us question his great prowess at the plate. His calling death "a fastball on the outside corner" (*F*, 10, 89) belies the truth that it's the inside fastball that's more likely to freeze a batter. An inside pitch is also harder to hit because the batter needs quicker reflexes to make up for his inability to extend his arms for a full swing. And even then, he's less likely to drive the ball than he'd be with a pitch farther away from his hands. By calling death a fastball on the outside corner, perhaps Troy means that he's not afraid of it, a possibility suggested by his calling "the outside part of the plate" the spot "where you can get the meat of the bat on [the ball]" (*F*, 10). But if this is his meaning, why does he keep comparing death to a turn at bat? He sounds like a man giving himself a much-needed pep talk. Were he certain of his superiority over death, he'd turn his mind to other matters.

These other matters are numerous and problematic, and they run deep. Ishmael Reed is correct in noting that Troy never commits "the ultimate sin" of deserting his family (96). Also to his credit is his honesty with money. But his belief that he can extend the bounds of his sexual freedom beyond marriage subverts his uprightness. For one thing, his infidelity distracts him from his family obligations; he buys his newly expanded freedom partly with Gabe's money. For another, this part of his life both excludes Rose and takes place behind her back. He has put himself at odds with his loved ones. Although self-deceiving, he does have a grim sense of how far he has sunk. His understanding that he has caused a crisis he can't alleviate but can't walk away from, either, gives *Fences* some of the heft of tragedy. Having indulged himself, he must now face some discomfiting truths that resist pat answers.

The force of his ensuing rage can make us shudder. Troy is exorbitant and outsize; everything about him is on a grand scale. Following Eugene O'Neill in *The Emperor Jones* (1921) and Peter Shaffer in *The Royal Hunt of the Sun* (1964), Wilson presents this bigness without apology or mockery. If Troy's bullying, vitriolic manner recalls O'Neill's Brutus Jones, the coarse grain of reality infusing his eloquence also turns the mind to Othello. The depth of his heartbreak, fracture, and sunken hopes lingers with the audience long past the final curtain. Troy had let us witness the inner workings of his progressive self-destruction, inviting us to share his downfall even when he was being selfish and cruel. This downfall occurred with relentless speed. Wilson built *Fences* around a conservative premise, an old-fashioned insistence upon responsibility and recoil. Because he usually concerns himself more with atmosphere and idiom than with the linearity of realpolitik, he may have written the play against the grain of his creativity. The difference in approach between *Fences* and Wilson's other work has already attracted attention. Savran calls *Fences* "his most structurally conservative work" (289), and Michael Awkward traces this conservatism to the play's origins: "The artistic ancestry of *Fences* is at least as much Euro-American as African, for the play's sensibilities . . . display . . . its creator's mastery of American theatrical structure, pace, and methodology" (213–14). The play's mixed bloodlines, no liability, have had an enriching effect, the conventional structure of *Fences* lending both shape and counterpoint to the darkness of its underhistory. Pleased by the play's "formulaic theatrical tidiness," Frank Rich credits the Wilson of *Fences* with "a sure instinct for crackling dramatic incident and a passionate commitment to a great subject".[5]

But the art of *Fences* can't be encompassed by the pay-as-you-earn ethic of the white industrial West. Although the characters and their complications are American, the play's resolution comes from Africa, specifically the black African faith in the continuity of man and nature Wilson would speak of in 1992 (Savran, 302). The play's epigraph alludes to the negating of both linearity and repercussion by benevolent spirits:

When the sins of our fathers visit us
We do not have to play host.
We can banish them with forgiveness
As God, in His Largeness and Laws.

(x)

Wilson believes that the divine attribute of forgiveness can wipe out the sins of our fathers but without eradicating our heritage in the process. Perhaps this feat of charity, though, can best be performed by children, and perhaps it needs to be performed through the vehicle of song, as opposed to that of rational discourse. Near the end of the play, Troy's youngest survivors, Raynell and Cory, hold the stage by themselves. Together they sing the hunting song that Troy learned from *his* father. Curbing their resentment has enabled them to take pride in a past that still thwarts and vexes their elders. Their duet radiates promise. But the actualization of that promise doesn't belong to them. A blessing is required. Into the yard comes Gabe, on leave from the mental home where Troy stowed him seven years before. This "disoriented and con-fused beautiful man," as Lloyd Richards calls him in the play's introduc-tion (*F*, viii), has come for his brother's funeral. The gathering is now complete. Everyone in the family will say farewell to Troy graveside, with Bono's absence from the stage clinching the impression of family unity.

In Gabe, Wilson chose the only person he could to focus the play's finale. "Gabriel replaces a failed Christianity with an empowering African spirituality," says Missy Dean Kubitschek, conveying the essence of Gabe's rare gift.[6] Whereas Troy courted the devil and Mr. Death, Gabe had mentioned eating biscuits with Saint Peter in heaven (*F*, 26). The song he sang when he first came on stage expresses the harmony with which he interacts with his surroundings (24). Voicing the wisdom reserved for the afflicted, he calls Lyons "King of the Jungle" and gives Rose a rose that he tells her is "the same rose as you is" (47). Madness and sanity may not have switched places on the set of *Fences,* but Wilson makes it clear that Gabe's aggrandizing, synthesizing vision is healthier than the demeaning, self-centered one of Troy.

Wilson also validates the centrality in the play's finale of this war vic-tim with a steel plate in his head. Gabe believes that he's going to see Troy into heaven by playing the battered trumpet that always hangs from his waist. Cory and Raynell have added *their* important share. But the next vital step is beyond their powers. Opening the gates of heaven for a treacherous brother constitutes an act of forgiveness so supreme that it can only be performed by a madman or a saint. Only a madman, a saint, or an August Wilson would deem Troy worthy of heaven. Forget that Gabe's trumpet makes no sound when blown into. So firm is Gabe's belief that Troy deserves salvation that, undaunted by this setback, he howls and dances a *"dance of atavistic signature"* that opens heaven's gates (101). He has redeemed Troy's betrayal of him by squiring his brother into the company of the saints.

The theology invoked by this finale is debatable. But Wilson won't debate it. Nor should he. Though his 1987 play treats big themes, it's neither grim nor heavy. Its craftsmanship blends with its vision, thanks to its discipline, quick thinking, and toughness. It also knows how to deploy its assets. Wilson can convey both poignancy and fun in two minutes of backyard joshing because he has a handle on the inner lives of his people, and he can do this important work without manhandling our emotions. *Fences* belongs on the top table. It's an ironclad, no-arguments classic, ranking alongside such American stage masterpieces of the post-Vietnam era as David Rabe's *Hurlyburly* (1984), David Henry Hwang's *M. Butterfly* (1988), and Terrence McNally's *Master Class* (1995).

Chapter Five

Songs That Bind and Glow

H. L. Gates Jr. calls the subject of *Joe Turner's Come and Gone* "the sense of cultural loss that accompanied the Great Migration" of rural southern blacks to the industrialized urban North, where, they believed, a better life awaited them (47). This belief, as Troy Maxson's youthful hardships in *Fences* showed, stemmed more from rumor and wishful thinking than from fact. The "displacement, alienation, and isolation" that Shannon speaks of afflicted many ex-sharecroppers who failed to find even the lowest paying work to earn train fare back to their southern families (121).

The August 1911 time setting of *Joe Turner* counterpoints this drama of dispossession with breakaway industrial expansion and growth. Wilson's prologue to his 1988 play notes Pittsburgh's steel mills working full throttle, new roads being laid, and tunnels being dug through nearby mountains to lure the workers that the mills needed to meet production demands. Many of the engineers who weren't tunneling through mountains were spanning the Monongahela with new bridges to attract labor to the mills (*JT*, prologue). A reference in the play to a black man who jumped to his death from Pittsburgh's Brady Street Bridge (under which a young Troy Maxson camped out) conveys the exclusion of blacks from both this industrial boom and the optimism it fostered (*JT*, 38). Unlike *Fences*, *Joe Turner* takes place indoors, but in a boardinghouse, which puts forth a greater sense of homelessness than *Fences* did. This homelessness has a stinger in its tail. The boarders, most of whom are jobless, all share the plight of having been set adrift by an intimate without apology.

Shannon yokes this displacement to the play's title. Joe Turner's practice of kidnapping blacks and then putting them to work on his Tennessee chain gang evokes the "cultural fragmentation, the disintegration of the black family, and the plight of the black man as social pariah" that haunt the action (Shannon, 124). This evocation is based on fact. Blues historian Paul Oliver cites the work song "Joe Turney," which centers on a "long-chain man" who brought prisoners to the Nashville city jail from Memphis in the 1890s (29). Then Oliver quotes W. C. Handy's

"Joe Turner's Blues," which treats the ordeals of black convicts serving time in a Nashville jail (29). The difference in the names of the blacks' captor, though small, deserves a look. Wilson claims that, after he wrote *Joe Turner,* he discovered that his eponym's name was "actually Turney" (Barbour, 10). Democratic governor of Tennessee between 1893 and 1897, Peter Turney (1827–1903) did have a brother named Joseph, the youngest of seven Turney sibs.[1] But calling him Turner rather than Turney suits the play's thematic intent so well that Wilson might have even let his mistake stand had he discovered it before opening night. The mistake evokes the famous Kansas City blues singer Big Joe Turner (1911–1985) in a play that not only relies heavily upon music but also includes, in Jeremy Furlow, a blues guitarist in its cast. The mostly itinerant characters filling out the cast enact, too, the popular blues tropes of wandering, homelessness, and lost love.

Besides the owners, the only fixture in the boardinghouse, a way station for the homeless and thus another blues standby, is the elderly Bynum Walker. But Bynum has settled in by default. His decades on the road have exhausted him. As his last name implies, he's no homebody. Only his age ended this rambler's rambling ways. A final point about the play's title: it is a misnomer. Joe Turner hasn't gone at all. His oppressiveness has left a strong residue. Embodying the arrogance of the white South, he caused terrible emotional damage, which he then left his victims to deal with. The ease with which he appropriated Herald Loomis for seven years still haunts Loomis. This former church deacon had been preaching to some gamblers in a small town near Memphis when Turney "swooped down" on them and put them all in custody (*JT,* 72).

This happened in 1901, since which time Loomis has become disoriented. Many of his problems stem from women. Paul Oliver quotes a lyric by the legendary blues singer Leadbelly, or Huddy Ledbetter (1888–1949), "We like for women to be aroun' cause when women's aroun' that bring men and that bring money" (37). Because money counts less in *Joe Turner* than either belonging or finding one's place in the world, Bynum modifies Leadbelly's sentiment thus: "Women be where the men is so they can find each other" (*JT,* 18). A play that includes a character called the People Finder, *Joe Turner* endorses the idea that people need other people. But the work also portrays the stubborn realities that keep people apart. First, the pairing or combining of people can't be arbitrary; it's better to be alone than with the wrong person or group. To cite the play's governing metaphor, the songs of the singers must fit. Which means, first, that the environment has to be free; a new tie can't be formed until closure is put on a previous one that could compete with it. Herald Loomis has spent the last four years looking for his wife so that he can farewell her and start anew.

Renewal, growth, and self-transcendence in *Joe Turner* often stem from music. "You bound to your song. . . . All you got to do is sing it. Then you be free" (*JT,* 91), Bynum tells Loomis. He speaks home. In act 2, scene 2, music shatters Loomis's reserves and breaks through to his core. This music comes from a Juba dance, an ancestral rite including Christian materials performed on Sunday evenings at the Hollys' as an act of communion. The Juba confirms the bond created by the fried chicken dinner the boarders have just finished. Augmented by hand clapping, shuffling, and shouting in a style *"as African as possible"* (52), this free-form musical celebration creates a powerful unity. So deep do the recognitions probed by the Juba drive that they melt the defining marks of the participants. Guitarist Jeremy Furlow says, "Don't need no guitar to Juba" (51), and his restrained, workaday, practical landlord, Seth Holly, takes his wife, Bertha, from her dishwashing to include her in the dance.

A communal song with deep cultural roots, the Juba joins its participants to their African roots. Blacks were Africans before coming to America. The Juba celebrates their acceptance of this heritage. But people have a private life as well as a collective one, part of which consists of a song unique to them. A vital principle, this song both shapes and confirms character. It's a pathway to growth and a sign of completeness. Pereira likens it to the Zen concept of karma: "The song is the music of each person's essential nature, his or her true identity. And that identity . . . dictates the course of each one's destiny" (63). It can take the form of a ruling passion or perhaps a vocation. The song may also be a special skill or an insight that constitutes a seeing beyond. In its purest form, it's a person's ultimate synthesis, bonding with its singer in a crescendo of both self-discovery and self-acceptance. Loomis's song is lost inside him. He just has to connect with it. It has been there all along waiting for him both to grasp its value and to vibrate in tune with its pulse.

Most Broadway audiences in 1988 had at least heard of plays like Clifford Odets's *Waiting for Lefty* (1935) and Samuel Beckett's *Waiting for Godot* (1952), the title figures of which never appear onstage. More surprising to them in *Joe Turner* would have been the greater prominence the play affords the instinct and the unconscious than did *Ma Rainey* or *Fences*. But the Wilson of *Joe Turner* isn't displaying a new flair for the subliminal, the camouflaged, and the enclosed. Loomis's statement to his daughter, Zonia, about her mother, "I can smell her" (30), puts him closer to his African origins than a Troy Maxson or a Levee Green. The others in *Joe Turner* share this proximity. Like the Jewish immigrants in Bernard Malamud or Saul Bellow, they enact their ethnic origins. As Wilson said to Kim Powers, *Joe Turner* shows black American speakers of English communicating their African worldview: "I set the play in 1911 to take advantage of some of the African retentions of the characters. The mysticism is a very large part of their world. My idea is that somewhere, sometime in the course of the play, the audience will discover these are African people. They're Black Americans . . . but their world view is African" (52). The audience's discovery of the characters' Africanness may not have produced the effect Wilson intended, if, in fact, the discovery ever happened. White America's search for the truth follows the path of the paternalism, the Calvinism, and the Newtonian physics that underlie the European mind-set. Any inheritor of this tradition will find the African folk spirit that rules Wilson's people confusing and baffling. The shade of a woman who has been dead for several years punishes a youngster for breaking a promise. The dialogue that ensues between the youngster and a girl of 11, which includes subjects like the physical sensation of death, has a purity and an intensity that few of their seniors could handle. This vigor serves an important end. As in *Fences,* this exchange between children comes in the play's next-to-last scene in order to set the mood for a finale African in both tone and sensibility. In 1996 M. C. Roudané acclaimed Wilson as "the first African-American to have [in *Fences* and *Joe Turner*] two plays showing simultaneously on Broadway" (97). This unique pairing was short-lived, *Joe Turner*'s run at the Ethel Barrymore Theater extending only 105 performances from 27 March to 26 June 1988 (Shannon, 133). Playgoers comfortable enough with the African retentions built into Wilson's two earlier plays recoiled from the ethnicity of *Joe Turner.* Berkowitz may have been voicing a popular stand in his claim that its "heavy reliance on mysticism" made *Joe Turner* "the least effective of [Wilson's] plays so far" (197).

Enter Herald Loomis

Some might also question Wilson's decision to build his 1988 play around Herald Loomis. Loomis allows himself to be press-ganged into a work crew, where he toils for seven years. He spends the next four years searching for his wife in the company of a daughter he has kept out of school. Then, after finding Martha, he orders Zonia to stay with her, even though Zonia clearly prefers *his* company. His need to own his soul (or find his song) counts more with him than the need to love. Loomis is on a mission. But besides being a hunter, he's also a frantic, hunted spirit, trapped in a gridlock of rictus and panic. Joe Turner captured part of his soul along with his body, which he needs to recover before he can live authentically. He looks out of sync. Taking advantage of the visual aspects of theater, Wilson brings Loomis on stage wearing a heavy coat even though the time of year is August.

Loomis does differ from the others in the play. Like the abject seated man in Romare Bearden's 1978 collage "Mill Hand's Lunch," he's depressed. Perhaps he's cold without his woman. His blood circulation might have also slowed down because his song is misplaced. His strangeness baffles the members of the Hollys' boardinghouse set. Nor will he help them know him. When asked where he came from, he responds enigmatically, "Come from all over. Whicheverway the road take us that's the way we go" (*JT,* 15). But his and Zonia's movements look random only when judged by standards based on reason alone. Cognition matters less to him than intuition or the instincts. An impulse from within has told him to turn Zonia over to her mother as soon as possible so that she can enjoy the benefits of being reared by two parents, even if the rearing occurs at different times.

This wild-eyed man is also a believer. Despite the hard rains that have washed out the nearby roads, he's sure that the white stranger who had taken his dollar to find Martha will turn up at the Hollys' on schedule. His faith is justified; Rutherford Selig, the People Finder, appears exactly on cue at the Hollys'. Was Loomis sure that Selig wouldn't let him down? At first appearance, Loomis exuded something like pugnacity or arrogance. He knew that his winter coat made him look odd. When he saw Seth Holly sizing him up after being asked about room availability, he told the dubious landlord, "Mister, if you ain't got no room we [he and Zonia] can go somewhere else" (*JT,* 14). He's serving notice that he doesn't need Seth, his querulousness, or his boardinghouse. He won't back down, either. He understands his rights and insists on them. To Seth's later attempt to evict him, he replies that his having paid for his room through the week entitles him to stay till week's end.

When asked by a theater critic from the *New York Post* about the origins of Loomis's name, Wilson said, "Herald, because he's a herald. Loomis because he's luminous" (Hill, 93). A herald proclaims momentous news. He can be a forerunner, harbinger, or precursor, like Elijah in the Old Testament or John the Baptist in the New. But what savior's or redeemer's coming has Loomis foretold? Both the line from a song of Bynum's, "I'm going to see the king" (*JT*, 58), and the new name taken by Loomis's wife, Martha Pentecost, suggest beginnings and ends. Putting closure on his tie with Martha gives Loomis a radiance that identifies him as the shiny man, "the One Who Goes Before and Shows the Way" (10), the man that the rootworker, or conjurer, Bynum has been seeking. Accompanying his new glow is the recovery of his song. After Joe Turner "swooped down" on Loomis (72), he told him he was worthless. But if the ex-deacon lacked worth, he'd not have been kept in Turner's custody for seven years. Turner wanted Loomis's song, his personal dynamic, even though he couldn't have applied it to himself.

Loomis's struggle to regain his song has drained him. He keeps insisting that he must say goodbye to Martha in person. His long search for her calls to mind a character in Edward Albee's *Zoo Story* (1958) who has to go far out of his way to cover a short distance correctly. When Loomis finally does rediscover Martha, he speaks first. He mentions twice his longstanding wish to see her face. No embrace is required. This main character in a play full of wild excesses has made very modest demands. "I just been waiting to look on your face to say goodbye" (*JT*, 90), he tells Martha. Conversely, Mattie Campbell, another boarder at the Hollys', he calls "a full woman" (77) whom he'd like to touch. But she finds him too intense. He burns so fiercely that she's afraid of fading in his fire. And though she'll later change her mind, she never does close with him during the course of the play. She has read him accurately; until he exorcises Martha, he can't approach another woman.

Besides, his song is that of self-sufficiency. A loner, he prizes autonomy and individuality over intimacy and bonding. When told that Zonia will profit from his discovery of Martha, he answers, "Got to find her for myself" (*JT*, 76). He must locate in Martha his lost half, but only to let it go so he can start over. "I ain't gonna let nobody bind me up" (91), he insists. Though "a good woman" whom he'll always cherish (90), Martha can't join him in his search for self-being. As in *Ma Rainey,* the main character of *Joe Turner* blasphemes near final curtain (Troy Maxson, the leading figure of *Fences,* broke a commandment and violated a sacrament). Loomis also follows Levee in pulling out a knife. Then, after reacting to Martha's imperative that he be washed in the blood of the lamb, he slashes his chest. He can lend meaning to his own life; Jesus needn't bleed for *him,* this herald of his own arrival. That he has redeemed himself shows in his exclamation, "My legs stood up!" (*JT,* 93). The salvation that has come to him in terror and pain hasn't immobilized him like the vision he had at the end of act 1. The difference between his two theophanies stems from his knife. In a December 1992 *Life* magazine article, Wilson reports that Malcolm X accused the same blacks who "shed blood for white America in defense of her honor and politics abroad" of fearing to bleed to gain justice and equality for *themselves.*[2]

Though Loomis renounces his Christian roots, he does keep his faith. Asked about what he'd do next if he failed to find Martha, he snaps, "Ain't no such thing as not finding her" (*JT,* 76). His search takes him to a local church. But this ex-deacon waits for Martha to come out rather than looking for her inside. Entering the church would confer a reality upon it that he's loath to do. This renegade's first clear act of apostasy comes in act 1, scene 4, where he interrupts the Sunday night Juba by shouting, "What's so holy about the Holy Ghost?" (52). His outburst provides one of the greatest shocks in the Wilson canon. To proclaim his equality with the Christian God, he shrills, "Why God got to be so big. . . .? How much big do you want?" (52) and then starts undoing his pants. This blasphemy swamps his renegade spirit. Out of control, he begins dancing around the room and speaking in tongues. And then he has his vision of disembodied bones rising from the sea. As Wilson says, this horrific vision gives him the self-knowledge he needs to continue his search (Savran, 289).

But the self-knowledge comes slowly. Bynum takes charge of Loomis during his trance, prompting, prodding, and guiding him in a combined catechism-exorcism. Loomis is in crisis. With his grounding in African juju, Bynum is the only person in the room who can break Loomis's spiritual deadlock. The break does occur. The sea-whitened bones of the slaves who died, mostly by drowning, during the notorious Middle Passage from Africa (which will reappear in Suzi-Lori Parks's *Imperceptible Mutabilities in the Third Kingdom* [1989]) take on flesh before reaching North America. Loomis identifies with these resurrected bones. "This is who you are. You are these bones" (Powers, 54), his vision tells him. He has survived an enslavement by Joe Turner that shouldn't have happened in the first place. His meekness in allowing Turner to control his life for seven years (unless Turner had a warrant to grab him up and then charge him with loitering and vagrancy) perpetuates the lawless tyranny with which Turner is identified. It also shows Loomis conniving in his own defeat.

Rejecting bondage, on the other hand, restores his song, that of self-sufficiency (*JT*, 93). But he's not yet ready to sing it. As has been seen, the first act of *Joe Turner* ends with him immobilized on the floor. Bynum has entered his vision but can't help him to his feet. "My legs won't stand up!" (56) Loomis screams as the stage darkens to end act 1. But unlike Troy's collapse in *Fences,* Loomis's is temporary. Whereas Troy keeps tailspinning, Loomis will rise. Then he'll walk a path he has charted for himself. This path will bypass the Christian ideology behind the system that supported Joe Turner's enslavement of free men. Walking it will certify Loomis as his own church. Like Troy Maxson, he shows that the black man in America can be responsible (Savran, 298). But he surpasses Troy by keeping focused on his goal. The steadiness with which he merges ends and means wins him the day. While this achievement looks small, *Joe Turner* magnifies it. The play, with its simple plot and plain language, is immensely moving.

African Retentions

The character most helpful to Loomis is, advisedly, the one most closely attuned to the mysticism undergirding his African cultural identity, Bynum Walker. Pereira has discussed the qualities that make Bynum so potent a force of renewal for Loomis: "Bynum is a rootworker, a conjurer with a special connection to nature. His strength derives from a tradition that stretches directly back through slavery to his African roots. He is a highly evolved descendant of the medicine man of African tribes and the conjurer of slave plantations" (64). This mojo man no doubt stirs the suspicions, if not the animosity, of many white playgoers with his herb garden, the dialogue he apparently holds with the wind (*JT*, 78), and the charms, or packets, he tells people to put under their pillows at night to reach their goals. Then there are his pigeons, which add a further element of strangeness and mystery along with a hint of transcendence. These pigeons he kills, making patterns on the ground with the blood he squeezes out of their slit throats. The flair with which he enters Loomis's trance, though, and helps him banish his demons should redeem this ritual violence in the minds of many. His conjury does work. Act 2, scene 2 opens with a domino game between him and his landlord, Seth Holly. Straightaway, he begins singing, apparently to himself, a song which opens with the words, "They tell me Joe Turner's come and gone" (*JT*, 67). This lyric, which also includes the words, "Come with forty links . . . /Got my man and gone" (67), raises some key questions: Did a suspicion of Loomis's tie to Joe Turner summon the song from the conjurer's memory? Has Bynum intuited Loomis's imminent arrival in the parlor where he and Seth are playing dominoes? and did the aura cast by the arriving Loomis dredge the Joe Turner lyric from Bynum's unconscious? If these questions can be answered yes, then the impulse behind them must be Bynum's conjury. As always, Bynum has used his special gift both wisely and sparingly. Hearing his Joe Turner song prompts Loomis by stages to go public with his abduction by Turner, a necessary step in his redemption; no crisis can be overcome that hasn't been first acknowledged.

Bynum's beliefs may seem fantastic, but he puts them to uses that are solid, practical, and benevolent. His sometimes aphoristic, sometimes oracular, speech serves a mentality rooted in both decency and common sense. "Now, I can look at you, Mr. Loomis, and see you a fellow who done forgot his song," he says in act 2, scene 2, just after luring Loomis into the Hollys' parlor. "Forgot how to sing it. A fellow forget that and he forget who he is" (*JT*, 71). Like the tact and the timing he displayed helping Loomis overcome the effects of the ancestral ordeal of the Middle Passage, his restoration of Loomis's song shows superb insight. Wilson's stage directions say of Bynum, *"he gives the impression of always being in control of everything"* (4). Nowhere is this control more evident than in the common sense and compassion with which he applies his mojo. Shannon speaks intriguingly of "Bynum's deceptively low-key role in the play" (136). Bynum *is* more of a catalyst than a creator. Mingling ancient lore and heart knowledge, he'll help people only when he can. His restraint is productive, blending in his psyche the African and black American experiences. Just as he helped Loomis sink the horrors of the Middle Passage, so does he relieve in the others some of the lostness caused by the Great Migration, which, having brought droves of blacks to the North in search of jobs, broke up so many black families.

As his name indicates, Bynum specializes in cohesion and closure, a gift or song he learned from his father. But his pairings aren't arbitrary or automatic; he'll only join people who belong together. "You can't bind what don't cling" (*JT*, 10, 91), he knows. He's guided by his intuitive grasp of the underlying fitness of things. Though he'll speed a friendly, productive pairing, he'll discourage one that's unsuitable. "A woman is everything a man need" (46), he claims, voicing his belief that people are better matched than alone. But, as he tells Mattie Campbell, the match has to be right. He also accepts the limits of his power.

Though capable of bringing people together, he can't *keep* them together, largely because he can't manufacture happiness. Restoring Mattie's departed lover to her, he knows, will cause her more grief than that created by his absence.

Jack Carper scarpered because he believed Mattie to be under "a curse prayer" (*JT,* 22), the sure sign of which was the deaths of the two babies they had together. "He ain't bound to you if the babies died" (23), Bynum tells her. The two deaths prove that she and Jack were mismatched. Honest and straightforward, Bynum won't profit from Mattie's misjudged longings. Investing her heart in the wrong person, he wants her to know, violates the fitness of things. But if he bruises Mattie's spirits, he also boosts them. The same intuitive stroke that told him she and Jack were incompatible tells him that a more suitable partner than Jack is nearby, "searching for your doorstep right now" so he can take Jack's place (*JT,* 23). Perhaps he has even crossed the doorstep. Though played against a vast cultural and geographical backdrop, *Joe Turner* corners very tightly in its plot lines. The people in the play can often meet their hopes by reaching out for something or someone close at hand. As in *Oedipus Rex,* home truths can often be found at home.

This law applies just as strictly to Bynum as to any of the others. "I'm looking for a shiny man" (*JT,* 70), he says minutes after riling Loomis with his Joe Turner song. What Bynum wants is a reunion. He already met the shiny man on a road near Johnstown, Pennsylvania. The radiance the stranger emitted, while exalting everything ("Sparrows big as eagles" [9]), prompted Bynum to call him "the One Who Goes Before and Shows the Way" (10). Loomis regains this power thanks to Bynum. It happens when, after rejecting the Lamb of God, he washes himself in his own blood, an act that helps Bynum, too. Everyone a shaman, claims the subtext of *Joe Turner.* The healer is healed by someone whose inner split *he* helped heal. In fact, he *had* to heal the split before reinstating the sheen, or glow, he wants to warm himself by. Bynum's efforts help two people. The reversible flow he induces confirms, as well, the vitality of the African folk spirit that still actuates the characters, none of whom was born in Africa.

The play's only character who might reject this truth is Seth Holly. Wilson has explained why Seth differs from the rest of the boarding-house set: "Seth is a northern free man. His father was not a slave. He was born in the north. So his experiences are totally different from those of the rest of the characters. The fact that he owns a boardinghouse and that he is a craftsman, that he has a skill other than farming, sets him

apart from the other characters" (Powers, 53). Wilson also says in his
stage directions of this northern-born craftsman and landlord, "*he has a
stability that none of the other characters have*" (*JT*, 1). This stability comes
from the secular pragmatism he has absorbed from the competitive
industrial society into which he was born. Having bought into that society's ethic of self-improvement, he has four jobs. Besides running the
boardinghouse where the action unfolds, he also holds a factory job,
grows vegetables, and makes pots and pans in a shed on his property.

Like any good American, Seth has set still higher goals for himself,
which he's willing to work hard to attain. Nor does he expect favors.
Invoking white man's logic, he wants to incorporate himself. But white
man's logic doesn't apply to him. He *can* increase his inventory, his pro-
ductivity, and thus his profits by starting his own smithy and hiring four
or five workers. First, though, he needs money for tools, materials, and a
new work space, and the only way he can borrow it is to sign over his
house to the lending agent, which he won't do. Meanwhile, he soldiers
on. He runs his boardinghouse efficiently. Each would-be boarder is
asked the proposed length of his or her stay. Each must pay in advance
for a week's lodging, food, and optional towel service. Each also learns of
his or her privileges and obligations; the latter, Seth insists, features
being "respectable" (*JT*, 5, 13, 48, 59).

Another middle-class value he sets store by is accountability. Though
he doesn't suspect his white business partner Rutherford Selig of cheating him, he does make sure that Selig gives him fair value for labor and
materials. Selig, by the way, would never cheat Seth. For one reason,
he'd be caught immediately because of Seth's ability to do sums quickly
and accurately in his head. For another, he values his partnership with
Seth. Though skilled at selling Seth's pots and pans, he can't make
them. Seth, who needs to be close to both his regular job and boardinghouse, values the partnership, as well, signs of which are the biscuits,
coffee, and cabbage he and Bertha give Selig when he returns from his
sales trips. Selig always accepts these gifts with courtesy and gratitude,
graces which might have encouraged Seth to help him carry his wares to
his wagon at the end of act 1, scene 2.

Wilson approves of Seth's bond with Selig, since, like the Loomis-
Bynum tie, it obviously helps both men. The good value Herald Loomis
gets from Selig, who brings Martha to him for a dollar, underscores Wilson's tolerance of interracial business ties. But the secularized Seth Holly
has been vibrating to the rhythms of his competitive machine-driven
society for so long that he has all but lost touch with his African roots. A

clue to this displacement comes in his regular job. Seth works nights, a
regimen dictated by his white boss, Mr. Olowski, and an inversion of
natural process. It's fitting that this denier of his roots should have as his
most longstanding tenant a rootworker, or herbalist. But he'll have to
overcome a great deal of Western conditioning before he can appreciate
Bynum's conjury. He calls the conjure man's daily rites "mumbo jumbo
nonsense" (*JT,* 1) and "heebie-jeebie stuff" (2), and he disclaims
Bynum's story about having met the shiny man.

Loomis, who carries just as strong a charge of African tradition as
Bynum, began flustering Seth from the start. Seth's first impression of
Loomis, "Something ain't right about that fellow" (*JT,* 19), conveys an
anxiety that will persist. Seth thinks that Loomis is lying about his
name. He's troubled by Loomis's supposedly mad, driven look. Worried
that Loomis has been acting "sneaky" (87), he believes Loomis has come
to town to rob a local church. And he won't help Loomis find Martha
because he's afraid that Loomis might hurt her. If he could legally do it,
he'd break his contract with Loomis and put him out of the boardinghouse on Juba Sunday, when Loomis's wild outburst ends the party. Yet
Seth hasn't assimilated completely into the urban North. Though dis-
paraging of Bynum's conjury, he also finds it fascinating. The same
mental split underlies his response to Selig, whom he values as a trading
partner but discounts as a people finder. Loomis, he'll always scorn as a
disturbance (*JT,* 69). But the ambiguity of his responses to both Selig
and Bynum suggests in him an openness to the spirit world he might be
unaware of himself. This suggestion takes on added credibility from his
last name. Not only is holly equated with Christmas, a day of revelation
and rejoicing. It's also central to Druidism, a pre-Christian form of wor-
ship that could both go as far back in time and rely as heavily upon mysticism as Bynum's African-based mojo.

Seth's wife, Bertha, shares his rational, secular outlook. She disavows
Selig's credentials as a people finder, and she attributes Loomis's wild-
ness on Juba Sunday to drink. But she's much more than a skeptic. Her
warmth and generosity recall Rose Maxson of *Fences.* Both she and her
husband call forth associations with food. Whereas Seth keeps a veg-
etable garden and makes pots and pans, she busies herself around the
stove. In fact, both acts of the two-act *Joe Turner* open with her in her
kitchen making breakfast while talking to Seth. This presumably childless couple have found an alternate way to sustain life—housing and
feeding their boarders—just as those boarders have been testing alternative lifestyles and systems of belief themselves. Bertha has stopped

searching. "I get along with everybody" (*JT,* 50), she says. One trait that wins her the trust and affection of others is her charity. Whereas Seth is brisk and efficient with the boarders, Bertha keeps them fed. She leaves a plate of yams, which she covers with a warming dish, for Loomis when he comes home late for dinner in act 2, scene 2. On the Saturday morning of Loomis's departure, she both tries to find him lodging elsewhere and tells him he's "welcome to some breakfast" rather than being entitled to it, before moving on (85). At the outset, she spotted his need for special care. Thus she reduces by 50¢ Seth's standard rate for room and board in exchange for Zonia's help with the housework. Another one of her defining moments occurs in the kitchen, as well. The dance she does near the end, "*a demonstration of her own magic*" (87), when she intuits the mutual attraction of Loomis and Mattie Campbell, expresses her faith in the triumph of love over cynicism and fragmentation.

Mattie is one of two women of 26 who move into the boardinghouse soon after Loomis's arrival there with Zonia, the other being Molly Cunningham. Being the same age and having the same initials makes them, if not alter egos, then possible directions for one another, a presumption given force by their nearly simultaneous arrival at the home of a couple who have been married for 27 years and who could thus be their parents. Finally, although both Mattie and Molly have suffered for love, they try to overcome heartache differently. Molly doesn't want to put down roots. She makes both Seth (*JT,* 48) and Bynum (*JT,* 62) repeat their names after being introduced to them because she's thinking of the next place her wanderlust will take her. By contrast, Mattie, who wants to settle in permanently with one man, has the nesting instinct.

Jeremy Furlow, a 25-year-old guitarist from North Carolina who can't hold a job or stay out of jail, talks Mattie into moving in with him. What Mattie likes in him is a gentle boyishness that will resurface in Lymon of *The Piano Lesson* and in Sterling of *Two Trains Running,* both of whom quicken the hearts of good women. But catching sight of Molly makes Jeremy forget Mattie immediately. Which is proper; the roving life he and Molly favor gives him a better shot at happiness than he would have had with Mattie. Neither is Mattie saddened by Jeremy's change of heart. Living with Jeremy might ease the sorrow caused by Jack Carper's flight, but at the cost of becoming emotionally involved with another temporary partner. Whatever her mixed feelings about Jeremy, Mattie forgets them soon after meeting Loomis. At first, Loomis's intensity scares her. Then she's excited by it; such dedication, she reasons, could support the domestic stability she craves. She also offers something *he* craves, something he's not ready to accept—the chance to flee the past's deadening grip through sexual renewal.

What's more, she makes sure that Loomis takes note of this chance. Near the end of act 2, scene 3, Loomis lets on that he's impressed by the color of her dress. Some days later, in act 2, scene 5, he and Zonia are making ready to look elsewhere for Martha. Mattie stops them on their way out of the boardinghouse. She's delaying their departure to give Zonia a ribbon, the whiteness of which matches her dress. Loomis's parting words to Mattie show that she has moved him again: "A man looking for a woman be lucky to find you. You a good woman, Mattie" (*JT,* 87). Perhaps her attentiveness to Zonia and her cleverness with color have also joined Zonia and Mattie in Loomis's psyche. He plans to give Zonia, clad in bridal white, as it turns out, to Martha as soon as he can. But losing Mattie, too, may be more than he can bear, now that she has shown him her goodness of heart. Bertha conveys her approval of his appreciation of Mattie by breaking into her magic dance. Mattie, who knows the pain of loneliness, is also willing to gamble on Loomis's reluctance to send her away. He speaks his last words in the play to Martha: "Goodbye, Martha" (*JT,* 94). Then he exits the house. Seizing her last chance to close with him, Mattie follows him, undeterred by the knife he's still holding. She knows that love is always dangerous. Besides, the autonomy he has gained by slashing his chest could have very well calmed his inner turbulence. Now that he has farewelled Martha, he can focus on nearest things. Why can't one of them be Mattie?

Mattie senses her chance to fill an important place in his life because of the void created in him by Martha's sudden reappearance and banishment. She owes her luck to Rutherford Selig, who justifies his epithet, the People Finder, by restoring Martha to Loomis, if only to be banished. Wilson said of Selig, "he's not evil at all. In fact, he's performing a valuable service for the community" (Powers, 53). This service consists of reuniting broken families. He makes it clear to Loomis that he can't promise to find Martha. Yet he not only finds her, but also brings her to Loomis at the most favorable time—when Loomis is leaving the Hollys' boardinghouse. This man who never applies the term People Finder to himself (Powers, 53) helps Bynum Walker differently. By identifying Loomis as Bynum's long-awaited shiny man, whose return Bynum had equated with salvation, Selig convinces Bynum that he's saved. Bynum accepts this blessing, as his upbeat curtain line indicates: "Herald Loomis, you shining! You shining like new money!" (*JT,* 94).

Making It Sing

There's evidence in *Joe Turner* to support Shannon's calling the play "a
patchwork of episodes" (120). Well-worked plans go awry; accidents
and twists of fate upset rational structures; as Bynum says, good luck
can descend on a person without his or her knowing it and then move
on (*JT,* 74). How to find one's song in such a climate? Fragmentation
and pain are everywhere. Molly, Mattie, Jeremy, and Loomis have all
been deserted by a lover or a mate. Selig had to leave *his* wife out of fear
that she'd kill him if he stayed. Bynum's statement in act 2, scene 2,
"Seem like everybody looking for something" (70), applies to all the
boarders, including Bynum himself. All feel rattled by the stress of living alone in an industrial northern city. Some are road weary. Loomis
comes from Tennessee, Jeremy from North Carolina, Mattie from Texas,
and the nonboarder Selig from Kentucky.

Except for Selig, who functions better on his own, as his traveling
salesman's job implies, all these others want to be paired off. The first
words Mattie speaks in our presence, "I'm looking for a man" (*JT,* 21),
foreshadow the truth that most of Wilson's people need other people.
The man she's looking for is Bynum. She wants him to help her reunite
with a departed lover. And perhaps she does regain love, but with a different man—thanks to Bynum *and* Selig, both of whom have made
careers of bringing people together. They also save these others a lot of
toil. Meaning and fulfillment are often nearby in *Joe Turner,* perhaps
inside the quester's very doorstep. Bertha tells Mattie in act 2, scene 3,
"You gonna look up one day and find everything you want standing
right in front of you" (*JT,* 75). The quest both starts and ends at home
for Wilson's widely traveled, road-weary people. Their collective problem consists mostly of attaining the presence of mind to act on this
truth.

Both the impulse that led Selig to go to the very church in which
Martha was worshipping and the beating given young Reuben Mercer
by a ghost show the action of *Joe Turner* to be governed by mystical
forces. But these forces create patterns that challenge Shannon's claim
that the play is episodic (120). A relentless interior logic and a carefully
regulated tempo direct the lives in *Joe Turner,* giving the work a continuity and closure rarely found in more conventional drama. Act 1, scene 1
introduces an irony that befits the pessimism of a Thomas Hardy.
Bynum tells Loomis that Selig will help him find his missing wife.
Bynum adds that he has hired Selig himself to find a missing person.

That person, as has been seen, is Loomis, whom Bynum is addressing at that very moment. Then it comes out that Loomis has just missed connecting with Selig. He'll have to wait a week for Selig's return. This delay, though, rather than defeating Loomis, allows issues to develop that lend impact to Selig's efforts on Loomis's behalf. Recalling a Bach invention, events unfold in the play's last scene right on cue. The play ends in the morning, as it began, creating the illusion of a single day. Loomis's departure from the boardinghouse coincides with his reunion with Martha. His mission has been fulfilled. He has no reason to stay at the Hollys' any longer, a development pleasing to Seth, who has been asking him to leave. As Bertha's dance of the blood's memory signifies (*JT*, 87), everything has worked out for the best. The laughter that follows the dance honors the coming union of Loomis and Mattie, which couldn't have occurred at the Hollys', anyway.

If *Joe Turner* is Wilson's "most complex play" (Pereira, 105), it also qualifies as his most tonic, normative, and corrective. Fusing the grubbily mundane and the airborne metaphysical, it puts forth a deep reading of life, one that's dark, rich, and symbolic. The characters' spirits haven't been crushed by the grinding northern city of Pittsburgh that has ignored their needs. They're creating traditions of their own. Skills and mind-sets pass from one generation to the next. "Most folks be what they daddy is" (*JT*, 61), says Molly in act 2, scene 1. She's right, if by "most people" she means the Hollys' circle. Seth's father taught him how to run a boardinghouse and how to work with tin. Bynum learned the art of binding from *his* father. Selig also carries forward his father's trade of people finding, which dates from the pre–Civil War plantation owners who wanted to recover their escaped slaves.

Wilson's people in *Joe Turner*, though displaced, are not defeated. The climactic Juba of act 1, scene 4 confirms their African heritage as a source of both energy and unity. The mythmaking continues. Characters like Bynum and Seth show traditions building from the boardinghouse, traditions flexible and open ended enough, moreover, to include the white traveling salesman Selig. Wilson takes his place in this process of tradition building. At the outset of the action, Mattie Campbell is living at 1727 Bedford Avenue (26). Wilson's stepfather was named David Bedford (Brown, 120), and Wilson once lived in a rooming house located at Pittsburgh's 1727 Bedford Avenue himself. This token of self-referentiality discloses in him a kinship with his materials, a bond underscored by his notes to the play's director. The stage directions in *Joe Turner* are longer and also more analytical and interpretive than those

of the two earlier Wilson scripts. It's no wonder that the play remains
his favorite in the canon (Shafer 1998, 12). This commitment to his
materials has helped Wilson avoid the trap of peddling either an ideology or a world-weary, disillusioned cynicism. The Christian elements of
the Juba that Loomis scorns warm and nourish some of the others. In *Joe
Turner*, he has written a play of both historical import and religious hope,
partly because his style reflects contemporary speech and partly because
his psyche is benevolent without being sentimental.

Chapter Six
Notes from the Past

Wilson's warrior spirits all yearn to connect with something or someone, even while perversely doing their utmost to deepen their isolation. Juncture is thus achieved but costively in the plays. In *The Piano Lesson* (1990), the family bond itself is threatened by the encroachments of business. Material interests invade and corrupt the most private corners of life, largely because these places have unwittingly invited corruption and invasion. The "sparsely furnished" Pittsburgh house where the action of *The Piano Lesson* unfolds lacks "warmth and vigor," Wilson says in the play's brief prologue. Then he shows why. Three people inhabit the house—Berniece Charles, a 35-year-old domestic, her 11-year-old daughter, Maretha, and Doaker, Berniece's uncle and the house's owner. Since Doaker's full-time job as a railway cook keeps him away from Pittsburgh much of the time, there's often no protective male presence in the house, creating a void that keeps Berniece on edge and thus blocks her ability to bestow or accept love.

Wining Boy, Doaker's brother, does visit the family sometimes. But this itinerant cadger of money, food, and drink provides little comfort or strength. Like Berniece, he's widowed, and he's likely to disappear without warning. Other signs of disconnection and collapse surface quickly. Doaker's wife has left him. James Sutter, a white landowner whose forebears owned the Charles family in antebellum Mississippi, has recently died. The truck that Berniece's brother, Boy Willie, drove up to Pittsburgh from Mississippi keeps breaking down. The Charles family needs a hefty grouting of solidness and self-worth. But at what price? Wilson wonders. In a 1987 *Chicago Tribune* interview he said, "The play asks two questions. . . . 'Can you acquire a sense of self-worth by denying your past?' and 'What can we do with our legacy?' " (Christiansen, 5). These questions pivot on a 137-year-old piano that Sandra Shannon calls "the center of the play's conflict as well as its symbolic core" (144).

Wilson wants us to decide whether such treasures should be enshrined to help people understand their heritage or whether they should be used to build a secure, prosperous future. Any claim that keeping the family piano would frustrate progress has to reckon with the images of Charles ancestors carved into it. Nor should it be forgotten that Berniece associates the piano with her memory of her dead mother. This Chekhovian conceit stokes the argument that the piano holds the collective spirit of the Charles clan. Perhaps in the minds of the less tenderhearted, though, that argument ignores the truth that the piano is basically a product of wood and wires. Difficult enough on their own, such conjectures take on frightening depths once ghosts enter the equation.

Ghostless, the equation is already steep. Having occupied black and white homes in both Mississippi and Pennsylvania, the piano bodies forth continuity. The music it makes implies a harmony absent from race relations in America. It also reminds us that Wilson's polemics can clash with his creativity. Despite his warnings that assimilation threatens the black identity of African Americans (Shafer 1989, 170), he showed in the Seth Holly–Rutherford Selig partnership in *Joe Turner* a happy fusion of black and white traditions. The black and white keys of the Charles's piano suggest the same optimism, but cautiously (Feingold, 118). Boy Willie Charles's dream of selling the piano could be kindled as much by protest against a slave past as by a vision of the future. Pereira has discussed both the positive and negative aspects of the piano's long history: "It is a sacred relic . . . a reminder of the misery [Berniece's] family endured; by keeping it she pays homage to their sacrifice. But she also keeps alive the anguish associated with the past" (90). This anguish is real. Though a memorial and a celebration, the piano has also caused several deaths. Doaker, who recently heard a ghost playing it, says, "Berniece need to go on and get rid of it. It ain't done nothing but cause trouble" (*PL*, 57). A local minister who tries in vain to bless it agrees. "Seems like that piano's causing all the trouble" (104), carps Avery Brown over his Bible and bottle of holy water.

The piano came to the Sutters in 1880 as a gift for a Miss Ophelia, whose name suggests, if not madness, then mental instability. The name of the piano's first owner, Mr. Nolander, invokes the disenfranchisement that still haunts the Charleses in 1936, the time setting of Wilson's play and the year before Joe Louis would become boxing's heavyweight champion. The piano's association with the ideas of combat and servitude moves forward through the generations. Boy Charles, the father of Berniece and Boy Willie, always groused that, even though slavery was long past, the Sutters still owned the Charleses because they owned the piano bearing several Charles images. On 4 July 1911 (*Joe Turner* took place in August 1911), his sons Doaker and Wining Boy took steps to end this symbolic thralldom. They stole the piano from the Sutter home and took it to the next county. The robbery reflects the Charles family's ongoing implication in crime (Wining Boy, Doaker, and Boy Willie would all do time between 1911 and 1936), and it also explores the link between crime and black America itself. If Boy Willie pushed James Sutter down the Mississippi well where he died, then the theft of the piano 26 years before sparked a series of violent crimes that have continued to hammer both families. The theft recoiled on the Charleses straightaway. Right after its occurrence, Boy Charles's home burned. Then the arsonists burned one of the yellow boxcars on the Yazoo and Mississippi Railroad, or Yellow Dog,[1] killing a fleeing Boy Charles along with four hobos who, like him, were trapped inside. The violence has persisted, James Sutter being the second of the suspected arsonists to fall down a well to his death. Local lore credits these two deaths to the Ghosts of the Yellow Dog, the spirits of the five black men who died in the boxcar that was torched the day the Sutters' piano left Sunflower County.

The violence surrounding the piano threatens to spread. Boy Willie wants to turn the piano into a cash asset. Doaker, though, has forbidden him to remove it from the house without Berniece's permission—which he'll never get; Berniece, who wants to keep the piano, orders Boy Willie out of the house when she learns of his intentions. But, because she's only a tenant in the house, rather than the owner, her eviction decree carries no force. Nor will Doaker, her uncle-landlord, support the decree. He has defined areas of domestic authority with a precision that thwarts the contending sibs. Though he has stopped Boy Willie from removing the piano, he won't oust his nephew from the house. This deadlock frustrates all. Terrific suspense uncoils from Berniece's reference to the handgun she keeps upstairs, the same handgun, incidentally, that caused her husband Crawley's death in Boy Willie's company three years before. Her appearance onstage with the gun presumably in her pocket rivets the audience. In the bobbing tidewake of the symbolic mother-son conflict of *Ma Rainey* and the literal father-son clash of *Fences,* fratricide has lurched to the center of *Piano Lesson.*

The process occurs in a climate of negritude, Wilson restoring the watermelon trope with which he raised the curtain on *Fences* ("The nigger had a watermelon this big" [*F,* 1] were Troy Maxson's first words spoken in our hearing). The watermelons Boy Willie has brought to Pittsburgh mask his seriousness of purpose. Like Tod Clifton's Sambo dolls in Ellison's *Invisible Man,* they're a means to an end—in Boy

Willie's case, the acquisition of a farm in Mississippi. His performance is well judged. By using the stereotype of the black watermelon peddler to misdirect his customers' attention, he revives in the Wilson canon the mischievous, unpredictable deity of African myth known as the trickster. Watermelons *are* bound up with blackness in America, if not in the easy, mindless way many believe.

Significantly, he wants to transport the piano, another vehicle of black tradition, in the same truck that carried the watermelons from Mississippi. In fact, he feels that the piano can fit comfortably in the truck alongside his unsold watermelons—as it should; the stack of watermelons and the piano both symbolize black America. One is stereotypical and degrading, the other noble and aggrandizing. Yet neither can be accepted without the other. By combining them imaginatively, Wilson shows his ability to mock while he celebrates. He had introduced this combination at great risk when he broke the dramatic flow of *Fences* at the play's most gripping moment to have Rose Maxson send Gabe into the house for a slice of watermelon (76). His strategy in *Piano Lesson,* though different, also pays tribute to the doubleness that for decades has helped black Americans survive. Boy Willie has come to Pittsburgh with two goals in mind. He wants to sell his truckload of watermelons, and he also hopes to sell the piano sitting in Doaker's parlor. But this hawker of watermelons shows the buying public only one of his aims. He has acted wisely. His riding the flow of energy created by a stereotype lodged in everybody's mind serves him well. By playing the grinning peddler of watermelons that grew in sugar-sweetened earth, he suppresses a side of himself that could give offense.

A Collision of Purposes

Wilson defines Boy Willie subtly. He's both an eccentric and an ordinary man who occupies space in the world without apologies. Boy Willie Charles is as demanding and difficult as Ma Rainey, Levee Green, or Troy Maxson before him. Both his blindness to the nuances of character and his hostility to the world's natural ambivalence have made him careless, arrogant, and willing to exploit others to advance himself. In the trademark warrior vein, he'll take what he believes he's entitled to, by force if necessary. Were he told that his society's laws were made by whites, are enforced by whites, and have been put in place to protect white interests, he would deny any difference between himself and the white man (*PL,* 38). In fact, were any difference to obtain, it would tilt in his favor.

This bizarre anarchist claims that he has the "power of death" (88) and that he was "born to a time of fire" (93). Thus he feels entitled to grab whatever pleases him. "I don't go by what the law say," he tells his uncle, adding, "I go by if it's right or not. It don't matter to me what the law say" (38).

Even his friend Lymon Jackson's reference to Parchman Farm, a Mississippi prison where Boy Willie has done hard time doesn't bridle his will. His dismissal of Lymon's reference to this prison that was run like a farm captures some of Boy Willie's doggedness. Spanning some 2,000 acres and 46 square miles in the Yazoo-Mississippi Delta, 90 miles south of Memphis, Parchman merits the title of David M. Oshinsky's harrowing 1996 book *"Worse than Slavery": Parchman Farm and the Ordeal of Jim Crow Justice.* Parchman's inmates had to work in blazing heat. Despite this constraint, failure to meet production quotas would incur punishments like torture, starvation, and being forced to eat contaminated food. Eager to avoid such brutality, some of the prisoners collapsed on the workfields from sunstroke or overwork; some died of malaria. Torment was unavoidable. "Escape attempts carried an unspeakable penalty: a whipping without limits."[2]

Only the most obdurate and headstrong would risk a second sentence in Parchman. Wilson accents Boy Willie's dash, brio, and defiance by contrasting him with Avery Brown, an ex-Mississippi farmer of 38 now living in Pittsburgh. Moving north has helped Avery. He holds a regular job as an elevator operator; he has become a preacher; he has managed to borrow enough money to start his own church. He has also proposed marriage to Berniece. Yet, even though the Christianity he has embraced has deep roots in black America, it fails to exorcise James Sutter's ghost in act 2, scene 5. The gains accrued by Avery's northern migration carry a deceptively high price. Perhaps it's small minded of Boy Willie to address Avery as "nigger" (e.g., *PL,* 22) to show him that he shouldn't be too impressed by his prospects as a Pittsburgh transplant. But having severed himself from his southern roots has already clipped Avery's wings. The Thanksgiving turkey his employer gives him every year symbolizes his vassalage as aptly as his elevator man's job conveys the illusion of progress. Regardless of the heights to which his elevator takes him, it always returns him to the ground floor. And because it only goes up and down, it also rules out forward progress.

Perhaps Berniece's reluctance to marry him stems from a suspicion that he's fighting his heritage. Insight into the tension inhibiting the growth of their love comes in act 2, scene 2, the only time in the play when they're alone together. Berniece invites him into the home just as she's about to take her bath, her invitation indicating that he has already seen her naked. He feels encouraged. But then she deflects his marriage proposal by saying, in terms that smack of 1990s feminism, "Everybody telling me I can't be a woman unless I got a man. Well, you tell me, Avery—you know—how much a woman am I?" (PL, 67). Yes, she and Avery have probably been lovers. But having sex with Avery might have left her feeling a bit flat. Several hours after he leaves her, she's charmed by Lymon. And she's never seen stepping into her tub, or taking her prenuptial ablutions, implying her continuing opposition to becoming Avery's wife.

Perhaps her reluctance hinges on the intimation that her brother, Boy Willie, would never rely on any white boss for *his* Thanksgiving turkey. The acquisition of land is a major accent in *Piano Lesson* (as opposed to Avery's wish to rent a storefront as a site for his church). Land not only offers the farmer a chance to be productive. It creates, as well, the opportunity to build a house and raise a family. Because each year brings a new rotation of crops and livestock, perhaps other families can live off it, too. This renewability opens up for growing numbers of people a sense of wholeness and rootedness that replaces the anxiety of homelessness and displacement.

An option to buy the same 100-acre farm where his family worked as slaves has given Boy Willie a chance to secure his future. He has two weeks in which to come up with $1,500 to buy the acreage. Yet no deal will have been clinched, even if Boy Willie does meet the Sutter family's deadline. First of all, the Sutters' asking price to Boy Willie was $2,000; the $1,500 figure was quoted to a white neighbor who had been asking about the land. Next, the Sutter clan may have already sold the land to another buyer during Boy Willie's absence, feeling no obligation to honor a casual oral agreement with a black. The land, finally, may be worthless, as Doaker claims (PL, 36). After all, the white neighbor who was offered the right of first refusal turned down the chance to buy it, at a lower price than that quoted to Boy Willie, as others may have, too. But Boy Willie won't be stopped, and Wilson admires his tenacity more than he condemns his ruthlessness. Having planned ahead, Boy Willie intends to tap three different sources to pay for the Sutter acreage: he has already saved $500, and the outstanding thousand will come, in more or less equal parts, from the profits amassed by selling both the watermelons and the family piano. He has been looking for a local buyer for the piano, perhaps the white man who has been trying to purchase old musical instruments from local blacks. But he suspects that finding the right buyer may take time. When Berniece asks him, the morning of his arrival, why he's not out in the street selling his watermelons, he responds with a lie, claiming that his wide-awake traveling mate, Lymon, is too sleepy from the long ride north. Lymon's innocent reaction to his fib, "I ain't sleepy" (*PL*, 26), points to Boy Willie's reluctance to sell all his watermelons before arranging the sale of the piano, as well.

Mei-Ling Ching sees value in Boy Willie's plan to convert the piano into a cash asset: "For Boy Willie, the piano is an antique souvenir with only a neutral spiritual value, hence a profitable object. To sell the piano is not to betray their family identity but to make it more productive."[3] Boy Willie believes that he owes his father, who died because of the piano, the opportunity to enfranchise the family. Besides being a farmer who wants to farm his own plot of land, Boy Willie feels he'd be dishonoring his father by letting the piano gather dust in Pittsburgh. Invoking Holloway's "stacking niggers" metaphor in *Two Trains Running* (35), Boy Willie tries to convince Berniece of the benefits of "building" on their joint legacy (*PL*, 51). Properly farmed, the Sutters' 100 acres will "give back to you" (51), he argues, growing crops and feeding livestock and thus creating a healthy, renewable interchange between the land and those who farm it.

The family piano, beautiful as it is, slights this functional ideal as long as it sits barely used. Its "sentimental value" (*PL*, 51), though fine and noble, represents a luxury the family can't afford. It has become an economic dead end at a time, 1936, when people are grabbing every available chance to recoup the heavy losses caused by the 1929 depression. Berniece hasn't played the piano for years. And since she doesn't give lessons on it, it neither brings in money nor helps anyone acquire a skill, except for 11-year-old Maretha, who could study on a new piano, which Berniece could easily buy with her half of the profits from the sale of the old one. Finally, moving the piano could end the round of thieving, killing, and well-falling that has been plaguing the Charleses for the past 25 years.

The commotion and confusion Boy Willie brings into the Charles house at opening curtain foreshadows his strong sense of purpose. He explodes into the house at five o'clock in the morning, expecting a grand welcome. Then, after waking everybody, he asks for food and drink. This disruptiveness typifies him. In act 2, scene 4, he tips a sleeping Lymon off a couch because he wants Lymon's immediate help loading the piano he sold behind Berniece's back. The previous scene saw him bringing home a local woman for sex even though the family, including Maretha, was sleeping upstairs. Wilson will use Maretha again to show Boy Willie's reluctance to curb his impulses for other people's good. By faulting Berniece in her disciplining of Maretha in act 2, scene 5, Boy Willie *is* overstepping, unlike Doaker, who never interferes with Maretha's rearing. Yet the little episode has some of Wilson's trademark ambiguity. Berniece has just chided Maretha for fidgeting during a hairdo. "If you was a boy I wouldn't be going through this" (*PL,* 90), she grumped. Boy Willie's reaction, "Don't you tell the girl that. Why you wanna tell her that?" (90), while possibly included in the play for its trendy feminism, does strike the proper moral note. It may have also been included because of the activity Berniece is performing— hot-combing grease into Maretha's hair to relax it and thus play down her ethnicity (she had already warned the girl not to "show . . . your color" [27]).

In this regard, Boy Willie may be extending more respect to the family's black southern heritage than Berniece. Perhaps her lapse explains why Wilson made her the first character in the play to report having sighted the ghost of James Sutter (*PL,* 12). She does need schooling in the lore of the black rural South. Despite her apparition, she keeps insisting that Boy Willie, and not the Ghosts of the Yellow Dog, pushed Sutter down the well (e.g., 14, 69). A Mississippi preacher who holds the ghosts to be agents of divine justice disagrees with her (69). And so might Wilson; he made Sutter a 340-pounder to support local legend. An avenging ghost could push a man this big down a well more easily than even a weight lifter in tournament trim.

Naturally, Boy Willie attributes Sutter's strange death to the Ghosts of the Yellow Dog, too (*PL,* 34). Whether he believes his attribution is another story; only *he* knows whether he killed Sutter. Like Sylvester of *Ma Rainey,* he'll blame his misdeeds on others, an example being his claim made to Lymon that Grace, the young woman he brought home for sex, and not he, broke Berniece's parlor lamp the night before. Though he'd never admit it, Boy Willie feels uneasy about Sutter's death. Beneath his braggadocio lurks guilt. Whether he killed Sutter will never be known. But he does stand to profit from Sutter's death because it has given him the chance to own his first farm.

Sutter's own feelings about seeing his Mississippi acreage turned over to Boy Willie also run high. Shannon has hinted at his centrality in the unfolding Charles family drama: "Not just a figment of imagination or hallucination, this spirit of the former 300-pound white landowner is a confirmed presence in Berniece's home as he is witnessed by each member of the Charles family" (160). As Shannon suggests, Sutter is a busy ghost, displaying himself to all of the members of Doaker's family circle before his climactic showdown with Boy Willie. Doaker, in fact, saw him about three weeks before the play's present-tense action "[']cause of the piano" (*PL,* 57), he claims. Obviously, the ghost knew that Boy Willie would be coming north to sell the instrument, and he wanted to stop him. Even though two Charleses, Doaker and his brother Wining Boy, stole it from the Sutters, the ghost of James Sutter wants it kept in Doaker's parlor rather than being moved to the home of a stranger. His appearing to both Doaker and Berniece with his hand atop his head (*PL,* 14, 57) reflects Wilson's belief that the dead have their duties just like the living. Sutter knows that the Holy Spirit will enter his body and redeem it only after he has foiled Boy Willie's projected piano heist. Sutter's bulk is more of a help than a hindrance in this regard. The outsize ghost will thwart Boy Willie and Lymon's attempts to remove the piano by simply sitting on it.

Wilson's ability to dramatize his belief in the power of the spirit world to intervene in the daily affairs of black Americans grew in the three years dividing *Piano Lesson* from *Fences.* Troy's wrestling match with Mr. Death both occurred while Troy was delirious and made itself known to us years after its occurrence. The Charles clan's encounters with Sutter's ghost, on the other hand, are both more extended and more carefully woven into the play's present-tense action. The ghost first reveals itself to Berniece "calling Boy Willie's name" (*PL,* 14). Thus Boy Willie is unnerved by it early in the action; he hasn't left it back in Mississippi, as he had hoped. His defenses having snapped quickly in place, he rejects its existence so vehemently that he denies Berniece the glass of water she needs to calm her nerves. Minutes later, though, sensing his implication in the ghostly drama, he contradicts himself. Perhaps he has remembered that ghosts materialize only in places to which they've been summoned. Hiding behind bluster, he says, "I wish I would see Sutter's ghost. Give me a chance to put a whupping on him" (*PL,* 17).

This reference to a "whupping" turns the mind to the black hero who made the term famous, Muhammad Ali, title figure of a poem of Wilson's that appeared in Chicago's *Black World* in September 1972 (60–61). It also ties in with the arrogance Boy Willie exhibits when he says later, "Ain't no mystery to life" (*PL,* 92). His swaggering continues: "You just got to meet it square on. . . . You can stand right up next to the white man and talk about the price of cotton" (92). His primordially American optimism confirms the dynamism of hard work, the ability to seize opportunity, and a pay-as-you-earn realpolitik that rewards industry and perseverance. Sutter's ghost has to teach him that this secular capitalism applies but barely to him because of its irrelevance to the collective unconscious of black America. Boy Willie's refutation of the ghost well into the play's last scene ("Ain't no ghost in this house" [96]) keeps him at cross-purposes with his heritage. But it also impresses us, its wrongheadedness invoking both the pride and desperation that misled Oedipus into denying the wisdom of the oracle.

The symptoms underlying Boy Willie's denial had already shown themselves. And he should have attended to them, as his statement "It's hard to figure out white folks sometimes" indicates (*PL,* 82). So impetuous is he that his arrival in Pittsburgh precedes that of the sun, under whose light most of his society's business takes place. He's often out of step with his surroundings. Rather than exulting in life's interconnectedness, he segments life. He's so keen to sell the family piano that, invoking the Biblical story of the false-hearted mother willing to rend her presumed child in two to guard her maternal rights (I Kings 3:16–28), he speaks of cutting the piano in half. His inability to see things whole also misleads him into accusing Berniece of interpreting the Bible "halfway" (*PL,* 89). Ironically, the "eye for an eye" (89) ethical system he supports falls short in its dismissal of mercy, charity, and the New Testament imperative to turn the other cheek. This same segmenting outlook prompts him to draw a line with his foot across the floor of Doaker's parlor to divide his part of the house from Berniece's. He's always dividing and subdividing. Characteristically, he tells Doaker to "mark down on the calendar" the date the family took possession of the much-coveted piano (91). "You ought to mark that day and draw a circle around it" (91), he adds, voicing the fragmenting mentality that blinds him to the organicity that has made the piano both an intimate family record and an expression of the family's soul.

On the other hand, his ability to be tender and sunny has helped earn him the ghost's (and Wilson's) attention. There's much in *Piano Lesson* that casts the overhyped Boy Willie in a soft light and makes him warmly human. His nearly obsessive sense of purpose, for instance, hasn't destroyed his good manners. He introduces his traveling mate, Lymon, to Doaker, Berniece, and Wining Boy at first opportunity. Thoughtfully, he shares with Lymon the bread that Doaker grills for him. This willingness to share without being prodded (which is light-years away from Levee's greediness around food) reflects a goodness of heart he discloses elsewhere. Within minutes of greeting them, he invites both Maretha and Avery Brown to help themselves to a watermelon from his truck. Then, after giving Maretha a dime to play a tune for him on the piano, he promises to buy her a guitar (with some of the profits he expects from selling the piano, no doubt). Nor does he try to defend himself from Berniece's blows when she strikes out at him for allegedly causing her husband Crawley's death.

Any actor playing the role of Boy Willie should convey this sensitivity. If not a soft man, Boy Willie has softness in him. The chance to buy the very land his ancestors toiled on as slaves represents such a gigantic breakthrough that it has scrambled his judgment. Jesse Owens's breaking of four track records in the 1936 Olympics may have tricked Boy Willie into believing that life's prizes are his for the taking. Like Chekhov's Lopakhin in *The Cherry Orchard,* he's more a victim of the acquisitive spirit of his day (in his case, the post-Depression decade) than of greed. When the play ends and Sutter's ghost has fled, it's Boy Willie we worry about more than the others.

Family Politics

Boy Willie's opposite number in the play, his sister, Berniece, knows him well enough to be warned by his unannounced arrival at Doaker's. Immediately, she suspects that both the truck he and Lymon drove from Mississippi and its contents were either stolen or paid for with stolen money. So nervous does Boy Willie's arrival make her that within moments of seeing him she asks him how long he plans to stay (*PL,* 7). Wilson speeds the action in the early going in order to sustain her anxiety. Having yoked the presence of Sutter's ghost in the house with that of Boy Willie, she asks her brother to leave (16). She's apprehensive because she wants to protect the domestic calm she has worked so hard to put in place since her husband's death. Central to this conservative mind-set is the truth that Crawley died committing a crime—alongside Lymon and Boy Willie. She hasn't seen her brother since Crawley's death, a calamity she blames on him, partly because he escaped it. On this issue, Wilson is deliberately vague. Though Boy Willie invited Crawley to commit the crime (a wood heist) that eventually took his life, he didn't pressure Crawley to join him and Lymon at the woodpile. Nor did he persuade Crawley to bring to the crime site the gun that frightened the investigating police into shooting him. These ambiguities have knotted Berniece's heart. Her inability to stop grieving over Crawley's death explains in part why Sutter's ghost appears to her; the ghost wants to shake her out of her doldrums in order to sensitize her to the attentions of an Avery or a Lymon.

Her intransigence includes the piano. Doaker (*PL,* 9, 12) and his brother Wining Boy (42) are both right in their belief that she'll never sell the piano. Ironically, though her ideas about the future of the piano clash with Boy Willie's, brother and sister are both driven by a loyalty to the past. Pitted against Boy Willie's claim that selling the piano would redeem the legacy of suffering it represents is Berniece's contention that the carvings on the piano make it unsellable; a family monument, the piano must stay at Doaker's. It's permeated with deposits of family experience. "Money can't buy what that piano cost. You can't sell your soul for money" (*PL,* 50), she insists.

Aggravating her opposition to Boy Willie on the issue of the piano is the death of her husband. Berniece believes that Crawley would still be alive if Boy Willie hadn't included him in the crime that took his life. She seems unmoved by Lymon's claim that, instead of surrendering to the police as he and Boy Willie did, Crawley opened fire and died from an answering volley of shots. So long as Crawley is dead and Boy Willie is alive, her resentment against her brother will persist. The bath she draws for herself but never takes at the start of act 2, scene 2, the play's midpoint, suggests that she never cleanses herself of this resentment during the play's time setting. Both her attitude and that of Boy Willie toward the piano are understandable. But they're also irreconcilable. As Frank Rich said in his *New York Times* review, "both characters are right—and wrong."[4] Which is as Wilson intended it; though a playwright needn't approve of his people's choices, he can sympathize with the motives underlying them. *Piano Lesson* doesn't assign blame. Instead, like Tennessee Williams's *Streetcar Named Desire,* it describes a tension both moral and emotional that acquires added sinew by unfolding within a family context.

Berniece snaps the tension when she sits at the piano she had neglected for years and, to the accompaniment of a simple tune, chants a litany made up of the names of her dead forebears (Shannon, 146). Because the spirits of these forebears pervade the piano, all she has to do to win their help is to ask for it. Because they love her, they oblige her gladly. Once more in August Wilson, the solution to an important problem lies nearby. An unseen hand led her to the piano. The person helped most by her impromptu chant, though he'd be loath to admit it, is Boy

Willie. The routing of Sutter's ghost by the spirits of his ancestors gives him the chance to do battle with it. Perhaps his seizing of this chance matters more than would have his selling of the piano. Regardless of how much land he owned, he could never buy freedom and equality by impersonating a white cotton farmer. But he *can* start the process. Wilson said that the disposal of the piano meant less to him than the spunk Boy Willie displayed fighting the ghost of Sutter, the white man whose slaveholding ancestors owned Boy Willie's people for generations ("How to Write a Play like August Wilson," 17).

This resolution has offended some playgoers. Berkowitz calls Boy Willie's fight with Sutter's ghost "a theatrically weak climax, since the mystical element seems imposed on the essentially realistic play" (198). Arguing in kind, Mimi Kramer complains that the play's ending "takes refuge in mysticism and melodramatic event" (83). Both critics can be answered by noting that Wilson's technique remains consistent throughout *Piano Lesson.* The work's climax *does* owe much to the intervention of the otherworldly. But the otherworldly also clarifies much that preceded it, particularly the Ghosts of the Yellow Dog, who for years have been scourging the white racist vigilantes of Mississippi's Sunflower County. The play's surprise ending convinces us of its inevitability. This is no small achievement. The "essentially realistic" (198) plotting elements of *Piano Lesson* cited by Berkowitz bespeak Wilson's sound understanding of human nature. The play's mysticism supports its realistic foreground rather than giving Wilson an easy way to resolve the plot. Without straining for profundity, his poignant inwardness of vision and shrewd knowing humor convey the tricky, unstable nature of identity in *Piano Lesson.* Nor does he forget the interplay of identities. Reflecting a Borgesian economy, his careful, moving attention to detail telescopes large fictions into a tiny space.

These fictions take life from Wilson's preference for the specifics of experience over the abstractions of rational planning. The climax of *Piano Lesson* starts building in the play's middle scene, act 2, scene 2, which takes its drive from Avery—his religious faith, his ministry, and his sexual attraction to Berniece. From this point forward, instinct and impulse will ride herd over the intellect. The two following scenes show Boy Willie's attempt to have sex with Grace on the parlor couch, and, in a gentler vein, to keep the play from peaking emotionally before the end, Lymon's more restrained charming of Berniece. By the play's last scene, which opens with Boy Willie's preparations to remove the piano from Doaker's parlor, life's absurdity is enjoying a merry romp. Boy Willie opens the front door from the inside expecting to greet Lymon, his supposed helper, but, instead, admits Avery into the house. This small reversal prefigures what ensues—the blocking of dramatic drive and closure and the dispersion of Boy Willie's ruling passion into low comedy.

When Lymon does show up at Doaker's, he's not thinking about moving any piano. Grace is waiting outside for him to take her to a movie. Wining Boy's entry into the house a few minutes later marks one more step in the shunting of Boy Willie's commanding sense of purpose into comic ambiguity. A drunken Wining Boy seats himself at the piano while Boy Willie is trying to move it, and, since he wrote the song he's singing and playing to honor the memory of his recently dead wife, he's allowed to perform as long as he likes. Then, transported by his music, he drapes his drunken self over the piano to stop Boy Willie from carting it away. Music has once again rerouted the dramatic flow of an August Wilson play.

And the naked upsurge of messy, unedited life has again stopped Boy Willie, a dynamic conveyed visually by a minor character. Thematically appropriate to Wilson's description of the contrariness and intractability of life is the appearance in the parlor of Grace, who had become bored with waiting for Lymon in the truck. She didn't hear Wining Boy's song. She didn't have to. With her red dress symbolizing the appetite that runs heroic action into a wall, her reentry into the same house she was put out of the previous night, when her sexual gropings with Boy Willie tipped over the parlor lamp, causes one more blurring of the hard focus Boy Willie has been trying to attain. Sutter's ghost is now ready to step in to serve one last lesson—on the pitfalls of pride.

A major player in Wilson's development of this cosmic comedy has been Lymon Jackson. Like Boy Willie and Wining Boy, he served time at Parchman Farm, and there's a good chance his convict days aren't over. Shot in the stomach in the same wood theft in which Crawley died and then sentenced to jail, he has already suffered. More suffering awaits him in Mississippi. No sooner was he released from jail than he was locked up again for vagrancy and fined $100. The same real-life Jim Stovall (Palmer, 100; *PL,* 36; cf. *2TR,* 72) who was given first-refusal rights on the Sutter acreage offered to pay Lymon's hundred-dollar fine so Lymon could repay the debt in kind by working overtime on Stovall's farm. Despite Lymon's preference for his 30-day sentence, the judge put him in Stovall's custody. Then Lymon fled to the North.

No warrior, the fugitive Lymon has an easygoing, loping charm that others find warmly engaging. His conversation often turns to the subject of women. Besides serving as a refuge from both Stovall and the sheriff of Sunflower County, Pittsburgh has attracted him because of its supposed abundance of available women. Soon after his arrival, he buys a suit and a pair of shoes to impress the ladies, and he wears them that very evening to trawl the local nightlife district. Whether it was his new togs or a reserved, respectful boyishness in his demeanor that charmed her, Grace liked him well enough to accept a movie date with him. Berniece had noticed him, too, perhaps because he—and not her uncle or her brother—offered her a glass of water after she was shocked by Sutter's ghost in act 1, scene 1 (*PL*, 13).

Wilson's giving Lymon and Berniece their own scene to play alone together (act 2, scene 3) expresses a newfound belief on his part that women are charmed more by the gentleness that Lymon (and that other ex-convict Sterling Johnson of *Two Trains Running*) displays than by the macho antics of a Troy, a Levee, or a Boy Willie. Lymon's wants are simple. A plain man with no illusions about himself, he tells Berniece that he's looking for both a job "unloading boxcars or something" and a woman to relieve his loneliness (*PL*, 77). The openness and innocence with which he rehearses these hopes charms Berniece as do his good manners. "Was you in bed? I don't mean to be keeping you up" (79), he says with his customary candor. Then with the same openness, this 29-year-old runaway whose life up to the present time has consisted mostly of false starts offers her a bottle of perfume.

His dabbing the back of her ear with a drop of the dollar perfume breaks her reserves. They kiss before she exits up the stairs, ending the play's most poignant, artistically nuanced scene. The moment is one of great tenderness. Lymon's loneliness has grazed that of Berniece. As is suggested by the six years that divide him from the older Berniece, Lymon isn't a suitable mate for her. But he needn't offer her the prospect of permanence to fulfill Wilson's dramatic intent. The brief spell he exerts on her shows that her heart isn't calcified. Despite the emotional chill caused in her by Crawley's death, she can still renew herself sexually. And perhaps the quiet glow Lymon feels after kissing her briefly certifies him as an agent of renewal.

Blending the Farflung

As in *Joe Turner*, the improbable and the unlikely both carry great weight in *Piano Lesson*. The scene following the tender, understated exchange between Berniece and Lymon opens noisily with Boy Willie bursting into Doaker's parlor and dumping a sleeping Lymon on the floor (*PL,* 81). It's also quite possible that James Sutter's brother did give Boy Willie two weeks to find the cash for the family acreage. Many stranger things happen in this play in which faith and intuition, omens and portents often assert their might at the expense of reason. Robert Brustein's verdict, that *Piano Lesson* is "the most poorly composed" of Wilson's four Broadway-produced works to date because of its "repetitiousness, crude plotting, and clumsy structure," falls wide of the truth.[5] Clever, determined, and visionary, *Piano Lesson* goes beyond even *Joe Turner* in yoking both the knockabout and the absurdity of daily life to the spirit world. Its avoidance of the stiff, the diagrammatic, and the simplistic helps the play achieve this bond. Each character adds something to the central conflict; each brings something subtle and interesting to the theme.

Piano Lesson profits from the clamor that runs through it. Perhaps Wilson's noisiest play, its shouts, chants, and drumbeats foreshadow the racket caused by Boy Willie's wrestling match with Sutter's ghost. Like Grace's red dress and the loud pink suit Lymon buys from Wining Boy, this uproar helps break down the threshold of rational response that Wilson deems irrelevant to the deeper meanings of his 1990 play. Tone and theme dovetail perfectly in *The Piano Lesson,* a fierce, wise, and gripping work that confirms the steady growth of a major American playwright.

GENEALOGY
The Charles Household

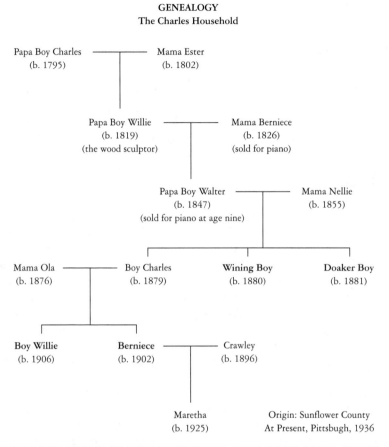

GENEALOGY OF THE CHARLES HOUSEHOLD, FROM THE PLAYBILL OF THE
NEW YORK PRODUCTION OF *THE PIANO LESSON*.
Reprinted by permission of August Wilson.

Chapter Seven

Forever under Attack

Set in 1969, *Two Trains Running* provides a gritty, unflinching look at the effects of a decade of great progress for black America. The progress covered many areas. The year 1962 saw the election of the first black man, Jackie Robinson, to baseball's Hall of Fame and, thanks to the efforts of the Student Nonviolent Coordinating Committee, new highs in black voter registration in the deep South. Two years later, Dr. Martin Luther King won the Nobel Peace Prize and, a year after that, more than 3,000 people marched the 54 miles between Selma and Montgomery, Alabama. The list of breakthroughs continues. Justice Thurgood Marshall became the first black member of the U.S. Supreme Court in 1967, and 1968 brought the passage of the Civil Rights Act. But many would feel let down by this landmark bill. The benefits of hindsight explains why. The failure of the act to create more equality and justice for blacks could have been predicted from the ugliness that preceded it. The murders of Malcolm X in 1965 and of Dr. King in 1968 belong in the same continuum as the slaying of civil rights workers in Mississippi in 1964 and the deaths caused by riots in Watts in 1965 and Detroit in 1967.

This violence erupted for a reason. Despite the Black Power activism and the progress in civil rights legislation since 1962, blacks in America were still oppressed. Their future looked bleak. In the air were signs of the coming of cities that would be too fast, too crowded, and too smart to be easily endured by the black underclass, cities also marred by growing numbers of glue sniffers, heroin addicts, and hookers living in condemned buildings without electricity or running water. Unfolding in a transitional era, *Two Trains Running* (1992) describes urban blacks caught in the wash of social change. It depicts the clash of old and new energies—the relative ease of an old order faced by the anarchy of a new social agenda that includes the militant politics of the Nation of Islam.

The ordeals of both the Middle Passage and the Great Migration have revived in the minds of Wilson's people. For another population displacement is at hand; city planners are razing Pittsburgh's Hill for an urban redevelopment plan without first providing for the residents' relocation.

There are other forebodings. Besides flattening a friendly, vibrant community that has meant home to many people, the proposed renewal scheme will create new, uglier slums that will aggravate Pittsburgh's present ghettoization—the division of the city's population by color and income. A large public works program will replace neighborhood continuity with "projects," big low-income, high-risk public housing. Symbolizing both the doomed organic community and the warm socializing buzz of the street is Memphis Lee's homestyle restaurant, the setting for Wilson's 1992 play. Like the jitney station in Wilson's unpublished 1982 *Jitney*, Lee's has been targeted for demolition by the city. Across the street from it stand a funeral home and a meat market, suggesting rapacity and even cannibalism. This looming devastation rivets us because the restaurant, it soon becomes clear, is more than a place of business. It's also a makeshift community center and social club. People drop in at all hours for coffee and conversation. Neighborly and charitable, these denizens of Lee's take up a collection to bail a local man out of jail so he can attend his wife's funeral (*2TR*, 55).

Yet Wilson is too ironic and socially aware to ride the flow of sentiment induced by the death of Bubba Boy's wife. Capable of being tender and tough minded at the same time, he deliberately sited *Trains* in a climate of "urban decay" (McDonough, 153). The local supermarket, the five-and-ten, two drugstores, and the local doctor and dentist, it comes out early, have all left the Hill or gone out of business. "Ain't nothing gonna be left but these niggers killing one another" (*2TR*, 9), says Memphis, forecasting the inevitable upshot of this erosion of amenities and services. Nor can he stop the slide. Once a thriving business, his diner now has a small clientele. At the time of the first act, its larder consists only of a little coffee, some beans, frozen hamburger, and a box of rice. Memphis goes shopping during the course of the action for limited quantities of chicken, meat loaf, and pie he'd have stocked—and sold—in abundance during the diner's earlier, palmier days.

On the subject of Memphis and his surviving clientele, Carla J. McDonough says, "a sense of detachment, decay, and dissolution pervades their talk. These men are separated from their families and are left very little in the way of companionship" (153). Marginalized and wounded they have become. West the mortician is the only local whose business has been thriving. He can forget the days when it took two weeks to get a broken toilet fixed. So lucrative is his mortuary that he no longer replaces broken window panes with wooden boards; his livery includes seven Cadillacs; looking to add to his millions, he has been buying up much of the real estate on the Hill so he can sell it back to the city at a profit before it's razed. Memphis has also known prosperity, if not recently. Like West, he's a property-owning driver of a Cadillac. But the devastation that has enriched West—including that caused by black-on-black crime—is threatening *him*. This wise investor sees the forced sale of the building he has divided into a diner and rental apartments taking away from him both a steady source of cash and a means of self-validation.

He and his cronies lead half lives, a sad truth suggested by their mostly being known by one name. Holloway has no woman, and West is a widower (widowers outnumber widows in Wilson). Hambone, Wolf, and Bubba Boy (another widower) are known only by their nicknames. Memphis Lee, whose first name is probably also a nickname, has a wife he rarely sees. Loneliness also frets the two characters who develop the play's love interest. By default, the orphan-turned-bank-robber Sterling Johnson took the last name of an adoptive family he no longer sees. His putative mate, Clarissa Thomas (*2TR*, 18), is always called Risa, denoting a loss of clarity or brightness in her life. The others share her plight. Gloom has gripped the doomed neighborhood with its shards of broken glass, thriving mortuary, and Bubba Boy's newly dead wife. Wilson told Mark William Rocha in a 1992 interview that his intention in *Two Trains Running* was to show "that by 1969 nothing . . . changed for the black man" (27). In 1969, the efforts of the deceased Malcolm X and Dr. King, like the high-profile 1968 Civil Rights Act, did look futile. But futility hasn't swallowed all, thanks to the synergy created by the play's fusion of vision and voice. Supported by dialogue sinewy, charged, and sometimes hilarious, the ambiguity that permeates Wilson's beliefs about social progress for blacks provokes more debate than grief.

Life on the Edge

By all reasonable standards, the people in *Trains* qualify as losers— depressing to think about and painful to watch. That they fuse as a winning, engaging group whose doings fascinate us counts as a small miracle. This feat hinges in part on the deft and always entertaining techniques Wilson uses to drive a grim story. In part it hinges on Wilson's belief in the inadequacy of reason to explain life's mysteries. This belief, if unoriginal, is both hard won and moving. Wilson is the opposite of an ideologue. He hates ideologies and dogmas. To him, they're narrow and partisan, and they do great harm. They also make politicians look clumsy and stupid at times when they need flexibility and breadth of outlook. This truth explains a great deal in *Trains*. A minute into the play a character says, "The NAACP got all kinds of lawyers. It don't do nobody no good" (*2TR*, 2). Wilson would probably approve this verdict. He's as hostile to collective solutions as was Ellison in *Invisible Man*. Pereira sees him directing that hostility toward recent attempts by black activists to improve their people's chances for justice and equality. The death of Wilson's Prophet Samuel, Pereira claims, coming soon after those of Malcolm X and Dr. King, signals the failure of the civil rights movement in the United States (6). The ballyhoo created by both Prophet Samuel's funeral and the monster rally for Malcolm X supports Pereira's claim.

Prophet Samuel confirms Wilson's genius for driving a plot with a character who never shows his face to the audience. That face *is* seen offstage, though mostly by the undertaker West, since the prophet died just before opening curtain. But others have been thronging not only to see that face but also to touch it. Prophet Samuel had enjoyed roaring success preaching the doctrine of freedom and dignity through the acquisition of wealth. Though this dovetailing of material and spiritual blessings squares with mainstream Yankee Protestantism, Wilson rejects it with the same scorn he aims at the Black Power movement. Signs that Prophet Samuel represents a false direction include his sleazy background. Like Rinehart in *Invisible Man*, he's a huckster of religion with a criminal past who bleeds his own people (*2TR*, 25–26). His death, which might have been caused by poison, suggests the same spiritual paralysis called forth by the dead priest in James Joyce's "The Sisters," from *Dubliners*. Sisters are what Prophet Samuel's devotees might have called themselves, but the bonds he had with them were rumored to have been sexual. In fact, the poison that may have killed him would have been fed to him by a jealous female retainer (*2TR*, 6).

Though based on hearsay, this possibility stays alive. For poison *could* have driven the disorder that follows his death: a fight caused by someone who tries to crash the line of mourners waiting to pay their last respects, an opportunist who would charge admission to see the corpse, and an attempted late-night burglary of the funeral parlor where the corpse was laid out all imply a poisoning of the social order Prophet Samuel had allegedly set out to redeem. He always walked with corruption and fraud. Shannon has discussed the carnival atmosphere he liked surrounding himself with both to amuse his followers and to distract them from his ignorance of the living God: "Even after his death,

Prophet Samuel is able to attract hordes of people—the hopeless, the desperate, or simply the curious. While alive, he enjoyed a popular ministry based upon a mixture of showbiz antics, con artistry, and an immodest display of religiosity: he wore robes, went shoeless, and with much fanfare, baptized converts in a nearby river" (188).

As is shown by the disruptions following Prophet Samuel's death, such extravaganza inhibits both social and spiritual uplift. Wilson, duly warned, resists imposing either an arbitrary aesthetic order or a political agenda on his materials. Reflecting the disarray he sees around him, his theater addresses the challenge of maintaining a belief that defies reason. Warrior spirits like Troy Maxson and Boy Willie Charles break so many rules making this provocative leap of faith that they foil themselves. The issue revives in *Trains,* a work that posits a new ontology with its fusions of logic and nonsense and of the outlandish and the factual. Defying huge odds, the number 621 hits for the second time within a week. Sterling's number will also win but with mixed results, since it's cut in half, paying only 300 to 1 rather than the customary 600 to 1. Reason and common sense come under question as early as midway through the first scene when, moments after claiming that she has been cleaning a chicken, Risa admits that the diner is out of chicken (*2TR,* 16). Undeterred, her boss, Memphis, will soon tell her to fry the nonexistent chicken, to which she replies that she's already frying it (19).

Obviously, the world of Wilson's people regulates itself by a mystique far removed from Western pragmatism. Embodying this mystique is a 322-year-old woman named Aunt Ester, who lives at 1839 Wylie, just minutes away from Memphis's diner, the Wylie Avenue address of which is 1621. But the August Wilson of *Trains* varies his usual practice of siting salvation close to the mise-en-scène. Though suggesting sexual passion, the red door of Aunt Ester's apartment leads to inner peace and self-acceptance. But these blessings aren't open to all. She speaks in riddles, and, like that of Bynum in *Joe Turner,* her wisdom is more of a challenge than a quick fix. She makes Sterling come to her three times before admitting him. Her standards are high. She *will* rid people like Sterling of their bad energy, but anyone who approaches her with selfish motives will walk away empty-handed. In particular, she refuses to help those who want her to show them how to get rich (*2TR,* 25). Indicative of the times they're living in, five characters in the play (four speaking parts and Prophet Samuel) ask her help. What she says to them reaches us only in rough outline, Wilson deliberately avoiding telling all. As he should; one of the privileges of being alive consists of moving forward in the dark. Were all life's riddles and mysteries disclosed to us, faith would be drained of meaning, and the afterlife would lack purpose. Thus Risa, a follower of the charlatan Prophet Samuel and a no-show at Aunt Ester's, gives Sterling his winning number, 781, but withholds its import from him. Defying reason, she also claims that the deranged Hambone has more sense than any of the other patrons of the diner (*2TR*, 45).

Perhaps insight into the play's larger meaning lies in its title. Memphis says that every day two trains run back to his hometown of Jackson, Mississippi. He hopes that he'll soon board one to reclaim the farm that was stolen from him in 1931. He has judged his prospects well. Any train is a blind, amoral force, like money, a subject the characters argue about often. Memphis could hop on either of the two trains that leave daily from Pittsburgh. The sense of mission impelling him will endow the morally neutral train he takes with value; the moral drama must come from him if it's to come at all. Observing unity of place, Wilson ends the play before Memphis's long-awaited train ride to Jackson. But he does talk about the play's title in terms applicable to Memphis. His words appear both on the back cover of the 1993 Plume paperback reprint of the play and in the playbill (p. 34) of the 1992 Broadway production at the Walter Kerr Theater: "There are always and only two trains running. There is life and there is death. Each of us rides them both. To live life with dignity, to celebrate and accept responsibility for your presence in the world is all that can be asked of anyone."

Dignity and personal responsibility are virtues that members of an underclass, particularly a transient one, can rarely afford to cultivate. The frequency in the canon of both trains and the blues, Wilson's main source of artistic inspiration, calls forth the idea of transience, specifically the Great Migration and the many family breakups it caused. Romare Bearden, the black American painter and collagist whose work inspired both *Joe Turner* and *The Piano Lesson,* referred to trains more gently when he said in 1977, "Negroes lived near the tracks, worked on the railroads, and trains carried them North during the migration."[1] Wilson prefers the darker tones. Doaker, who spent 27 years working on the railroad, says in *Piano Lesson* about train passengers, "They leaving cause they can't get satisfied" (18). To him, trains symbolize failure to cope. Rather than staying home and trying to solve their problems, the fainthearted think that riding a train to a new town will make them go away.

They're wrong. Rather than staying behind in Mississippi, Sutter's ghost spent the three weeks before the opening curtain preparing for Boy Willie's arrival in Pittsburgh. Moreover, a train *will* sooner or later carry Boy Willie back to the Mississippi town where his journey began (*PL,* 19). Both the sound made by an approaching train at the end of the play (107) and Boy Willie's last question "Hey, Doaker, what time the train leave?" (108) reinstate the realities that rule most of Wilson's people—anxiety and the illusion of freedom.

A character whose financial and emotional distress converts to physical disquiet in *Trains* is Sterling. Recalling Wilson's other jobless young men just out of jail, such as Booster in *Jitney* and Lymon in *Piano Lesson,* Sterling is afraid that his new freedom offers no promise of a happy, productive life. So haunted is he by the fear of returning to jail that at times he seems to be inviting arrest. Self-preservation has never been his forte. Ten minutes after he robbed a bank, he was spending the stolen money. Yet, as Shannon says, he's no more of a monster than was the boyishly endearing Lymon: "Sterling is a strangely off-beat character. Far from presenting the hard-core image one might expect, he appears painfully naive—almost childlike" (180–81). The good luck he claims to have been born with (*2TR,* 21) has deserted him. Unable to find work, he tries in vain to sell his watch. The job he held after his release from prison lasted only a week, at which time he was laid off. Or so he says (20); according to Memphis, Sterling quit. Holloway, the play's griot figure, agrees; if Sterling wanted to work, he'd have a job, Holloway believes (52–53). Holloway and Memphis could be right. It's possible that Sterling's youthful charm stems from his immaturity. One of the most intriguing questions posed by *Trains* is whether Sterling (the Laurence Fishburne role in the 1992 Walter Kerr Theater production) can ever become a contented, peaceable member of society.

Alas, most of the evidence is negative. Lacking a sense of process, the boyish Sterling wants the rewards of labor without the toil: he steals some flowers from a memorial to give Risa because "it's silly to buy flowers" (*2TR,* 61); he also steals a five-gallon can full of gasoline. And it may also have been Sterling who broke West's window while trying to burglarize the mortuary after dark (he'll break a storefront window later in the play). Spending five years in prison didn't wipe out his criminal streak. Giving up his job search quickly, he buys a handgun, which he believes will help him access the material goods he wants but lacks the patience to work for. Holloway (52) and Memphis (79) both judge well when they envision him back in jail within weeks. Judging from his recklessness, they've skewed their timetables in his favor.

The person he'd sadden most by returning to prison is Risa. Like Lymon of *Piano Lesson,* he charms women rather than trying to overpower them. Risa is moved by his gentleness. He rejects her offer of beans in act 1, scene 1, explaining that he has been eating beans for the past five years. But a couple of days later, he gladly eats the beans she serves him, even asking for a second bowl. He has touched Risa. Within minutes, she twice uses the phrase "the right person" while discussing dancing partners (*2TR,* 46–47), implying that she might welcome his attentions. But what kind of future would these attentions foster? Though uneducated, Risa is both sharp and caring. Other characters have misread this beguiling combination. Memphis miscues when he calls her "a mixed-up personality" (32), and the numbers runner Wolf falls just as wide of the mark with his reductive summary, "all she need is a man" (32). Risa defies definitions and formulas. Although constantly rebuked by Memphis, she's confident she won't be fired (18). She and Memphis both know that the diner is more than just a business establishment. To maintain its status as a surrogate home, it needs the female presence she gives it. Thus, without admitting it, Memphis prizes her kindness and warmth. What's more, the success he attains could well come from the wisdom he exercises by emulating her rarest quality—a fierce independence.

Like the others in the play, Risa is a lonely person awaiting redemption through love. But she wants love on her own strict terms, and it can only be shared with "the right person." Wilson fills in the background to the formation of these requirements. Some time before the play's present-tense action, perhaps as long as six years ago, she slashed her legs (*2TR,* 32). Her scars depict her protest to being classified sexually or appraised as a possible bedmate. In the interest of building a long-term bond, she wants to turn the attention of any would-be male admirer to her inner self. She doesn't regret the 15 scars on her legs. To her, they still express a wish to be appreciated in her totality. There's much in her to appreciate. She speaks gently to Hambone, gives him a coat to wear, and feeds him whenever he comes into the diner. Though a follower of the Prophet Samuel, she'll attend neither his funeral nor the big rally for Malcolm X. She doesn't need the support of crowds to shore up her beliefs. Her values are personal, not collective, and she rates any leader's example over his mortal remains. (She will skip Hambone's funeral, too.)

Like everybody else, she knows, too, that love on one's own terms misses love. Thus she'll have to relax her agenda, fine as it is. Without protesting, she hears both Wolf and Sterling call her "baby" (*2TR,* 21). Protests wouldn't help her, anyway. She wants to share a special bond with a man she hopes might be Sterling. But she sees with a sinking heart that Sterling's sexual interest in her has put him on a par with all the other men who have courted her for the past six years; "You just want what everybody else want" (100), she tells him. She wasn't expecting the reply she gets from him. By slashing her legs, he says, she violated nature. What's natural, he continues, is for a man to notice the charms of a pretty woman and then take steps to enjoy them. Instead of marring her legs, she should have simply used them to walk away from any man whose advances she found unwelcome.

Whether this argument convinces her is not clear. More obvious is her inability to fight the attraction she feels for him. Her reason tells her to resist him: "You ain't got no job. You going back to the penitentiary. I don't want to be tied up with nobody I got to be worrying is they gonna rob another bank or something" (*2TR,* 100). Her message is clear. She's doomed if she builds her life around an ex-con who doesn't know right from wrong. But within minutes of explaining to Sterling his unfitness as a mate, she's dancing with him and then kissing him. Her instincts have defeated her judgment. Wilson supplies the foreshadowing to show that Sterling has been wearing down her judgment longer than she suspects. Just as she violated her principles by accepting his bouquet of stolen flowers, so will she later accept him as a lover.

This cautious, self-protective woman's worst nightmare threatens to burst into reality. As has been seen, Sterling and the job that was waiting for him after he served his jail sentence parted company after a week. Nor has he learned from this setback. When told that he lacks the education to get "one of them white folks' jobs making eight or nine thousand dollars a year," he replies in terms redolent of Troy Maxson or Boy Willie: "I can do anything the white man can do. If the truth be told . . . most things I can do better" (*2TR,* 52). This arrogance can only land him back in jail. Within moments of voicing it, he starts shopping for a handgun. And not only is the handgun he buys illegal; it's also one he had already owned and gotten rid of because it malfunctioned (53). Spending five years in prison hasn't improved his judgment. Later, he takes the gun to the racketeer who halved the payout for the number that hit on the day Sterling bet on it. The four or five gorillas, or bodyguards, surrounding Mr. Albert show Sterling that his unannounced

visit to the crime boss was a bad mistake. Wisely, he didn't start brandishing his gun in Albert's stronghold. He's probably as ready for an
audience with Aunt Ester as he'll ever be.

Rocha says of this ancient conjuress whom death seems to have forgotten, "Aunt Ester is to be taken as the original African American, as
old as the black experience in America" (Nadel, 128). Regardless of her
exact age (three figures are mooted, ranging from 300 to 349), it
approximates the length of time that Africans have been living in North
America. The matriarch of the Charles family of Sunflower County, Mississippi, in *Piano Lesson* has the name Mama Ester. Perhaps the two like-
named women embody the same ancestral wisdom. Holloway's claim
regarding Aunt Ester, "She ain't gonna die, I can guarantee you that"
(*2TR,* 40), besides reflecting a Borgesian acceptance of the bizarre, puts
her beyond human processes. Her exemption from the categories that
define the rest of us empowers her to boost Sterling's spirits. Before
meeting her, Sterling believed that the world was about to end (87–88).
Afterwards, he determines to marry Risa. Aunt Ester vitalizes him by
advising him to be the best person he can, using the qualities given him.
These qualities, she believes, will suffice him. If he stays within himself
and cultivates what he finds there, he'll prosper. She closes their session
with her usual mandate—that he throw $20 into the Monongahela
River.

The session helps him, perhaps most of all because he obeys her mandate. Soon after returning to the diner, he sings. Then he and Risa dance
and kiss to the accompaniment of an Aretha Franklin tune coming from
the diner's recently repaired jukebox. Music has again promoted uplift
and cheer in a Wilson playscript. But how long will its happy sway last?
The next morning, Sterling robs a local store, reopening a path for himself to the jail where he just served time. He no longer regrets having
been born (*2TR,* 52). He'll even help further the continuance of the
world he thought was about to end by having the children he had earlier
forsworn. In fact, he may have fathered one in the hours that lapsed
between the torrid kiss he shared with Risa at the end of act 2, scene 4,
and the opening of the play's final scene the next morning.

But the criminal streak he discloses several times during the action
implies that Risa will have to raise any offspring she has with Sterling
alone. Having gone six years without sex (*2TR,* 32), this paradigm of
restraint and integrity finally lowers her guard for an amoral adolescent.
His not being a Black Power activist has made him an anomaly among
his peers. What brings this 30-year-old into the mainstream is his law-

lessness. The numbers runner Wolf's comment, "every nigger you see done been to jail one time or another" (54), applies more strictly to Sterling than to anyone else in the play. Unfortunately, the person who stands to suffer the most from its recoil action is Risa. In a truth borne out by Rose in *Fences* and Berniece in *Piano Lesson,* the women in Wilson's plays often suffer the most for the misdeeds of their men.

Varieties of Love and Justice

Risa's boss, Memphis, tries her differently. Forever ordering her around or grumbling about her alleged inefficiency, he views Risa, says Sandra Shannon, as "the epitome of incompetence" (*2TR,* 176). But he's more than a scold. Like his faithful customer West, he starts out as a curmudgeon whose future behavior proclaims him a nice guy deep down. Gruff yet kindly, he has suffered in the past. Trouble with the law drove him from Mississippi in 1931. He had bought a tract of land from the same Jim Stovall who bullyragged Lymon in *Piano Lesson.* When, against all odds, he found underground water beneath his new property that would help him grow crops, Stovall got a local judge to void the sale. Memphis could only buy land from him that was arid and thus worthless. To clinch the point, Stovall killed Memphis's mule and set fire to his crop. These wrongs rattled Memphis but without corrupting him. Despite all his complaints about Risa, he'd never fire her, as they both know. The same inconstancy governs his behavior with the unfortunate Hambone. Cruelly, he whisks Hambone's coffee away from him, pours it out, and then pushes him into the street (*2TR,* 43). But then he regrets his cruelty. On Hambone's next visit, he tells Hambone to finish his beans quickly and leave the diner as soon as possible, but then, in a gentler vein, he tells Risa to give him another muffin. Beneath Memphis's brusque facade lies a sweet nature. And a font of good sense; it looks curious, in view of his man's rudeness with Hambone and Risa, that Wilson says of Memphis in his stage directions, "*His greatest asset is his impeccable logic*" (*2TR,* 1). Deepening our puzzlement is his illogical behavior with Wolf. Though he forbids Wolf to take bets on the diner's telephone, he plays the numbers himself, using Wolf as his agent.

And he'll continue booking his bets through Wolf. He's one of the few people in Wilson's plays who have beaten the odds. "It wasn't till I hit the numbers eight or nine years ago that I got to the point where I could change my clothes every day" (*2TR,* 3), he tells Wolf. He also used his winnings to buy the building where the diner now stands, an act that opened new vistas for him. The vistas came into view quickly. The day after buying the Wylie Avenue building for $5,500, he was offered $8,000 for it—a figure he turned down. For one thing, owning real estate won him the immediate benefit of shedding the pistol he used to wear all the time. Robbers tempted by the $400 he used to keep in his pocket would have no interest in stealing his new deed of ownership. He has been enjoying his safety. Rather than analyzing the good luck that brought it about, he accepts it, knowing that life laughs at rational formulas. He's logical because his belief in second chances has put him on a level field with the caprice ruling the world. His wife's having left him 20 years ago soured him on women but without chilling his heart. He nags Risa because he's shocked that he has been so deeply moved by her. Though he doesn't want her sexually, neither does he want her to stop working for him. Thus, to strengthen his hold on her, he'll malign Sterling, whom he sees as a threat to Risa's continued presence in the diner.

His belief in patience and perseverance usually serves him well, a sign of which is the Cadillac he drives. Though he can't offer Risa the excitement that Sterling represents, he surpasses Sterling in both his staying power and breadth of vision, virtues that could help him outlast his rival, would he ever own to himself that a rivalry between him and Sterling exists. Surviving misfortune has taught him how to cope. Whereas younger Wilson protagonists like Levee, Boy Willie, and Floyd Barton of *Seven Guitars* enact the trademark Jamesian (and Chekhovian) drama of contemplating with great passion an outcome that will be aborted, Memphis sees *his* hopes bear fruit. That his bonanza comes on the same day that both Prophet Samuel and Hambone are buried shows this surge of new life blossoming from death. West violated what looked like "*impeccable logic*" (*2TR,* 1) when he offered Memphis $15,000 and then $20,000 for a building that cost him only $5,500. By accepting either of West's offers, Memphis would be more than doubling his investment; besides, says West, he'd not get a better price from the city council, whose "right of eminent domain" (39) frees them to place any value they want on a piece of condemned property under their control. But Memphis, who has a logic of his own, won't budge. Wilson's giving him the closing words of act 1, "they got to meet my price" (60), shows the centrality of this logic to the play. Memphis has dug in his heels at $25,000. And even though he mentions the figure of $30,000, he does so whimsically, never believing that his decaying building would fetch such a fortune.

He'll also say in a different context, "Ain't no justice. That's why they got the statue of her . . . blindfolded. . . . You can't do nothing without a gun. . . . That's the only kind of power the white man understand" (*2TR,* 42). Yet the patience he exercises pursuing his goals gives the lie to this militancy; as in the plays of Brecht, the words of an August Wilson character can clash with his deeds. The warrior ethic Memphis proclaims endorses the belief that only those willing to bleed to secure justice deserve to be called agents of progress. The scars on the bodies of Risa and Hambone and the fresh wounds on Sterling's hands and face at the end convey this willingness. But to what avail? It comes to little, at least within the time frame of the play. First, Sterling still believes that violence will solve his problems; by becoming involved with him, Risa has saddled herself to precisely the kind of man she had vowed to shun. Second, Hambone's ham arrives too late for him to eat it.

The $35,000 Memphis gets for his condemned building represents a shocking turnabout for Wilson. A black man has surpassed his dizziest goals by working within the system. And perhaps therein lies the logic Wilson credits him with. Though justice is blind, sooner or later her scales may swing in the black man's favor. And once they do, they set a useful precedent. Memphis's unlikely bonanza could make it easier for other blacks to get fair value—or better—from Pittsburgh's civil justice system. His tenacity also opens doors for *him.* He resolves to reclaim his land from Jim Stovall near Jackson, Mississippi, after which he'll return to Pittsburgh and open a big new restaurant in a fancy neighborhood.

But Wilson doesn't completely demystify his success. First of all, the play ends before Memphis sets out for Mississippi; we never learn how well he fares in his action against Stovall. Next, he owes much of his success to Aunt Ester, whose contempt for money had first frightened him by moving her beyond the pale of his value system. Yet not only does he visit her. He also obeys her imperative to throw $20 off the Brady Street Bridge (*2TR,* 108). The $50 he spends at the end on a funeral bouquet for Hambone shows that he has absorbed Aunt Ester's wisdom: anyone fixated on money forfeits happiness.

Like Memphis, the funeral director West knows about deferring gratification. Like him, too, he visits Aunt Ester because he wants to improve his life. But because he can't bring himself to throw away money, he misses something more valuable—the chance to enrich his spirit. Now Wilson deliberately avoids portraying West as simply a money grabber. The many shadings, ambiguities, and even redeeming traits built into West's character credit him with having incurred fewer emotional scars building a strong inner-city business than would have most black entrepreneurs in his place. Naturally, his success has made him the butt of nasty rumors, his envious detractors claiming that, to save money, he recycles both the caskets and the burial clothes of the cadavers that pass through his mortuary. These charges are ridiculous. West has earned millions by taking his part of the world on its own gritty terms.

One *can* argue that he's not creatively linked to the neighborhood his millions came from. This connoisseur of death has been recently buying up condemned buildings. And the source of the capital behind this new venture is death. It follows that death is the best business in a neighborhood where all the stores have shut down and where most of the young men carry weapons. Speaking of the dearth of amenities, services, and jobs on the Hill, Memphis says, "Ain't nothing gonna be left but these niggers killing one another. That don't never go out of style. West gonna get richer and everybody else gonna get poorer" (*2TR,* 9). Though this insight discloses the upshot of the sad economic polarization dividing blacks and whites, it also gives a distorted picture of West. Granted, he can't escape the deathliness that has made him rich. He wears gloves all the time to cover the hands that prepare his corpses for burial; he has also been wearing the same pair of shoes for three years, suggesting that his steps have been taking him in the same deathly grooves and paths. This suggestion is valid; less free than his fortune might lead one to imagine, he lives in rooms above his mortuary.

But if he can't shake off death, he resists being absorbed by it. The black clothes that Wolf condemns him for wearing are standard garb for his trade (*2TR,* 11). "That's what he's supposed to wear" (11), says Holloway, who also de-demonizes West by noting his courtesy, punctuality, and compassion (12). West deserves Holloway's tribute. No cheat or robber, he maintains high professional standards. He keeps his hearses clean and smoothly running. When one of his window panes breaks, he replaces it as soon as he can with plate glass, avoiding the wooden boards that would make his funeral home look tawdry and low class. Besides keeping the home open longer than usual to give Prophet Samuel's followers the chance of a final glimpse, he also stops a would-be mourner from charging the followers money to see the dead prophet. *Trains,* unlike *Ma Rainey* or *Fences,* emphasizes the commonplace over the extraordinary, a truth borne out by the splitting of the archetypal warrior-hero's role between the unwarriorlike Sterling and the aging Memphis, a tactic that helps Wilson explore the archetype from different angles. As an ordinary guy looking to make the best deal for himself in an uncaring, sometimes brutal, world, West contributes to this artistic intent.

He can't be blamed for offering to buy Memphis's property at a price that will work to his advantage. Commercial transactions are supposed to profit both buyer and seller, and Memphis would profit immediately from the $15,000 West is ready to put into his hands. It's easy to snipe at West. Risa winces when she hears of Hambone's upcoming burial in a welfare casket, as do we. But we can't fault West, as she does, for refusing to spend $700 of his own money to buy Hambone a brass casket. He had already displayed Hambone's body in one of the mortuary's chapels at no charge. The compliment Sterling pays him for the "good job" he did laying out Hambone is probably well deserved (*2TR*, 106). No scrooge, West is but one of two people Holloway believes to have focused all his energies on his love for a woman, his late wife (103).

The death of Mrs. West before opening curtain omitted several big technical problems for Wilson. But it does raise questions about her widower's heart. Wilson's reference to West's *"love of money"* chimes with the playwright's practice of disallowing him a first name (*2TR*, 36). Though the mercenary streak of this half-lifer may not have cut across his love for his wife, it *has* marred his widowhood. His belief that death joins the dying person to the rich panorama of history both discloses in him a mystical bent and lends his mortician's job a priestly aspect (76). But his love of money distracts him from the meaning of this role. His statement, "life's hard but it ain't impossible" (93), shows him to be in tune with reality. He'd rather walk through life carrying a little cup than a 10-gallon bucket because, being easier to fill, it improves his chances for happiness (94).

His willingness to stay on the Hill, rather than expanding his power base, shows that he has taken this lesson to heart. His having rejected an American success ethic built on abundance bespeaks his integrity. But it also suggests a narrowness of vision. West represents a false direction, as is seen in his visit to Aunt Ester. The visit took place 22 years ago, when he was reeling from his wife's recent death. His refusal to go along with Aunt Ester's injunction to throw $20 into the river foiled any chance he had to rebuild his psyche. He'll only act in ways that make sense to *him*, even when his welfare is at stake. It was a failure of imagination that prompted him to offer the $20 he was told to throw into the river to Aunt Ester. He didn't see that she already had something more valuable than money. Nor did he understand that his salvation entailed being shaken out of the mind-set imbued in him by his job.

One of those who hears about his audience with Aunt Ester is the retired roofer Holloway. Called by Rocha "the community elder and oral historian" (Nadel, 116), Holloway generates most of the play's sharpest insights. He's also the one who sends Sterling to Aunt Ester. He does this because he appreciates the value of Aunt Ester's therapy, namely, the inner peace and self-acceptance without which life's blessings dry up. Holloway recalls the sensation of having his soul cleansed when Aunt Ester put her hands on his head. Memphis, who's still ignorant of the uses of passivity, answers, "I'd rather believe if I rubbed Prophet Samuel's head I'd be rich" (2TR, 24). But he does take an open mind to Aunt Ester later in the play, which helps him heed her advice, and, as a result, his ensuing good fortune joins with the affirmations that surface at the end.

These affirmations cluster around the deranged Hambone. Hambone's mental problems aren't new. In 1960 or so, he painted the fence of a local butcher named Lutz. Though the years have clouded the exact terms of the contract struck by the two men (2TR, 23–24, 28), it seems that Hambone agreed to accept a chicken upon completing the job. But the contract included an added incentive; for doing a good job, he'd be given a ham. At job's end, Hambone was offered a chicken, which he turned down, insisting that his efforts deserved a ham. He still believes it. Every day, including Sunday, he waits outside Lutz's store, demanding his ham. In fact, the ham he never received has wrecked his mind. The first words he speaks in our presence are "He gonna give me my ham. . . . I want my ham. He gonna give me my ham" (2TR, 14). He will say little else. But even though his talk is limited to these two statements, it evokes the flair of the fool saint or the idiot savant. The play's action supports this evocation. First, Holloway praises Hambone's idiotic intransigence. Speaking of him, Holloway says, "He might have more sense than any of us" (2TR, 29). By accepting Lutz's chicken, Holloway argues, Hambone would have wronged himself. Not only would the chicken have tasted rank; eating it would have spoiled the taste of every chicken he'd sample in the future.

What's more, Lutz set the terms for his contract with Hambone. Agreeing to them is as much of a concession as Hambone can make. Having made it, he must stand fast. Accepting a chicken he doesn't want would both confirm his inferiority to Lutz and show him conspiring in his own shame. His dissent, on the other hand, earns him a freakish half victory. His self-respect has held firm. There are other rewards. As Sterling says, his holdout gives him a purpose, helping him start each day with a sense of expectation: "He have more cause to get up out of the bed in the morning than I do" (*2TR,* 50). A good existentialist, the means-oriented Hambone knows that the value of any endeavor consists chiefly of the energy and commitment poured into it. By withholding the ham Hambone believes he deserves, Lutz sustains this flow. Nobody in the play besides the offstage Lutz has his perseverance or dedication. "He let Lutz drive him crazy" (*2TR,* 44), says Memphis. There's more to say on the subject. It's just as likely that Hambone has addled Lutz's wits by forcing him into a moral corner; Lutz can't extend him kindness or charity without losing face. But Hambone's impact extends beyond the disbursement of meat products. As is reflected by the Aunt Ester subplot, truth surfaces in obscure, unlikely places in *Trains.* Lutz's appearance at West's the day of Hambone's pauper's funeral counts as a tribute. Though at odds with Hambone, Lutz secretly admired him. He may have even envied him, this madman who has the truth.

Hambone's thematic importance builds in the play's second half. The end of act 2, scene 1 marked the midpoint of *Trains;* four scenes have been played, and four will follow. Act 2, scene 2 begins with Holloway's asking Risa if she has seen Hambone (79). She couldn't have, not on that day, anyway. He died in a welfare rooming house. He was broke; presumably, he had no family; nobody knew his name. Yet this outcast's death causes a greater stir in the diner than Prophet Samuel's, a high-profile event that backs up traffic for two miles and forces the police to use helicopters for crowd control. Though only three or four people signed the funeral book in the chapel where Hambone was laid out, he was, as Wilson said in 1992, "the soul of the community" (Rocha, 26). All the patrons at Lee's are changed by him, a sign of which is his modest funeral. Whereas the diner stayed open during both Prophet Samuel's funeral and the gala for Malcolm X, an event that drew 3,000 people, it closes the afternoon of Hambone's memorial service. This stroke, all the more impressive for the muted tones with which it reaches us, calls forth the life and beauty that overtake the fragile boundaries of art.

It also adds iron to the play's upbeat finale. As has been seen, the city council has given Memphis more money than he ever dreamed his sagging old building was worth. Still euphoric from his bonanza, he gives Risa $50 to buy flowers for Hambone, who taught him the importance of deferring gratification. Then Sterling bursts into the diner, holding a ham in his bleeding hands. He has just crashed through the window of Lutz's meat shop and stolen the ham, which he wants West to put in Hambone's coffin. Memphis's euphoria has spread. Inspired by Aunt Ester, Sterling has shown his willingness to bleed to gain justice, enacting his author's claim that black people won't wait any longer for their ham. McDonough praises Sterling's act of bringing Hambone the ham that he coveted but was bilked of for the past nine and a half years: "Unlike the robbery that landed [Sterling] in jail, this robbery is committed out of a sense of justice—to at last give Hambone what he earned in life" (156).

This note of triumph takes its force from Wilson's trademark motifs, conceits, and social beliefs. But just as typical of Wilson are the ambiguities underlying it. While muting the drum-and-bugle music of a happy finale, these ambiguities foster dialogue. The ending of *Trains* opens up many areas for discussion and disagreement. Yes, Sterling vindicates Hambone's sense of justice. But need he have bothered? Hambone may not have deserved his ham. Siding with Lutz, Memphis said he wouldn't have given Hambone a ham either (*2TR,* 28). Besides, now that Hambone's dead, he's past caring. Risa may be right in her belief that Lutz is going to rot in hell (107). But he won't rot as quickly as Hambone's ham. Acting with his usual recklessness, Sterling may have risked another jail term for nothing. Even when driven by a refusal to settle for less than is fair and just, crime in Wilson always creates problems rather than solving them. It's doubtful that when Aunt Ester told Sterling to focus his energies on the goal of self-improvement she meant for him to polish his skills as a crook. His code of justice, however admirable, has led him down the wrong road.

Enriching the Mosaic

But this problematic code doesn't derail the play. Any cavils aimed at *Trains* don't diminish its remarkable achievement. As in any other good play, its ending supplies no tidy moral, no easy justice, no pure motives. Deftly modulated and psychologically rich, what precedes the finale abounds in vivid moments and moods that replace linear development. *Trains* subordinates plot to situation. Its leisurely tempo and relaxed way with its people suggest a play with time to spare. A casual conversation may meander, giving every appearance of aimlessness. But this apparent waywardness contains careful irrelevancies and memories that disclose the inner dynamics of Memphis's social set. Any production of *Trains* should be sensitive to these dynamics. The play will work best if the actors synchronize their styles, adapting to one another's gestures and words in order to blend as a well-tuned, quietly efficient ensemble.

Unstructured drama can be disconcerting, incoherent, and dull to watch. Yet *Trains* flows with an ease and grace that stems in part from scenes loosely joined by recurring images and familiar characters schmoozing in a friendly environment where food is served. The play's greatest rewards don't stem from any urge Wilson creates in us to discover what happens next but, rather, from sound characterization, a fluid progression of scenes, and pitch-perfect dialogue. Wilson is a superb stylist with an uncanny ear for parody and comic dialogue. These gifts make *Trains* a play of high ambition couched in a style that's non-rhetorical and rhythmically demotic. The play's loose structure—with its digressions, random comings and goings, and detachable vignettes—focuses Wilson's best energies. Some of the comic scenes, including the one in which Sterling tries in vain to teach Hambone the slogans of the Black Power movement (*2TR*, 57), are hilarious. False notes are few and far between in *Two Trains Running,* a work that describes transformations occurring in tandem, jostling one another, and grazing metaphysical heights while they shake our sides with laughter.

Chapter Eight
All Right with Whom?

Seven Guitars should be more comforting than it is, considering how profusely it's covered with Wilson's fingerprints. Some of the prints that identify the work as a product of his sensibility can be found in the area of style. When the blues harmonica player Canewell grumbles about an ex-employer's mistreatment of him, he's told, "He don't have to care nothing about you. You all doing business. He ain't got to like you" (*7G,* 47). Troy Maxson spoke in similar terms to his son Cory in *Fences* when he told the boy that he feeds and clothes him out of duty, not affection: "I ain't got to like you. Mr. Rand [Troy's boss] don't give me money come payday cause he likes me" (*F,* 38). There are other echoes. Like Hambone of *Two Trains Running,* the mother of Floyd Barton in *Seven Guitars* lies in a pauper's grave (*7G,* 50). Following the lead of Boy Willie Charles of *Piano Lesson,* Floyd plans to leave Pittsburgh for good after performing an important errand. Floyd also proves as dangerous a companion as Boy Willie, as the violent death of an offstage character shows. Like Crawley, Berniece's husband in *Piano Lesson,* Poochie Tillery dies while committing a crime engineered by the play's leading character, in this case, Floyd. The bullet that kills Poochie is fired by a policeman offstage, as in Crawley's shooting death. Wilson only depicts blade deaths. He does it again in *Guitars,* where the victim is another bluesman; just as the pianist Toledo was fatally stabbed in *Ma Rainey,* so does the blues singer and guitarist Floyd "Schoolboy" Barton of Wilson's 1996 play have his windpipe slashed. Perhaps his death ties in with his plans to go to Chicago. Louise, the rooming house manager of Wilson's *Guitars,* believes, like Doaker of *Piano Lesson* (*PL,* 18), that travel can't help people solve their problems (*7G,* 72).

Whites still wring Wilson's people without appearing on stage. Hedley, the fundamentalist firebrand, blames all his problems on whitey even though he has very little personal contact with him. Floyd's professional ties with whites do put Floyd at a disadvantage. As Hambone did for Lutz in *Trains,* Floyd works for a white man (in his case, a Chicago recording executive) who dictates the terms of their partnership. Floyd apparently didn't learn from his mistake of accepting a flat fee for his hit record "That's All Right" instead of demanding royalties based on sales. He's now returning to Chicago without first spelling out the details of his recording date there (7G, 22). His mistreatment at the hands of his manager is still worse. The white T. L. Hall steals the advance paid to Floyd from a local club for contracting to play at a dance. Floyd needs this money to redeem not only his guitar but also the instruments of two of his sidemen from a pawnshop. He'll never get the money owed him, Hall having been arrested for insurance fraud after pocketing it. The ensuing crisis faced by Floyd turns on Wilson's trademark moral complexity. For even though Hall cheated Floyd, he didn't force the bluesman to commit the robbery that led to his death two or three days later. Floyd slipped up badly by trusting Hall to begin with. He and his kind inhabit a world of risk. Poochie, his unemployed accomplice in the robbery, though only 27, looked older than his years (7G, 96), implying that survival itself goes hard with young inner-city blacks. There's no relief in sight for them. As in *Ma Rainey*, the plight of the black man is worse at the end of *Seven Guitars* than it was at the play's outset. And it was grim enough during the play's time frame, about a week in May 1948.

The United States was enjoying prosperity at this time, nearly three years after the end of World War II. The economy was flourishing, and both personal disposable income and consumer confidence were rising. Yet Wilson's people grub along in a rough part of Pittsburgh. They all live alone, too, and several of them have either just arrived or are planning to leave, making, as the play's backyard setting suggests, insecurity and displacement serious threats to their welfare. The vulnerability motif comes to the fore quickly. Floyd's drummer says of him, "He was staying in Chicago. Sometimes he was staying here. Next time he'll be staying around the corner somewhere" (7G, 3). Floyd's music spells out the stress this transience induces. Thus he and the others, gropers all for stability and status, relish Joe Louis's knockout victory over Billy Conn (a fellow Pittsburgher of Wilson's but also an Irish American, which is why the hometown bond goes unmentioned in the play). Red Carter's woman named their baby Mister to disconcert the white men who'll have to do him the honor of calling him Mister in their dealings with him. Going the Carters one step better, Ruby, the 24-year-old transplant from Birmingham, plans to name her baby King if it's a boy.

Ends and Means

The familiarity of the materials comprising *Seven Guitars,* though abrasive, puts the reader or playgoer on sociable turf. Both the Hill setting and the recognizable character types (e.g., blues musicians, a landlady, and a twenty-something woman from other parts whose first appearance well into the action redirects the action's emotional flow) also open our sensibilities. Already acquainted with the social background of the play, we can attune ourselves quickly to the plot. And if that plot is dark and disturbing, it probably won't prove more transgressive than any of its forebears in the Wilson canon. This coziness dissolves quickly. The dissolution, in fact, is hinted at before the houselights dim. Wilson's "Note from the Playwright," or prologue, rates culture (which traffics in constants) over history (the main subject of which is change). Perhaps Wilson has in mind the archetype of the savior whose physical death ushers in his spiritual rebirth. The dramatic climax of *Guitars,* Floyd's death, could represent for Wilson one of those "many things that threaten to pull them [his people] asunder" in "their struggle to remain whole" (*7G,* prologue). Wholeness can be slippery and evasive. As he showed in *Ma Rainey,* the artist is always a selfish monster. He or she also lies because the artistic imagination will distort or even deny reality in its search for deeper meanings. The trickster's disruptive psyche challenges us with both new truths and new ways to find the truth. It can also help establish this truth as the basis of a set of social guidelines and codes once we recover from the impact created by its newness.

His dying at 35 stops Floyd from easing us through the recovery. *Guitars* is ambitious and bold but also darkly enigmatic. Reviewing the play in the *New Yorker,* John Lahr called its May 1948 time setting "a pivotal, ironic moment in black American history, when African-Americans were poised between their greatest hope and their greatest heartbreak" (99). Young blacks had just fought and died for their country. Their patriotism sparked some major advances. Besides integrating the armed forces, President Harry Truman proposed antilynching legislation in 1948. But these actions did little to raise either the standard of living or the economic outlook of most African Americans, a truth Wilson conveys by siting his play in a cultural void. There's no reference in *Guitars* to World War II, to the death of Franklin Roosevelt, to the atom bomb, to the cold war, or to Jackie Robinson's feats as a Brooklyn Dodger. The sole reference to the world of public events pertains to the heavyweight title fight between Joe Louis and Billy Conn. Intriguingly, Wilson's treatment of the first fight in which ringside seats cost $100 apiece violates literal truth. Though Louis did knock Conn out in the eighth round as Wilson says, the two men fought on 19 June 1946, well after Mother's Day, and the referee was Eddie Joseph, not Marty Blaine (7*G*, 52). Louis did fight in June 1948. But his opponent, an 11th-round knockout victim, was Joe Walcott, and the fight took place in Yankee Stadium (Goldman, 92), not Madison Square Garden (7*G*, 51).

Wilson skewed this episode in boxing history in order to channel the Louis-Conn fight into the cultural milieu of 1948; Louis's successful title defense creates one more occasion for black joy that the coming months will sour. Coming late in act 1 (7*G*, 51–54), it also foreshadows and balances a moment of brightness in act 2, scene 7, where Ruby announces that her unborn baby will be named after the local man she'll credit with fathering it. Another sign of Wilson's respect for artistic symmetry comes in the play's title. Lawrence Bommer notes that the title of *Seven Guitars* "reflects all seven characters of the play" (16). Now *Fences* and *Two Trains* also had seven speaking parts. But perhaps *Guitars* marks a greater attempt on Wilson's part to distribute his theme more evenly among the different roles. It's fitting that Wilson's most introspective play should feature in its title the number seven. Seven fuses four (the seasons, humors, elements, and points on the compass) and three (the Trinity). This fusion of spirit and matter, in turn, focuses a work whose author has inscribed into it motifs and ideas from his earlier career for purposes of self-appraisal. Ideally, this appraisal would work best if the play's seven characters voiced seven different songs as well as seven different ways of looking at reality (in Wilson's seventh Broadway play, rather than his sixth). But the script that housed them would look too stiff and schematic unless it ran the length of, say, Eugene O'Neill's *The Iceman Cometh* (1946).

No, the seven speaking parts in Wilson's 1996 play don't claim our attention equally. But Wilson also avoids giving the play's main figure, Floyd Barton, the prominence enjoyed by a Troy Maxson, a Herald Loomis, or a Boy Willie Charles. Floyd has fewer lines than these men, and he'll leave the scene for 10 or 15 minutes at a time (e.g., 7*G*, 82–90), creating the flexibility that will allow other characters to drive the plot. The collaborative technique featured in *Guitars* evokes Wilson's racial past, particularly the call-and-response style of black preaching and the answering bebop riffs of a tune like Dexter Gordon and

Wardell Gray's "The Chase" (MCA Jazz Heritage LP Series, vol. 37, no. 1336). More noticeable still, though, is the paucity of stage directions following Wilson's "Note." The characters aren't described or discussed anywhere near as much as those in *Trains*, Wilson hoping in his reticence to free up the ancestral retentions of the actors. *Guitars* includes some maverick ideas about large subjects like love and death that could gain, in Wilson's eyes, new levels of expression voiced by actors given the freedom both to explore and interpret their roles. These ideas take on religious drive from both Floyd's singing of the Lord's Prayer (*7G*, 53) and his last public appearance. He sings at a club managed by one J. C. that draws such crowds that the club's roof and floor both appear ready to "cave in" from the big Sunday audience who came to the show (100–101).

Wilson keeps the play's form supple and limber in order to accommodate those set pieces that bypass the plot but give insight into the people and their daily routines. These vignettes include a recipe for cooking greens (*7G*, 35), a discussion of the relative merits of a knife and a handgun (42–43), and a meditation on roosters (60). Nor are the two roosters that inspire the meditation the only animals that play a part in *Guitars*. Besides Miss Tillery's duck and dog (her son is also called Poochie), there are the chickens Hedley kills and cooks before making sandwiches of them. But we're not finished with fowl. There's also the Blue Goose, site of the sold-out Mother's Day dance where Floyd performs. The characters' collective fear of poverty and loneliness has created a virtual Hobbesian war of all against all that can take on some of the frenzy of a barnyard squabble. This fighting and the pecking order it presupposes both remain a threat. No sooner does Miss Tillery's rooster die than she buys another, whose crowing sets her neighbors on edge. This edginess invokes their vulnerability to danger and loss. So long as they're onstage, they're also outdoors, as if bereft of clean, comfortable indoor snugs.

The supernatural, or fantastic, intrudes itself early, as several of the mourners at Floyd's funeral in act 1, scene 1, speak of seeing six black-hatted angels dropping from the sky to take Floyd to heaven (*7G*, 2–3). These celestial coffin-bearers are mentioned again at the end (106), showing the play's first and last scenes (act 2, scene 9) to be continuous in time with one another. In addition, the opening words of the short last scene, "Floyd 'Schoolboy' Barton" (104), spoken by Red Carter, are the same as those spoken by Red at the end of act 1, scene 1 (6). What happens between these utterances constitutes a time glide covering

Floyd's release from a Pittsburgh jail to his death. Our foreknowledge of his death creates a ritualistic aura that invokes the plot's reliance on fantasy and primitivism. *Guitars* is Wilson's strangest play to date. Written with an atypical flatness to go along with its fatalistic bias, it's as riveting as it is eerie and disturbing.

When Two Bulls Collide

Warm, ebullient, and robust, Floyd Barton has just spent 90 days in jail on a phony vagrancy charge. Like Sterling of *Two Trains Running,* another freshly discharged ex-con, Floyd learned very little behind bars about social adaptation. "You one of them special people who is supposed to have everything just the way they want it" (*7G,* 13), he's told in act 2, scene 2. Mindful of his welfare he is. His having put on weight in jail (15) reflects both his enormous appetite for experience and his tendency to temper defeat or setback. Though broke, he looks prosperous. And he does believe that his being a bluesman entitles him to privileges. The second scene of *Guitars* finds him preparing to parlay his inflated self-image into a fortune. He falls short of his goal. Like Levee, Troy, and Boy Willie, he enacts the Joycean flight of "almosting it." In "That's All Right," he has a hit record but none of the trappings of a recording star because the contract he signed with the record's producer brought him little money. So poor is he at the time of the play, in fact, that he has to pawn his favorite guitar to make the down payment on his mother's headstone.

The music he's getting ready to record in Chicago could both make him rich and boost his career. Bounties await him. Chicago is his earthly paradise. It's full of beautiful women; it's the place where the great blues artist Muddy Waters plays and lives; because of its size, it offers so many opportunities for success that Floyd can't help but thrive there. But he'll never enjoy this bonanza. Blocking his way to it is an elitist's contempt for fundamentals. This man who sees himself as both a musical genius and a streetwise hipster who knows all the angles hasn't paid his share of the grocery or the light bill. Vera Dotson, his fiancée, has noted his tendency to squander opportunity: "Everything keep slipping out of his hands," she says. "Seem like he stumble over everything" (*7G,* 31). Her friend Louise, who has seen Floyd hurt her in the past, agrees: "Floyd is the kind of man can do the right thing for a little while. But then that little while run out" (72), she says in act 2, scene 2.

Blessings elude Floyd because, as one of life's self-styled aristocrats, he scorns control and constraint. Flouting civilized process, he has put his faith in the Smith and Wesson .38 he carries with him. "I don't want to hear nothing about no Bible" (7G, 40), he growls. Like Wilson's other warrior spirits, he follows his impulses and lives by his own rules. If rebels like him create breakthroughs in politics and art, they're also great nuisances. For instance, when he left the prison workhouse, he was given a voucher entitling him to 30¢ a day for each of the 90 days of his sentence. But he lost the voucher. When he goes to the city finance office with the envelope the voucher came in, he expects to be paid. He also fails to redeem in a timely way his pledge to the pawnbroker who has his guitar. But, because he has been in jail, he claims that the deadline stipulated on his pawn ticket should be waived.

His belief that he can defy the rules other people live by extends to his private life. Unlike Sterling and Risa, who fall in love near the end of *Trains,* Floyd and Vera have been close for some time. He has already betrayed her and, the first time he's seen with her, he's asking her to forgive him. He wants Vera to go to Chicago with him, even though the last time he went there he took another woman and then broke his promise to send for Vera soon after settling in. Now, 18 months later, he expects her both to trust him and to do his bidding. Common sense tells her to deny him. Besides having deceived her in the past, he mentions in her presence the abundance of pretty women in Chicago (7G, 34), one of whom could easily turn his head. As her name suggests, Vera stands for the truth. But nobody can possess the whole truth, which is always glimpsed in fragments. The rakish Floyd hardly glimpses it at all. While supposedly spellbound by Vera's charms, he takes Ruby, the sexy newcomer from Alabama, to a local club. His hit record, "That's All Right," does win him popularity, which he parlays into another triumph, the rousing Mother's Day dance at the Blue Goose. But these gains are short lived. He buys himself a new guitar and a new suit along with a new dress for Vera with stolen money, the theft of which leads to his death within hours of the Blue Goose revels.

As Risa did with Sterling, Vera disobeys her better judgment by agreeing to marry Floyd. He had already failed her after raising her hopes, defecting first to another city with another woman and then to jail. His final defection—to death—shouldn't surprise her. As in life, Wilson's people, particularly his warrior spirits, never reform. They become intensified versions of their earlier selves, with all their traits

augmented, especially their faults. Floyd's inability to pay attention
during a card game he's playing and the ease with which a crowing
rooster unsettles him disclose in this "big man" (7G, 79) an anxiety he
can't repress. Several times in the play he lets on that he needs a supportive woman. He's wrong. The presence in his life of a woman who
believes in him will never give him the self-confidence he needs to be
happy.

"I believe every man knows something, but most times they don't
pay attention to it" (7G, 5), says Red Carter the day of Floyd's funeral.
This vital proposition says more about Floyd than it does about any of
the other characters in the play. As usually happens in a Wilson play,
though, whenever an important issue comes to the fore in *Guitars,*
ambiguity soon clouds the picture. An instructive precedent that will
blow away some of the drifts comes in the shooting death of Crawley by
the police during a crime Crawley was caught committing in *Piano Lesson.* Now even though Boy Willie told Crawley about the proposed theft
of some fallen timber and then invited him to participate in it, he disclaims responsibility for Crawley's death, insisting that he never coerced
Crawley into joining him. The ambiguity differs somewhat in *Guitars,*
probably because Floyd has no one like Berniece, Crawley's widow, to
goad him into protesting his innocence. No Berniece is needed, though.
His conscience is sterner and less forgiving than Boy Willie's, as his
words to Vera in act 2, scene 7, about personal responsibility, show:
"Maybe all the times we don't know the effect of what we do. But we
cause what happens to us. Sometimes even in little ways we can't see"
(7G, 92).

Can't see, but can perhaps intuit; *Guitars* is rich in subtext. Floyd
knows that he shouldn't have reacted to his agent T. L. Hall's theft of
the advance the Blue Goose paid before the Mother's Day dance by
committing a theft of his own. As he admits, though the link between
events can defy analysis, it operates, anyway, and its ineluctable opera-
tion can be both expected and prepared for. The robbery he commits
with Poochie invites moral inferences he has chosen to quash, and now
his conscience demands that accounts be squared, particularly because
his collaborator in the robbery is dead. First, Floyd could have found a
better place to hide his remaining share of the take than in the ground
below a freshly planted goldenseal. The carelessness with which he
replanted the goldenseal, exposing its roots, conveys the same impulse
to self-punishment. He's acting like a crook who wants to be caught.

He feels guilty because he robbed the finance company to begin with, because Poochie died committing a crime that was his, Floyd's, idea, and because he knows, despite his resolve to be faithful, that he'll deceive Vera in Chicago, just as he did the last time he went there. He didn't have to be within earshot to heed the wisdom of Louise's words in act 2, scene 2: "You ain't gonna all of a sudden be a different person just cause you in a different city" (7G, 72). Although this logic hasn't yet registered clearly with him, his suspicion that his forthcoming trip to Chicago, a venture financed in part by a friend's death, will renew Vera's sorrow prompts him to leave himself unprotected from the machete that cuts his throat.

Ironically, none of Floyd's misdeeds, past or imagined, motivate his attacker. Corroded by suspicion and fear, the 59-year-old Hedley is brimming with masculine anxieties. He never won the esteem of his mad, abusive father. (Ben Brantley had Hedley on his mind when he said in February 1995, "the theme of coming to terms with one's father echoes throughout Mr. Wilson's plays."[1]) He has never been athletic. Despite his grandiose ambitions, his attainments are slight. His defining and debilitating mark is a morbid self-preoccupation. His reference to his father's having worked as a stable groom ("My father . . . take care of the horses" [7G, 76]) invokes Freud's famous case study of Hans and the castrating father. Hans's vision of his father as a horse refers to the boy's fear that the father will castrate him for desiring his mother. Wilson omits the part of the archetype that leads to the growth of a conscience and, with it, the repression of the pleasure principle. What he does do is pit Hedley's castration fear against Floyd's need for women. Freud's statement about the artist, though voiced in a different context, "He has not far to go to become neurotic,"[2] discloses in Floyd a vulnerability he should have reckoned with in his dealings with Hedley.

Both men are individualists who accept the consequences of their choices, even when those consequences are destructive. The self-doubt that leads Floyd to sabotage his dream of becoming a premier bluesman runs just as strong in Hedley, who talks about being "a big man" (e.g., 7G, 18, 24, 67) but can't manage the basics of life, like paying his rent on time. This poultry merchant fancies himself a righteous soul who's looking for some ennobling cause that will support his fight against the forces of evil as he defines them. He imagines himself under constant assault. His lifelong fear of sterility accounts for his never having married. It also underlies his choice of a livelihood. Most of the chickens and turkeys he prepares for the pot on his "primitive mortician table" (7G, prologue) are female, over whom he exerts near total power. This dominance comforts him. Thus, like Floyd, he's both distracted and threatened by the rooster who lives next door. This is the rooster the others equate with the freshness and innocence of America's rural past (7G, 20, 82); by rousing farmers from sleep in the morning, the rooster helps them to an early start on their chores. It's also a rooster that an anxious Floyd throws a stone at. But Hedley's anxiety runs deeper than Floyd's because it includes Floyd along with Miss Tillery's rooster. It's also more sharply focused. Rather than accepting the rooster as nature's alarm clock (7G, 98), Hedley imparts a sexual coloring to it that recalls its use in *Ma Rainey's Black Bottom.* Toledo's statement in *Ma Rainey,* "Levee think he the king of the barnyard. He thinks he's the only rooster know how to crow" (59), prefigures Levee's rank overture to Dussie Mae: "[C]an I introduce my red rooster to your brown hen?" (82).

It follows that the strong sexuality Hedley has invested in the rooster next door compels him to kill it, which he does at the very end of act 1 (7G, 64). This beheading, which climaxes the play's first act, also foreshadows the resolution of the play. *Guitars* peaks when Hedley slits Floyd's windpipe in act 2, scene 8, an act he performs with the same assurance he displayed killing that other would-be cock-of-the-walk in act 1, scene 5. This assurance leaks quickly out of Hedley. Though sensational, both of his acts of slaughter lack effect, reviving the argument that violence in Wilson is always a pointless waste. Within days of the death of her pet rooster, Miss Tillery replaces it. Nor will Floyd's death silence his music; his songs will continue to find audiences both on the radio and in private record collections. Hedley's machete accomplished nothing. Floyd had angered Hedley by flirting with Ruby and inviting her to go out with him at the very moment Hedley appeared in the yard with some candy he had bought for her. But any rage he may have felt over being thwarted by Floyd should have waned. Floyd's plan to take Vera to Chicago puts him beyond dating range of Ruby, who has, in any case, decided to fulfill Hedley's greatest wish by telling him that he fathered the baby she was carrying when she came to Pittsburgh. The man Vera accused of living in the past (7G, 77) can look to a glorious future. Besides, Floyd, who should have been riding a Chicago-bound bus, likes and respects Hedley, commending the older man's refusal to be treated for TB since the refusal rings true with his value system (77).

But Floyd doesn't even have to threaten Hedley to die at his hand. The two men are so similar that in Hedley's mind there's only room for one of them on the Hill. Brandishing his machete at the end of act 2, scene 4, he says, "Now Hedley ready for the white man when he come to take him away" (*7G,* 87). His forecast is only marginally correct. He *will* use his machete. Yet by killing Floyd with it, he'll use it on the attack rather than in self-defense, and his victim will be black, not white. Once cast by Hedley in the role of sexual rival, Floyd was doomed. It doesn't matter that, besides harboring no plans to relocate Hedley, Floyd has arranged to relocate himself. Even the style of his murder could have been foreseen, decapitation symbolizing emasculation in the Freudian system that says so much about the play. The dust jacket illustration for *Guitars,* which depicts Floyd (whose name sounds like that of Freud) standing in the same pool of blood as a rooster, sharpens the identification in Hedley's mind that causes the play's two onstage beheadings.

The Wings of Ethiopia

The psychological, spiritual, and political energies infusing *Seven Guitars* all converge in Hedley in a context of Shakespearean anxiety about nature robbed of its order. Hedley's suspicion that he serves this disorder has heightened his anxiety. Instead of using Christianity's moral foundations to uphold the dignity of black America, he revels in slaughter, damning to endless torment anyone who gets in his way. A major component of his mind-set is the belief that the soil soaked with the blood of his forebears will enrich his soul. It's inevitable that he hates whites because *their* blood and *their* collective memories both bar them from his messianic fantasy.

Neither clown nor demon, this troubled, complex man drips death. He first appears right after the funeral of his murder victim, which he attended, and two scenes later he's making the chicken sandwiches he hopes to sell to the guests at another funeral service (*7G,* 18). The same death that helps his business has marked him. What keeps him in death's domain is his pentecostal fury. This would-be figure of wrath and destruction calls himself a hurricane, a lion, and a warrior (88–89). His creed is one of blood and thunder: " 'Ethiopia shall stretch forth her wings and every abomination shall be brought low' " (19), he raves, paraphrasing Psalms 68:31. This scourge (whom Shafer calls "a mystic" [1998, 37]) sees himself as larger than life, comparing himself to Toussaint L'Ouverture, Marcus Garvey, and Joe Louis. His heroic self-image declares itself in the opening words of the song he chants to begin act 2,

scene 5: "Ain't no grave . . . can hold my body down" (*7G,* 88). To ratify
his exalted self-concept, he traces a circle in the yard with his steps as
soon as he finishes his song, repeating the circular pattern he made with
the blood he squeezed from the neck of the rooster he killed in act 1,
scene 5. (The lack of authorial squeamishness Trudier Harris noted in
Bynum's sacrificial pigeons in *Joe Turner*[3] intensifies with the rooster in
Seven Guitars, the slaying of which isn't merely described but, rather,
portrayed.)

As has been seen, the eternity symbolized by these circles excludes
white people. It's therefore bogus. Defining conflict racially, he warns
the others, "The white man got a big plan" (*7G,* 69). This plan, if it
exists, can't be any uglier than his. Just as his black father nearly kicked
him to death, he, Hedley, had already killed one black man before the
play's continuous action, and he kills another during it. If anything, he
does the white man's dirty work of annihilating black people. The born
ruler's persona he affects while singing and making sandwiches in the
scene immediately before the one where he kills the rooster is fatuous.
This renegade who refuses to be treated by white doctors and tries to
sneak out of paying his rent is strictly small-time.

His legacy of wrongdoing extends most clearly from his father.
Besides being mad, Hedley Sr. named his son King, after Charles
"Buddy" Bolden (1877–1931), founder of New Orleans's first jazz band
and also the first king in a line of New Orleans cornetists that included
Joseph "King" Oliver and Louis Armstrong. Madness darkened
Bolden's last years, which suggests that Hedley Sr. might have disclosed
in himself a prophetic streak when he named his son. Bolden, "a riveting
performer of personal charisma and crowd-pleasing musical power,"[4]
had to be institutionalized after going "spectacularly insane" during a
street parade (Carr, Fairweather, and Priestley, 66). The insanity that
caused this flare-up worsened. After drunkenly attacking both his
mother and his mother-in-law, Bolden spent his last 24 years in a mental home (Carr, Fairweather, and Priestley, 66).

Hedley regrets having been named after this mad jazz king. The hon-
orific name has pumped him up with so many delusions of grandeur
that, when a fellow black refused to call him King, Hedley murdered
the man. His grandiose self-image still clings to him, but in an altered
form: though he'll still compare himself to Moses and Jesus, he's ready
to settle for becoming the father of the Messiah; his monumental impact
on posterity will occur through his son. The allure created by this
impact consumes him. Though impelled by apocalyptic visions, he takes

the initiative rather than waiting for the divine will to express itself. His lust roused by his messianic gabble, he has sex with Ruby. The next scene starts with Floyd alone on stage burying the money the theft of which will soon cost him his life. Death has become the offspring of Hedley's rut with Ruby. And logic decrees that more death will follow, an idea supported by the play's color symbolism. Besides expressing itself in the blood shed by Hedley's two victims, red, the color of martyrdom, asserts its might in the roses engraved on Floyd's mother's headstone, in the papier-mâché floral decorations Louise makes for Mother's Day, and in the flaming red dress Ruby (whose name denotes red) wears to the big dance.

Hedley traduced nature by fucking Ruby, a woman 35 years his junior, just as his fantasy of starting a plantation in Pittsburgh (7G, 24) traduces reason. Not only does Pittsburgh lack the climate, the available land, and the workforce to support a plantation; any farm Hedley installed there, against all odds, with its crops of tobacco and oats, would turn him into a facsimile southern white landlord. He would thus be one with his sworn foe. But as he did in *Trains* with the sale of Memphis's building to the city, Wilson again invites the possibility that the black man can beat the odds, even when he seems to have no chance. Granted, Hedley's turbulence and extravagance have raised the odds against him. But this excessiveness hasn't killed hope. Most of Wilson's plays end on a note of guarded acceptance, the pulse of life continuing to throb in a painful, frightening, yet beautiful world. Sometimes the throbbing will seem like a descent of grace or a divine intercession, ironically those very mercies that Hedley, who could profit a great deal from them, has banished from his militant theology.

The closing scenes of the three plays separating *Fences* from *Guitars* include the muted promise of renewal through sexual love. In *Guitars* the promise, though present, is even more muted. The prospect of fathering the Messiah seems to have humanized Hedley. He agrees to go to the sanitarium for treatment, and he also attends church—as does Ruby, for the first time in 20 years. Another ray of hope glances from the child she's carrying. Plays like *Fences, Joe Turner,* and *Piano Lesson* featured children in scenes near final blackout to signal hope. Perhaps Ruby's unborn child augurs the same brightness and cheer. When it's born, Hedley will be too euphoric to count the months since he first lay with her. But the future holds dangers, too. How will Hedley react if she has a girl? And even if a boy is born to her, the ordeal he faces as Hedley's son could thwart his healthy growth. Violent fathers inscribe violence into their sons. Also, as Hedley's burdensome first name shows, his father had the same wild hopes for him that he has for *his* unborn son. And Hedley became a murderer.

His murdering days may not be over. He and Floyd have the following exchange in act 1, scene 3:

FLOYD: "I thought I heard Buddy Bolden say . . ."

HEDLEY: What he say?

FLOYD: He said, "Wake up and give me the money."

HEDLEY: Naw. Naw. He say, "Come here. Here go the money."

FLOYD: Well . . . what he give you?

HEDLEY: He give me ashes.

FLOYD: Tell him to give you the money. (*7G,* 23 –24)

Their exchange recurs with variations three more times (*7G,* 39, 70, 103 –104). The last of them begins with Wilson saying of a drunken Hedley, *"He has waited many years for this moment"* (103). Hedley has stumbled into the yard at the very moment when Floyd is burying the remainder of his stolen cash. In his stupor Hedley mistakes Floyd for Buddy Bolden (Lahr, 101). Hedley's father had told him years before that one day Buddy would bring him the money to buy his plantation. When Floyd refuses to give Hedley the loot, he's killed. Hedley still has it in his pocket the day after Floyd's funeral. In the play's dying moments, he and Canewell do their own version of the litany Hedley had performed four times with Floyd. Canewell's taking Floyd's part in the litany implies that he'll become Hedley's next victim, an outcome darker and more wrenching than that of the last scene of *Ma Rainey,* which depicted the slaughter of one musician by another. The final exchange between Canewell and Hedley and the latter's response to it reveal that Canewell's life may be hanging by a thread:

CANEWELL (*singing*): "I thought I heard Buddy Bolden say . . ."

HEDLEY: What he say?

CANEWELL: He say, "Wake up and give me the money."

HEDLEY: Naw. Naw. He say, "Come here, here go the money."

CANEWELL: What he give you?

HEDLEY: He give me this.

    (HEDLEY *holds up a handful of crumpled bills. They slip from his fingers and fall to the ground like ashes.*) (*7G,* 106 –107)

Hedley won't profit materially from his murder of Floyd because he knows that money won't buy what he needs. He craves power. If he had the chance, he'd kill the great black heroes of the past because he wants to take their place. He even says of the just-slain rooster to the six characters assembled in the yard at the end of act 1, scene 5 (the only time in the play that the whole cast appears on stage together), "This rooster too good for your black asses" (7G, 64). The mythical grandeur building from the sexual symbolism of the rooster has dwarfed him. Hedley has always hated the masculine power he pretends to admire because it reminds him of his puniness. This childless man resents the rooster for the same reason. His stand in both cases is that of the loser. Knowing he can never attain the eminence of paragons like Joe Louis or Marcus Garvey, Hedley would kill them if he could. Only by destroying them can he wipe out the reproach they threaten him with.

One of these paragons is Canewell, Floyd's harmonica player and the script's griot, or raisonneur. Canewell's name suggests his and the other characters' rural southern origins, and it's Canewell who brings Vera the medicinal goldenseal plant Floyd will later uproot while hiding the money he stole. It's through Canewell, too, that Wilson rehearses some of the play's most disturbing ideas. For instance, Canewell faults Jesus for raising Lazarus from the dead. Life's laws, Canewell believes, are intrinsic. Besides violating this self-sustaining order, Jesus exposed the resurrected Lazarus to more of the pain he had put behind him by dying (7G, 25–26). Voicing an attitude conveyed by Floyd's hit song, Canewell will also claim that love that's not appreciated or returned still has value. Sufficient unto itself, love need pay no dividends. Perhaps he means that life is so bitter that any outgoing of the heart will redeem it. It's difficult to say because his role is much more rhetorical than it is dramatic. Wilson put him in the play to talk. Perhaps talk is all he's good for besides playing the harmonica. At the play's outset, a more opportunistic, alert character grabs a piece of pie Canewell had singled out for himself.

Distaffers

The homage Wilson pays to his mother in his unpaged "Note from the Playwright" reveals in him a sharpened awareness of women as a source of both wisdom and goodness. Women provide the play's clearest link to reality. As Hedley showed, they also furnish access to being. They can't be escaped by any seeker of wholeness and truth. Floyd shares Wilson's

mindfulness of mothers. He only feels free to leave Pittsburgh after buying a headstone for his mother's grave, and his recent jail sentence
began the day he buried his mother. He'll soon be back at her side. A
couple of days after performing at the Mother's Day dance (on 9 May
1948), he's buried in the same graveyard where he put her to rest three
months before. Ironically, his mother's death had freed him to live for
the first time. Moved by his weakness as much as by his strength, Vera
was ready to give herself totally to him before he took Pearl Brown to
Chicago, as she says in one of the play's most moving passages: "I
wanted to know where you was bruised at. . . . So I could touch you
there. So I could spread myself all over you and know that I was a
woman" (7G, 13).

Yet he only showed her a thin edge of himself, and now, 18 months
later, he's still oblivious to the value of her special gift to him: "I ain't
too good at talking all this out" (7G, 14), he blurts, claiming only that
he needs her more than he has ever needed any woman. But this is
rhetoric. It's only when Vera rejects him in spite of his having a hit
record that he perceives her worth. Her rejection of his suit shows him
that she values her heart's convictions more than the dazzle of fame.

But her heart is tender besides being tough. Sensing that Vera will
cave in to him, Louise winces at the prospect of seeing her friend
wronged and hurt again by Floyd. "She be better off with the iceman"
(7G, 17), Louise claims because of the womanizing Floyd's history of
squandering opportunities to better himself. This distrust typifies her.
Like Bertha of *Joe Turner* and Berniece of *Piano Lesson,* she has survived in
Pittsburgh by keeping her guard up. She also helps spell out the contrast, present in all of Wilson's plays, between both city and country and
North and South. This ex-Alabamian has retained enough of her old
homegirl ways to be defensive about them. Thus she snipes at her
neighbor Miss Tillery's pastime of keeping a rooster. This protective
loyal friend also ignores the dynamism exerted by her African roots.
When Hedley explains how goldenseal leaves helped his grandfather,
she tells him that if he's sick he should visit the local doctor. Perhaps she
has hardened her focus because the Hedleys and the Canewells she has
known, though rich in folk wisdom, often shirk their household duties.
Coping with the rigors of rooming-house management has toughened
her. It has also killed her appetite for men. Some time ago, a live-in
lover of 12 years' standing walked out on her, and she hasn't looked at
another man since.

Her self-imposed abstinence (a reprise of Risa's in *Trains*) has kept pain at bay. The more open-minded and thus woundable Vera says in act 1, scene 4, "Love don't know no age and it don't know no experience" (*7G*, 31). Yet intergenerational sex, a spin-off of intergenerational love, caused havoc in both *Jitney* and *Fences,* and it casts ugly shadows here in *Guitars* with the shaky union of Ruby and Hedley. What love does know in Wilson's works is discord and pain. A good example in *Guitars* is the "experience" (31) of the love triangle. Several love triangles form in the play (involving Red Carter, Vera, and Floyd; Floyd, Ruby, and Hedley; Floyd, Vera, and Canewell; and Vera, Floyd, and Ruby). Though none of them reaches the depth or provokes the heartache of the one yoking Rose, Troy, and Alberta in *Fences,* all of them cause friction; all threaten to erupt.

Inciting much of the play's erotic turmoil is Ruby, Louise's niece. Ruby has brought "her fast little behind" to Pittsburgh from Birmingham because of man trouble (*7G*, 30, 58, 71). In an offstage love triangle that predates the continuous action of the play, two boyfriends, one of whom got her pregnant, fought over her, and one of them was killed. It's appropriate that the rooster next door crows profusely during the scene in which the electrically sensuous Ruby first takes the stage (25). He's heralding the arrival of a kindred spirit. Logic also decrees that the rooster die at scene's end. Hedley, already inflamed by Ruby, wants to destroy whatever signs of male sexuality he can detect. Next, the atmosphere can only contain so much of the raw impulse her sensuality has introduced. This disruptiveness is felt immediately. Canewell and Red Carter are ready to fight for the privilege of carrying her suitcase upstairs. Noticing their rivalry, Louise sends a thirsty Ruby upstairs for a glass of water rather than letting one of her overheated admirers fetch it for her.

She even distracts Floyd. Despite Vera's presence at the card table, he's unable to concentrate on the whist game he's supposedly playing. Ruby continues to turn his head. At the same time he's trying to convince Vera to go to Chicago with him, he takes Ruby out for drinks. Ironically, this development influences Vera more than all of Floyd's blandishments. Up to this point, she had been deflecting his pleas. Having noticed Ruby's strong effect on him, though, she tells Louise, "I might just go on up to Chicago" (*7G*, 71). The competition for Floyd's attention suddenly created by Ruby's appearance has changed Vera's outlook on her options. Accepting, in Troy Maxson's words, the crookeds with the straights (*F*, 37), she sees that, in a world where feelings are often compromised or diverted (*7G*, 97–98; *2TR*, 103), love deserves her efforts. To share a life with Floyd, she'll have to pay the price of forgetting his misdeeds (*2TR*, 103). Love is so rare and ennobling that any chance to build a future on it must be grabbed.

Transgressive, challenging, and difficult, *Seven Guitars* is Wilson's most bewildering, threatening play. It's unlikely to gain the popularity of *Ma Rainey's Black Bottom* or *Fences*. The in-your-face writing is more demanding and takes more risks. Also, theme and character both depend on unpopular Old Testament ideas about obedience, patriarchy, and retribution. Driven by wounded pride and the cathartic allure of violence, Hedley takes the Lord's work of vengeance into his hands at the worst possible time. Yet his victim, Floyd, an armed robber, might merit the punishment Hedley inflicts upon him. What does God's choice of Hedley as an agent of natural justice say about divine wisdom, though? By withholding comment on Floyd's death, Wilson heightens its ravishing, terrifying force. But the best art always challenges definitions and judgments. A moving, courageous work, *Seven Guitars* shows misery spreading and getting absorbed into the collective black psyche. Sophisticated at one level and deliberately primitive and naive at another, the play crackles with invention and insight. This abrasive, illuminating work also argues that Wilson is the best kind of teacher—the one who, by withholding answers, encourages us to look for them ourselves.

Conclusion

August Wilson is patently American in the doggedness of his search for the meaning of life. As an artist, though, he inscribes his polemic into his art (Bigsby 291–92). There's nothing misty or wet eyed in his compassion. It's cool, fierce, hard, and gentle. In its restraint, it's also just and equal. He has framed his vision against a backdrop of an American ideal that has failed blacks, giving them poverty and humiliation rather than neat suburban homes enclosed by well-trimmed lawns. Exploding stereotypes of the ghetto poor, his juxtapositions of the ordinary and the African-American surreal evoke anger, affection, and, sometimes, a little hope. Rather than debating social issues, he concerns himself with the salvation of black Americans. His people defy both liberal pieties and the reductive conservative arguments about the poor. Young men like Cory Maxson of *Fences*, Boy Willie Charles of *The Piano Lesson*, and Sterling Johnson of *Two Trains Running* lack a trade, a formal education, and the mind-set to build happy, productive futures. The cartoonish names they often have, like Levee or Poochie, defy white audiences to sympathize with them or take them seriously. But these victims deserve everyone's serious attention. In naming them, Wilson has issued two challenges—an artistic one to himself to gain that attention and a moral one to us to heed the issues he's dramatizing.

This regard may not come easily. Black-white relationships in the plays sound a note of stalemate and resignation. As Wilson told Bill Moyers in 1989, blacks have been thwarted in their wish to be part of something important in America: "The social contract that White America has given blacks is that if you want to participate in society, you have to deny who you are. You cannot participate in this society as Africans" (177). An empiricist, Wilson doesn't subject black Pittsburgh to cubist fragmentation or dislocation in his treatment of black exclusion. The same culture that's haunted by white racism also suffers from self-division. Both the members of Memphis Lee's set in *Trains* and Ma Rainey's musicians fret each others' nerves. The violence that explodes at the end of *Ma Rainey*, *Trains*, and *Guitars* also refers to the emergence in urban America of street gangs, drug traffickers, and police violence. Yet the interplay of constants and variables in Wilson's work rules out pessimism. Muddles, evasions, and deceptions abound in the plays

147

together with violence. But *Joe Turner,* the Wilson script with the earliest time setting, 1911, shows, in Seth Bynum and Rutherford Selig, a productive, smooth-running black-white business partnership grounded in mutual respect. *Trains,* the Broadway-produced script set most recently in time, 1969, shows in Memphis a black man defeating city hall despite working within a system concocted to favor whites.

Then there's that side of Wilson that gives blacks no chance to attain justice and equality. This Wilson scorns the perversities of twentieth-century capitalism—the greed, squalor, and escalating inequities that have widened the gap between rich and poor. Particularly loathsome to him is the truth that many of his fellow blacks have bought into this system of competition and striving. Better for them, he believes, to return to the rural South and a way of life that bypasses the cynicism, sterility, and disillusionment of the industrial North (Pettengill 215 –18).[1] Like the feudal baronies of yore, the rural South can offer security and identity in exchange for a willingness to build one's life around an ethos of limited expectations. But how limited and for how long? one wonders. The collective willingness to settle for less that Wilson alludes to has helped sustain the larger mysteries of black life by cheating and exploiting blacks. The "attitude of brutal reductionism" (46) that Gates finds in Wilson's work is politically naive. It may also be rearguard. The urbanization of the South has softened the demarcation lines that governed attitudes about North and South before World War II. This softening, or blurring, has created new opportunities, some of which have removed those barriers that blocked Levee's stardom as a jazz artist or Troy's career as a major leaguer.

But black enterprise can transcend the urges of time. A development like the $35,000 the city council of Pittsburgh gives Memphis for his condemned building forecasts a future in which black families will dine on ham. Wilson offers no agenda for this boon, though, at least in his plays. His distinctive voice and vision blend the strange and the commonplace, the straight-faced and the playful. Building his plays in layers, he'll use a comic plot to develop a period piece and then refract the finished product through a prism of racial prejudice. The light emitted by this prism depends on its source. Which can change; rather than providing formulas, Wilson dramatizes his reading of the human condition in ways that make it accessible, plausible, and exciting. The black and white keys of the piano in *Piano Lesson* symbolize a direction for racial harmony (Feingold, 118). The song that brings about this harmony may still be both unwritten and unsung. But Wilson has been teaching us how to recognize it when we hear it. His beam of refracted light stops here. Taking care not to overexpose his poetic conceits, he builds provocative encounters around ordinary, yet high-tension, ingredients and then invites us into the force field they have created. It's our choice to view the Charles family piano as a product of wood and wires or as a font of pride, hope, and courage.

But recognitions that incite resolve must also incite positive action lest they run to waste. This conversion can plague Wilson's people. For them, beginnings spawn memories and regrets. In Wilson's dramas of ripe condition, serious damage has occurred before the houselights darken for the first act. The childhood traumas suffered by Levee, Troy, and Hedley induced in the three men feelings of guilt and anger that have warped their development. Wilson's people always face more crookeds than straights. Wilson will put a Sterling Johnson before us soon after getting out of jail in order to evoke the racial prejudice and economic hardship young blacks must surmount to gain a foothold in their competitive society. Remote from the classic comedy of manners, Wilson's plays convey the sense of life not quite lived, of the gap between hope and achievement, a gap usually unmediated by irony. These works deny the comic affirmation of life as potential, development, and discovery. The characters in them are outsiders, often unable either to grasp or enjoy life.

Aching with reality, the plays invite Chekhovian parallels. Every warrior spirit in Wilson wants something he's clearly not going to get, whether it's greatness (Hedley), musical fame (Levee and Floyd), or a farm (Hedley again and Boy Willie). Wilson takes the emotional temperature of these men by granting them glimpses of better days. But the glimpses flicker and fade. Except in the case of Memphis, the wished-for breakthrough never occurs; at age 53, Troy knows he'll never be a major leaguer. He's not alone in his bitterness. Isolation pervades both tone and subject in Wilson's theater despite his Dickensian gift for hurling us into the thick of things. The speed with which the reserve of a Wilson character can shatter gives the plays the ambience of a nightmare. Usually sited in stable social units, including families, the plays abound in images of domesticity. But these images have loneliness as their subtext, reminding us of the prominence of family strife in Greek myth, like the woes of Agamemnon and Oedipus, Medea and Hippolytus.

Family is a caution in the plays of Wilson, who is an expert in the rhythms and nuances of black households. Taking up from Chekhov and Terence Rattigan, he writes about family members who either put up with each other or destroy each other out of motives of love or loneliness. The clash of desires and aims moves quickly to the fore of the family-based *Fences* and *Piano Lesson*. What follows the clash exhibits healthy artistic vital signs. It would be hard to know what to add to a Wilson play and, after seeing or reading it again, still harder to know what to take out. His women seem less fully imagined than his men because he sometimes seems more interested in the effect a Martha Pentecost (of *Joe Turner*) will have on her man than in her individuality. (In Alberta of *Fences* and Aunt Ester of *Trains,* he conceived two important female characters who never appear onstage.) Yet these women have a complexity and an ambiguity that raises them above the level of caricature.

What's more, they exercise the power of choice. Martha disclaimed her marriage to Loomis after his disappearance from home went into its third year. After learning of Troy's infidelity, Rose rears his child by another woman but banishes him from her bed. Ma fires Levee. The decisiveness displayed by these three women often stems from a richness of heart knowledge and an intuitive wisdom lacking in the warrior spirit. Wilson celebrated these gifts as far back as 1971 in the poems "Bessie" and "Morning Song," both of which focus on long-dead women whom posterity has unjustly forgotten.[2] Wilson's appreciation of the female sensibility can express itself technically. Berniece Charles is the only female role of any size in *Piano Lesson,* and *Trains* includes but one female role, period. But these roles are among the choicest in the last 20 years of American drama, and the actresses playing them on Broadway all won acclaim that has helped their stage careers. *Joe Turner* and *Guitars* include several women whom Wilson leaves on the stage for extended periods without feeling compelled to intrude a man in their midst.

Often, one of these women will drive the plot. But in what direction? Because Wilson portrays life as a multifaceted mystery, his plot dynamics include shocks. One of his most striking features is the artistic control that makes these shocks memorable. He refuses to heat up his scripts with special effects, mawkishness, or a knowing irony that's sometimes called "attitude." The scripts are precise, elegant, and economical. Telling incidentals like Levee's new Florsheims, Seth Holly's tin sheets, and the sugar dispenser in Memphis Lee's diner help steer us through a complex of feelings. This sharpness and economy also improve the plays, Wilson's fastidiousness with detail shearing away the fat that could pad both the obsessiveness of his themes and the intensity informing his vision.

Sometimes, this vision discloses the larger truth. A family historian and a social chronicler both, Wilson can also rise to tragedy, the spiritual grace and incandescent beauty of his prose lifting a script to sudden heights. Recalling Plato's cave allegory (from *The Republic*), which confuses shadow with substance, Wilson's familiarity with both the sinister and the seriously strange convolutes surface and interior. Exteriors can count a great deal in a world that disavows a clean split between mind and body, a world, moreover, in which a person is judged by his or her skin color. The emergence of Sutter's ghost in the Charles home in *Piano Lesson* posits a reality behind language that keeps eluding us but that can be sensed through an ancestral retention. Wilson is a religious writer. He portrays the designs of the black people's God in both man and nature. He writes of the afterlife, of sin and redemption, of faith, forgiveness, and retribution. He's also sure that his people have souls, convincing us of their soul's existence by grounding an important event, like the advent of Loomis's wife in *Joe Turner,* in the supernatural (Martha is discovered in a church).

The issues rising from the event enact themselves as blood and sinew. No sooner does Wilson raise the knout of polemic than he goes straight for the guts. He'll look at the grossest aspects of his people's lives with such discrimination that the people attain rather than lose stature as they try to span the breach between what's right and what they're afraid they're going to do. Nearly every Wilson playscript turns on this paradox—that the more we learn about a character, the more mysterious the character becomes. Wilson's deviation from both the American norm of practicality and the American democratic manner creates much of his charisma. An internal mechanism buried so deeply inside his people that all they can say about it is that it's there imbues the everyday life of the plays with the possibility of the miraculous. This possibility stems from the collective unconscious, and it can be intuited through an awareness of motifs beating up from African-based myth and folklore, particularly the blues. The blues links Wilson to the great fund of wisdom and connection seated in his African origins.

All this makes up the theoretical background. The foreground consists of fragmentation, decay, and violence, with the violence often referring to the blues, a tradition and a value system Wilson ironically posits as a source of wholeness and joy. That his only two onstage murder victims are both blues musicians marks the distance between the actual and the ideal. Slow Drag and Floyd Barton also convey Wilson's commitment to the complexities nourishing his art. Fantastic but rooted in solid emotional reality, his plays evoke rather than argue or cast blame. He trusts his own private way of looking at things. Capable of being irreverent and traditional at the same time, he knows how to trade on the direct, the vivid, and the raw without forgetting how they're nuanced by subtlety and ambiguity. Through it all, the precision of his prose and his slanting shafts of humor keep sentimentality and despair at bay. He writes with deceptive fluency; Gates calls his "great gift" an "unruly luxuriance of language—an ability to ease between trash talk and near-choral transport" (47). An extraordinarily gifted stylist Wilson is, conveying, again and again, in sharp, often funny dialogue the exact words for his characters' half-formulated thoughts.

Full of peopled space, his plays stand their own ground. He's an authentic black American artist whose dedication precludes any ambitions to play the virtuoso, the cosmopolite, or the scourge. Nor has this creator of stunning linguistic effects and delicately shaded roles melted into his public image. The plays keep coming. For this, we should feel both exhilarated and grateful. August Wilson is a remarkable playwright who merits the superlatives that have been lavished on him. He has also bequeathed to his successors, regardless of race, an awful lot to live up to.

Notes and References

Chapter One

1. Gerald M. Berkowitz, *American Drama of the Twentieth Century* (London: Longman, 1992), 194.

2. Eric Bergesen and William M. Demastes, "The Limits of African-American Political Realism: Baraka's *Dutchman* and Wilson's *Ma Rainey's Black Bottom*," in *Realism and the American Dramatic Tradition,* ed. William M. Demastes (Tuscaloosa: University of Alabama Press, 1996), 218.

3. Liz Smith, review of *Joe Turner's Come and Gone, New York Daily News,* 28 March 1988, 8.

4. Richard Christiansen, "Artist of the Year: August Wilson's Plays Reveal What It Means to Be Black in This Century," *Chicago Tribune,* 27 December 1987, sec. 13, p. 4.

5. Sandra G. Shannon, *The Dramatic Vision of August Wilson* (Washington, D.C.: Howard University Press, 1995), 199.

6. Samuel G. Freedman, "A Voice from the Streets," *New York Times Magazine,* 15 March 1987, 36, 40, 49, 50; Chip Brown, "The Light in August," *Esquire,* April 1989, 116–25; Henry Louis Gates Jr., "Department of Disputation: The Chitlin' Circuit," *New Yorker,* 3 February 1997, 44–55.

7. Alan Nadel, ed., *May All Your Fences Have Gates: Essays on the Drama of August Wilson* (Iowa City: University of Iowa Press, 1994).

8. David Barbour, "August Wilson's Here to Stay," *Theater Week,* 25 April 1988, 8.

9. John Lahr, "Black and Blue," *New Yorker,* 15 April 1996, 101.

10. Lawrence Bommer, "A Keeper of Dreams," *Chicago Tribune,* 15 January 1995, 16.

11. Michael Feingold, "August Wilson's Bottomless Blackness," *Village Voice,* 27 November 1984, 117.

12. August Wilson, *Fences* (New York: New American Library [Plume], 1987), 23; hereafter cited in text as *F.*

13. August Wilson, preface to *Three Plays* (Pittsburgh: University of Pittsburgh Press, 1991), 9; hereafter cited in text as Preface.

14. Ed Bullins, introduction to *The Theme Is Blackness: The Corner and Other Plays* (New York: Morrow, 1973), 14.

15. David Savran, "August Wilson," in *In Their Own Words: Contemporary American Playwrights* (New York: Theatre Communications Groups, 1988), 294.

16. August Wilson, *Ma Rainey's Black Bottom* (New York: New American Library [Plume], 1985), 33; hereafter cited in text as *MR*.

17. Jay Plum, "Blues, History, and the Dramaturgy of August Wilson," *African American Review* 27 (Winter 1993): 561.

18. August Wilson, *Seven Guitars* (New York: Dutton, 1996), 1; hereafter cited in text as *7G*.

19. Paul Carter Harrison, "August Wilson's Blues Poetics," in *Three Plays,* by August Wilson, 294.

20. Paul Oliver, *The Story of the Blues* (Philadelphia: Chilton, 1969), 30; hereafter cited in text as Oliver 1969.

21. Robert Palmer, *Deep Blues* (New York: Viking, 1981), 17.

22. Albert Murray, *The Hero and the Blues* (Columbia: University of Missouri Press, 1973), 38.

23. Bill Moyers, "August Wilson: Playwright," *A World of Ideas* (New York: Doubleday, 1989), 168.

24. Kim Powers, "An Interview with August Wilson," *Theater* 16 (Fall/Winter 1984): 52.

25. August Wilson, *The Janitor,* in *Literature and Its Writers: An Introduction,* ed. Ann Charters and Samuel Charters (Boston: Bedford, 1997), 1901; hereafter cited in text as *J*.

26. August Wilson, "I Want a Black Director," in *May All Your Fences Have Gates,* ed. Nadel, 200–204.

27. Herbert G. Goldman, ed., *Ring Record Book and Boxing Encyclopedia, 1986–87* (New York: Ring Publishing, 1987), 568.

28. Holly Hill, "Black Theater into the Mainstream," in *Contemporary American Theater,* ed. Bruce King (New York: St. Martins, 1991), 88.

29. Kim Pereira, *August Wilson and the African-American Odyssey* (Urbana: University of Illinois Press, 1995), x.

30. C. W. E. Bigsby, *Modern American Drama, 1945–1990* (Cambridge: Cambridge University Press, 1992), 287.

31. Yvonne Shafer, *August Wilson: A Research and Production Sourcebook* (Westport, Conn.: Greenwood Press, 1998), 6; hereafter cited in the text as Shafer 1998.

32. Alan Nadel, introduction to *May All Your Fences Have Gates,* ed. Nadel, 5.

33. Matthew C. Roudané, *American Drama since 1960: A Critical History* (New York: Twayne, 1996), 98–99.

34. Richard Pettengill, "The Historical Perspective," in *August Wilson: A Casebook,* ed. Marilyn Elkins, Garland Reference Library of the Humanities, vol. 1626 (New York: Garland, 1994), 297.

35. Joe Pollack, "Dramatic Disunity," *{St. Louis} Riverfront Times,* 5–11 March 1997, 38.

36. Joan Fishman, "Romare Bearden, August Wilson, and the Traditions of African Performance," in *May All Your Fences Have Gates,* ed. Nadel, 141.

37. Mimi Kramer, "Travelling Man and Hesitating Woman," *New Yorker,* 30 April 1990, 83.

38. Ralph Ellison, *Shadow and Act* (New York: Random House, 1964), 85.

39. August Wilson, *The Piano Lesson* (New York: Plume, 1990), 31; hereafter cited in text as *PL.*

40. August Wilson, *Joe Turner's Come and Gone* (New York: New American Library [Plume], 1988), 87; hereafter cited in text as *JT.*

41. Yvonne Shafer, "An Interview with August Wilson," *Journal of Dramatic Theory and Criticism,* 4 (Fall 1989): 170; hereafter cited in text as Shafer 1989.

42. Ishmael Reed, "In Search of August Wilson: A Shy Genius Transforms the American Theater," *Connoisseur* 217 (March 1987): 95.

Chapter Two

1. Carla J. McDonough, *Staging Masculinity: Male Identity in Contemporary American Drama* (Jefferson, N.C.: McFarland, 1997), 38.

2. August Wilson, *Two Trains Running* (New York: Plume, 1993), 42; hereafter cited in text as *2TR.*

3. Jerry Tallmer, " 'Fences': Anguish of Wasted Talent," *New York Post,* 26 March 1987, C4.

4. From the typescript of Wilson's working draft of *Jitney* (provided by August Wilson), 55.

5. Mark William Rocha, "A Conversation with August Wilson," *Diversity* (Fall 1992): 35; hereafter cited in text as Rocha 1992.

6. Clifford Mason, *Gabriel,* in *Black Drama Anthology*, ed. Woodie King and Ron Milner (New York: Penguin, Meridian, 1986), 193–94.

7. Norine Dworkin, "Blood on the Tracks," *American Theater,* May 1990, 8.

8. Mark William Rocha, "American History as 'Loud Talking' in *Two Trains Running,"* in *May All Your Fences Have Gates,* ed. Nadel, 127; hereafter cited in text as Rocha 1994.

9. August Wilson, "How to Write a Play like August Wilson," *New York Times,* 10 March 1991, sec. 2, p. 5.

Chapter Three

1. Lois Gordon and Alan Gordon, *American Chronicle: Six Decades in American Life 1920–1980* (New York: Atheneum, 1987), 69–77.

2. Frank Rich, "Theater: Ma Rainey's Black Bottom," *New York Times,* 11 April 1984, C19; hereafter cited in text as Rich 1984.

3. Arnold Shaw, *Black Popular Music in America* (New York: Schirmer, 1986), 101.

4.   Philip E. Smith II, "Ma Rainey's Black Bottom: Playing the Blues as Equipment for Living," in *Within the Dramatic Spectrum,* vol. 6, ed. Karelisa V. Hartigan (New York: University Press of America, 1986), 182.

Chapter Four

1.   Joseph Reichler, ed., *The Baseball Encyclopedia: The Complete and Official Record of Major League Baseball,* 7th ed. (New York: Macmillan, 1988), 1444.

2.   George Vecsey, "Ray Dandridge, the Hall of Famer and 'Fences,' " *New York Times,* 10 May 1987, V3.

3.   Robert Peterson, *Only the Ball Was White: A History of Legendary Black Players* (New York: McGraw-Hill, 1970), 235–36.

4.   Edith Oliver, "Interlude 1987: 'Fences,' " *New Yorker,* 31 May 1993, 136.

5.   Frank Rich, "Theater: Family Ties in Wilson's 'Fences,' " *New York Times,* 27 March 1987, C3.

6.   Missy Dean Kubitschek, "August Wilson's Gender Lesson," in *May All Your Fences Have Gates,* ed. Nadel, 189.

Chapter Five

1.   Robert Sobel and John Raimo, eds., *Biographical Directory of Governors of the United States, 1789–1978,* vol. 4 (Westport, Conn.: Meckler Books, 1978), 1491–92.

2.   August Wilson, "The Legacy of Malcolm X," *Life,* December 1992, 89.

Chapter Six

1.   Hugh Merrill, *The Blues Route* (New York: William Morrow, 1992), 14.

2.   David M. Oshinsky, *"Worse Than Slavery": Parchman Farm and the Ordeal of Jim Crow Justice* (New York: Free Press, 1996),150.

3.   Mei-Ling Ching, "Wrestling against History," *Theater* 20 (Summer-Fall 1988): 71.

4.   Frank Rich, "A Family Confronts Its History in August Wilson's 'Piano Lesson,' " *New York Times,* 17 April 1990, C13.

5.   Robert Brustein, "The Lesson of 'The Piano Lesson,' " *New Republic,* 21 May 1990, 28.

Chapter Seven

1.   Calvin Tomkins, "Putting Something over Something Else," *New Yorker,* 28 November 1977, 60.

Chapter Eight

1.   Ben Brantley, "The World That Created August Wilson," *New York Times,* sec. 2, p. 5.

2. Sigmund Freud, *A General Introduction to Psychoanalysis,* trans. and rev. Joan Riviere (New York: Liveright, 1935), 327.

3. Trudier Harris, "August Wilson's Folk Traditions," in *August Wilson: A Casebook,* ed. Elkins, 64.

4. Ian Carr, Digby Fairweather, and Brian Priestley, *Jazz: The Rough Guide* (London: Rough Guides, 1995), 66.

Conclusion

1. Mervyn Rothstein, "Round Five for the Theatrical Heavyweight," *New York Times,* 15 April 1990, sec. 2, p. 8.

2. August Wilson, "Bessie," *Black Lines* 1 (Summer 1971): 68; August Wilson, "Morning Song," *Black Lines* 1 (Summer 1971): 68.

Selected Bibliography

PRIMARY SOURCES

Collection

Three Plays. Pittsburgh: University of Pittsburgh Press, 1991. Includes *Ma Rainey's Black Bottom, Fences,* and *Joe Turner's Come and Gone.*

Individual Plays

Fences. New York: New American Library [Plume], 1987.
The Janitor. In *Literature and Its Writers: An Introduction,* by Ann Charters and Samuel Charters, 1901–2. Boston: Bedford, 1997.
Joe Turner's Come and Gone. New York: New American Library [Plume], 1988.
Ma Rainey's Black Bottom. New York: New American Library [Plume], 1985.
The Piano Lesson. New York: Plume, 1990.
Seven Guitars. New York: Dutton, 1996.
Testimonies. In *Antaeus* 66 (Spring 1991): 474–79.
Two Trains Running. New York: Plume, 1993.

Unpublished Plays

Black Bart and the Sacred Hills. Written 1977; produced 1978.
The Homecoming. Written 1976; produced 1989.
Jitney. Written 1979; produced 1982, 1983 (rev. ed. 1997).

Essays

"How to Write a Play like August Wilson." *New York Times,* 10 March 1991, sec. 2, pp. 5, 17.
"I Want a Black Director." In *May All Your Fences Have Gates,* ed. Alan Nadel, 200–204. Iowa City: University of Iowa Press, 1994.
"The Legacy of Malcolm X." *Life,* December 1992, 84–94.
Preface to *Three Plays,* by August Wilson. Pittsburgh: University of Pittsburgh Press, 1991.

Poems

"Bessie." *Black Lines* I (Summer 1971): 68.
"Morning Song." *Black Lines* I (Summer, 1971): 68.
"Muhammad Ali." *Black World* I (September 1972): 60–61.

Interviews

De Vries, Hilary. "August Wilson—A New Voice for Black American Theater." *Christian Science Monitor,* 18 October 1984, 51–54. Details Wilson's ability to go beyond racial questions and stereotypes to universalize the issues he writes about.

Lyons, Bonnie. "An Interview with August Wilson." *Contemporary Literature* 40, no.1 (Spring 1999):1–21. Discusses Wilson's belief that black people are worse off today in the United States than they were 40 years ago. Describes the moral and technical problems of writing about "black Americans having uniquely African ways of participating in the world." Provides intriguing insights into the way Wilson writes.

Moyers, Bill. "August Wilson: Playwright." In *A World of Ideas,* 167–80. New York: Doubleday, 1989. Provides key insights into Wilson's ideas about the blues, the social contract that white America has given blacks ("You cannot participate in this society as Africans"), and *The Cosby Show* as a depiction of black American family life.

Powers, Kim. "An Interview with August Wilson." *Theater* 16 (Fall/Winter 1984): 50–55. Includes Wilson's remarks about the recurring father-son conflict in his work along with his intentions to convey in *Joe Turner* an African worldview through black American speakers of English.

Pettengill, Richard. "The Historical Perspective." In *August Wilson: A Casebook,* ed. Marilyn Elkins, Garland Reference Library of the Humanities, vol. 1626, 207–26. New York: Garland, 1994. Contains valuable commentary about the characters' attempts to reclaim the past in *Two Trains,* Wilson's use of historical perspective, and what Wilson attempted and believes he accomplished in his work.

Rocha, Mark William. "A Conversation with August Wilson." *Diversity* 1 (Fall 1992): 24–42. Particularly valuable for its insights into Wilson's masculinist ethos, its comments on *Two Trains,* and the influence upon Wilson of artist Romare Bearden.

Savran, David. "August Wilson." In *In Their Own Words*: *Contemporary American Playwrights,* 288–305. New York: Theatre Communications Group, 1988. Rehearses the motif of accepting moral responsibility in works like *Joe Turner* and the important aesthetic question in Wilson's work of Western theatrical influences like the well-made play.

Shafer, Yvonne. "An Interview with August Wilson." *Journal of Dramatic Theory and Criticism* 4 (Fall 1989): 161–73. Valuable discussion of Wilson's development as a playwright, with emphasis on his relationship with Lloyd Richards.

Shannon, Sandra G. "August Wilson Explains His Dramatic Vision: An Interview." In *The Dramatic Vision of August Wilson,* 201–35. Washington, D.C.: Howard University Press, 1995. An excellent account of the significance of scars, names, and the role of the unconscious as a shaping force in the plays. Also includes valuable commentary on the vicissitudes of the plays' marketing and staging.

Tallmer, Jerry. " 'Fences': Anguish of Wasted Talent." *New York Post,* 26 March 1987, C4. Looks at the effects of racial injustice and inequality upon young urban blacks.

SECONDARY SOURCES

Books

Elkins, Marilyn, ed. *August Wilson: A Casebook,* Garland Reference Library of the Humanities, vol. 1626. New York: Garland, 1994. Witty, penetrating discussions by young scholars on subjects such as influences, the deployment of African-American culture in the work, and the value of studying the canon in the light of contemporary critical theory.

Nadel, Alan, ed. *May All Your Fences Have Gates: Essays on the Drama of August Wilson.* Iowa City: University of Iowa Press, 1994. A valuable collection of essays on political, historical, gender, and artistic issues raised by the plays.

Pereira, Kim. *August Wilson and the African-American Odyssey.* Urbana: University of Illinois Press, 1995. Explains persuasively how Wilson's characters reinvent both themselves and their cultural legacy in order to survive in America's industrial North.

Shafer, Yvonne. *August Wilson: A Research and Production Sourcebook.* Westport, Conn.: Greenwood Press, 1998. Essential. Surveys the life and career; summarizes and provides critical overviews of the plays; includes a detailed, exhaustive bibliography with sharp critical insights accompanying each entry.

Shannon, Sandra G. *The Dramatic Vision of August Wilson.* Washington, D.C.: Howard University Press, 1995. A valuable, illuminating study of the formation of Wilson's artistic sensibility; also includes an interview (201–35) in which Wilson discusses the forces underlying his dramatic vision.

Bibliography

Shafer, Yvonne. *August Wilson: A Research and Production Sourcebook*, 51–121. Westport, Conn.: Greenwood Press, 1998.

Shannon, Sandra G. "Annotated Bibliography of Works by and about August Wilson." In *May All Your Fences Have Gates: Essays on the Drama of August Wilson,* ed. Alan Nadel, 230–66. Iowa City: University of Iowa Press, 1994.

Articles, Sections of Books, Reviews, and Reference Works

Adell, Sandra. "Speaking of Ma Rainey/Talking about the Blues." In *May All Your Fences Have Gates,* ed. Nadel, 50–66. Cogently relates Ma Rainey's life, the motif of the phonograph record, and the threat of incarceration to the motivations undergirding Wilson's 1984 play.

Awkward, Michael. "The Crookeds and the Straights: *Fences,* Race, and the Politics of Adaptation." In *May All Your Fences Have Gates,* ed. Nadel, 204–29. Finds Euro-American theatrical conventions informing the "structure, pace, and methodology" in *Fences.*

Backalenick, Irene. "A Lesson from Lloyd Richards." *Theater Week,* 16–22 April 1992, 17–19. Summarizes high spots of Richards's career as both director of the Yale Repertory Theater and dean of the Yale School of Drama.

Baker, Houston A. Jr. *Blues, Ideology, and Afro-American Literature.* Chicago: University of Chicago Press, 1984.

Barbour, David. "August Wilson's Here to Stay." *Theater Week,* 25 April 1988, 8–14. Discusses the influence of Borges and Marquez on *Joe Turner.*

Bergesen, Eric and William W. Demastes. "The Limits of African-American Political Realism: Baraka's *Dutchman* and Wilson's *Ma Rainey's Black Bottom.*" In *Realism and the American Dramatic Tradition,* ed. William M. Demastes, 218–34. Tuscaloosa: University of Alabama Press, 1996. Very useful insights into the impact of the visual effects created by staging in *Ma Rainey.*

Berkowitz, Gerald M. *American Drama of the Twentieth Century.* London: Longman, 1992. A friendly study that nonetheless faults both *Joe Turner* and *Piano Lesson.*

Bernstein, Richard. "August Wilson's Voices from the Past." *New York Times,* 27 March 1988, sec. 2, pp. 1, 34. An excellent examination of the deep structure of Wilson's early plays.

Bigsby, C. W. E. *Modern American Drama, 1945–1990.* Cambridge: Cambridge University Press, 1992. Explains how superior technique saves Wilson's moral passion from deteriorating into harangue in the plays.

Bommer, Lawrence. "A Keeper of Dreams." *Chicago Tribune,* 15 January 1995, 16–21. Recounts the centrality of the African American oral tradition in the plays.

Brantley, Ben. "The World That Created August Wilson." *New York Times,* sec. 2, pp. 1, 5. An intelligent look at the recurring father-son conflict in Wilson's plays.

Brown, Chip. "The Light in August." *Esquire,* April 1989, 116–25. An important study of Wilson's early years and the growth of his artistic imagination.

Brustein, Robert. "The Lesson of 'The Piano Lesson.'" *New Republic,* 21 May 1990, 28–30.

Bullins, Ed. Introduction to *The Theme Is Blackness: The Corner and Other Plays.* New York: Morrow, 1973.

Carr, Ian, Digby Fairweather, and Brian Priestley. *Jazz: The Rough Guide.* London: Rough Guides, 1995.

Ching, Mei-Lei. "Wrestling against History." *Theater* 20 (Summer-Fall 1988): 70–71. Discusses Wilson's blend of Christianity and "African cosmogony" in *Piano Lesson.*

Christiansen, Richard. "Artist of the Year: August Wilson's Plays Reveal What It Means to Be Black in This Century." *Chicago Tribune,* 27 December 1987, sec. 13, pp. 4–5. An illuminating biographical sketch and appreciation.

De Vries, Hilary. "A Song in Search of Itself." *American Theater,* January 1987, 22–25. Shows how Wilson's indebtedness to Ed Bullins and Amiri Baraka is tempered by his historical sense and his poetic imagination.

Dworkin, Norine. "Blood on the Tracks." *American Theater,* May 1990, 8. Contains sharp insights into *Two Trains.*

Ellison, Ralph. *Shadow and Act.* New York: Random House, 1964.

Feingold, Michael. "August Wilson's Bottomless Blackness." *Village Voice,* 27 November 1984, 117–18. Very strong on biographical background.

Fishman, Joan. "Romare Bearden, August Wilson, and the Traditions of African Performance." In *May All Your Fences Have Gates,* ed. Nadel, 133–49. Includes helpful insights into the influence exerted upon Wilson by his older fellow Pittsburgher. Includes valuable illustrations.

Freedman, Samuel G. "A Voice from the Streets." *New York Times Magazine,* 15 March 1987, 36, 40, 49, 50. Very strong on the Pittsburgh background; includes material on Wilson's plans for his future as a writer.

Freud, Sigmund. *A General Introduction to Psychoanalysis.* Trans. and rev. Joan Riviere. New York: Liveright, 1935.

Gates, Henry Louis Jr. "Department of Disputation: The Chitlin' Circuit." *New Yorker,* 3 February 1997, 44–55. A brilliant discussion of the thematic and stylistic features that set Wilson off from the commercial black dramatists of today along with some words about Wilson's bias for race-based casting.

Goldman, Herbert G., ed. *Ring Record Book and Boxing Encyclopedia, 1986–87.* New York: Ring Publishing, 1987.

Gordon, Lois, and Alan Gordon. *American Chronicle: Six Decades in American Life 1920–1980.* New York: Atheneum, 1987.

Harris, Trudier. "August Wilson's Folk Traditions." In *August Wilson: A Casebook,* ed. Elkins, 49–67. Analyzes Wilson's use of African American folklore to merge the secular and the sacred in *Joe Turner* and the other plays.

Harrison, Paul Carter. "August Wilson's Blues Poetics." In *Three Plays,* by August Wilson, 291–318. Pittsburgh: University of Pittsburgh Press, 1991. An illuminating discussion of "the panoply of expressive strategies" from non-Euro-American sources underlying Wilson's thought.

Hill, Holly. "Black Theatre into the Mainstream." In *Contemporary American Theatre,* ed. Bruce King, 81–96. New York: St. Martins, 1991. Important for its discussion of black-on-black tension in the Wilson plays.

Kramer, Mimi. "Travelling Man and Hesitating Woman." *New Yorker,* 30 April 1990, 82–83. Spells out significant differences between male and female outlooks, expectations, and experiences of life in Wilson's work.

Kroll, Jack. "Theater: And in This Corner." *Newsweek* 10 February 1997, 65. A humorous discussion of Wilson's February 1997 debate with Robert Brustein at New York's Town Hall on the question of race-based casting, production, and direction in the theater.

Kubitschek, Missy Dean. "August Wilson's Gender Lesson." In *May All Your Fences Have Gates,* ed. Nadel, 183–99. A convincing study of gender freedom and gender interaction in the plays.

Lahr, John. "Black and Blues." *New Yorker,* 15 April 1996, 99–101.

McDonough, Carla J. *Staging Masculinity: Male Identity in Contemporary American Drama.* Jefferson, N.C.: McFarland, 1997. An insightful sociological reading of Wilson, emphasizing the incidence of unemployment, crime, and firearm possession among urban black males in the Wilson canon.

Merrill, Hugh. *The Blues Route.* New York: William Morrow, 1992.

Murray, Albert. *The Hero and the Blues.* Columbia: University of Missouri Press, 1973.

Nadel, Alan. "Boundaries, Logistics, and Identity: The Property of Metaphor in *Fences* and *Joe Turner's Come and Gone.*" In *May All Your Fences Have Gates,* 86–104. Investigates with impressive intellectual rigor both literal and figurative discourse in Wilson's work.

Oliver, Edith. "Interlude 1987: 'Fences.' " *New Yorker,* 31 May 1993, 136.

Oliver, Paul. *The Story of the Blues.* Philadelphia: Chilton, 1969.

Oshinsky, David M. *"Worse Than Slavery": Parchman Farm and the Ordeal of Jim Crow Justice.* New York: Free Press, 1996.

Palmer, Robert. *Deep Blues.* New York: Viking, 1981.

Peterson, Robert. *Only the Ball Was White: A History of Legendary Black Players.* New York: McGraw-Hill, 1970.

Plum, Jay. "Blues, History, and the Dramaturgy of August Wilson." *African American Review* 27 (Winter 1993): 561–67. Discusses the blues as an agent of black self-awareness in the plays.

Pollack, Joe. "Dramatic Disunity." {*St. Louis} Riverfront Times,* 5–11 March 1997, 37–38. Sees signs of the influence of the Western theater on Wilson's plays.

Reed, Ishmael. "In Search of August Wilson: A Shy Genius Transforms the American Theater." *Connoisseur* 217 (March 1987): 92–97. Very helpful on the Wilson-Lloyd Richards collaboration.

Reichler, Joseph L., ed. *The Baseball Encyclopedia: The Complete and Official Record of Major League Baseball,* 7th ed. New York: Macmillan, 1988.

Rich, Frank. "A Family Confronts Its History in August Wilson's 'Piano Lesson.' " *New York Times,* 17 April 1990, C13, C15.

———. "Panoramic History of Blacks in America in Wilson's 'Joe Turner.' " *New York Times,* 28 March 1988, C15.

———. "Theater: Family Ties in Wilson's 'Fences.' " *New York Times,* 27 March 1987, C 3.

———. 'Theater: 'Ma Rainey's Black Bottom.' " *New York Times,* 11 April 1984, C19.

Richards, Lloyd. Introduction to *Fences,* by August Wilson, vii–viii. New York: New American Library [Plume], 1987.

Rocha, Mark William. "American History as 'Loud Talking' in *Two Trains Running.*" In *May All Your Fences Have Gates,* ed. Nadel, 116–32. Relates the interpersonal dynamics displayed in *Two Trains* to conventions of black speech.

Rothstein, Mervyn. "Round Five for the Theatrical Heavyweight." *New York Times,* 15 April 1990, sec. 2, pp. 1, 8. A riveting discussion of Wilson's awareness of the black diaspora.

Roudané, Matthew C. *American Drama since 1960: A Critical History.* New York: Twayne, 1996. Highly supportive study of Wilson, which includes valuable commentary about the "warrior spirit" in the plays.

Shaw, Arnold. *Black Popular Music in America.* New York: Schirmer, 1986.

Smith, Liz. Review of *Joe Turner. New York Daily News,* 28 March 1988, 8.

Smith, Philip E., II. "*Ma Rainey's Black Bottom*: Playing the Blues as Equipment for Living." In *Within the Dramatic Spectrum,* vol. 6, ed. Karelisa V. Hartigan, 177–86. New York: University Press of America, 1986. Argues cogently that Levee is the play's villain.

Sobel, Robert, and John Raimo, eds. *Biographical Directory of the Governors of the United States, 1789–1978,* vol. 4, 1491–92. Westport, Conn.: Meckler Books, 1978.

Tomkins, Calvin. "Putting Something over Something Else." *New Yorker,* 28 November 1977, 53–61. A useful overview of Romare Bearden's life and career.

Vecsey, George. "Ray Dandridge, the Hall of Famer and 'Fences.' " *New York Times,* 10 May 1987, sec. 5, p. 3.

Werner, Craig. "August Wilson's Burden: The Function of Neoclassical Jazz." In *May All Your Fences Have Gates,* ed. Nadel, 21–50. Shows Wilson's drama wresting lyrical expression and affirmation out of the ugliness of daily living in America's decaying inner cities.

Index

The Author

The author of 16 published books and shorter pieces that have appeared in places like the *New York Times Book Review, New Republic, Modern Fiction Studies,* the *Calcutta Statesman,* and the *Sydney Morning Herald,* Peter Wolfe teaches English at the University of Missouri-St. Louis. Winner of an NEH Award and two Fulbrights, Wolfe has held guest professorships at universities in Canada, New Zealand, Australia, Russia, Taiwan, India, and Poland. His book *Alarms and Epitaphs: The Art of Eric Ambler* won the Armchair Detective Award for the best scholarly work in the mystery genre for 1993, and in 1995 he won the University of Missouri President's Award for Research and Creativity. His previous books in the Twayne series deal with Mary Renault (1969) and Jean Rhys (1980).

The Editor

Frank Day is a professor of English and head of the English Department at Clemson University. He is the author of *Sir William Empson: An Annotated Bibliography* (1984) and *Arthur Koestler: A Guide to Research* (1985). He was a Fulbright lecturer in American literature in Romania (1980–1981) and in Bangladesh (1986–1987).